Space and Social Theory

BSA *New Horizons in Sociology*

The British Sociological Association is publishing a series of books to review the state of the discipline at the beginning of the millennium. New Horizons in Sociology also seeks to locate the contribution of British scholarship to the wider development of sociology. Sociology is taught in all the major institutions of higher education in the United Kingdom as well as throughout North America and the Europe of the former western bloc. Sociology is now establishing itself in the former eastern bloc. But it was only in the second half of the twentieth century that sociology moved from the fringes of UK academic life into the mainstream. British sociology has also provided a home for movements that have renewed and challenged the discipline; the revival of academic Marxism, the renaissance in feminist theory, the rise of cultural studies, for example. Some of these developments have become sub-disciplines whilst yet others have challenged the very basis of the sociological enterprise. Each has left their mark. Now therefore is a good time both to take stock and to scan the horizon, looking back and looking forward.

Series Editor: Bridget Fowler, *University of Glasgow*

Published titles include:

Nationalism and Soical Theory
Gerard Delanty and Patrick O'Mahoney

Interactionism
Paul Atkinson and William Housley

Feminist Sociology
Sara Delamont

The New Sociology of Economic Behaviour
Ralph Fevre

The Sociology of Religion
Grace Davie

Space and Social Theory

Andrzej Zieleniec

SAGE Publications
Los Angeles · London · New Delhi · Singapore

SAGE Publications Ltd
1 Oliver's Yard
55 City Road
London EC1Y 1SP

SAGE Publications Inc.
2455 Teller Road
Thousand Oaks, California 91320

SAGE Publications India Pvt Ltd
B 1/I 1 Mohan Cooperative Industrial Area
Mathura Road
New Delhi 110 044

SAGE Publications Asia-Pacific Pte Ltd
33 Pekin Street #02-01
Far East Square
Singapore 048763

Library of Congress Control Number: 2006940062

British Library Cataloguing in Publication data

A catalogue record for this book is available from
the British Library

ISBN 978–0–7619–4447–8

Typeset by Newgen Imaging System (P) Ltd, Chennai, India
Printed in India at Replika Press Pvt. Ltd.
Printed on paper from sustainable resources

**For Kasia,
Rowan and Audrey**

contents

preface

Space is or has been all too often taken for granted and assumed as a relatively unacknowledged aspect or backdrop to life. It is just there to be filled up, used, crossed over or negotiated in everyday life. In this it is much the same with much social theory. There is or has been an apparent neglect of the detailed consideration of space as an issue or a factor worthy of systematic analysis at least that is, until the last quarter of the twentieth century. Since then and with the publication of a number of influential texts and studies, particularly in the realm of a re-imagined human or cultural geography, space has become increasingly acknowledged as a fundamental and crucial area for social enquiry and analysis.

Space and spatial analysis are now increasingly being considered as an essential element in the development of theoretical knowledge and understanding as well as empirical investigations in a range of social scientific disciplines. No longer is the consideration and analysis of space deemed the preserve of geographical perspectives on the interplay between the human and 'natural' environments. Human-made environments and the social relations that made them as well as the interactions that occur in and through them is now the subject of critical and detailed analysis. Due credit then must be given to human and social geographers for their role in promoting and furthering the reprioritisation of space as a fundamental element for a comprehensive understanding of the complexity of social relations. However, in this new climate of inter-disciplinary activity there is the potential for an expansion in distinctly spatial analyses that should provide not only new horizons but also new directions for a variety of disciplines. Such a fecund future is premised on the recognition of the development and applicability of theories of space and spatial theories.

The aim of this book is to present some of these theoretical perspectives and to highlight their importance for the development of a more inclusive and accepted social theory of space. In this the intention is not to present a comprehensive overview of all the contributions to the corpus of knowledge that constitutes the field of social theories of space. Instead the objective is to be necessarily selective and approach the development of 'thinking on space' in a somewhat chronological manner. Similarly, the impacts and influence of such theories and analyses are to provide an indication of the fruitfulness of incorporating a social theory of space into empirical and theoretical investigations of the complex social relations that constitutes, in various forms, the investigation of social reality. In particular, but not exclusively, these theories are important for providing an understanding of the city and the urban which has and continues to be the focus of much social analysis of modernity. It is perhaps instructive to give some personal details of my own 'coming to terms' with space as a fundamental importance for social analysis and investigation.

As an undergraduate I was encouraged in the development of my own 'sociological imagination' through instruction in the classical theoretical foundations of the discipline (of Marx, Weber, Durkheim, Simmel, Comte, Saint Simon, Tonnies, etc.) and the development of contemporary theoretical approaches, perspectives, paradigms (from C. W. Mills, Williams, Elias, E. P. Thompson, Goffman, Popper, Kuhn, Bauman, Bourdieu, Foucault, Giddens, Beck, the post-modern debates of Jameson, Lyotard, Baudrillard, etc.). These provided the epistemological and ontological foundations of the discipline as well as its subsequent development and which informed the study of substantive areas including the urban, modernity, mass media, culture, consumption, stratification, work, literature and informed the detailed exploration of the methodological practice of sociology as well as its intellectual framework. In retrospect, it is perhaps easier to identify omissions than accentuate the positive aspects of my own foundation in sociology. In this, I could highlight the lack of an appreciation of the importance of a sociological analysis and understanding of the spatial dimension of the structure, organisation and experience of social relations and activities in the various 'specialisms' that were covered.

This relative lack of focus on space in sociological analysis and in my own knowledge only became apparent when conducting doctoral thesis research necessitated understanding of the problematics of space. My thesis research involved the analysis of the origins and development of urban public parks as inherent features of the social and physical landscape of the city of modernity. What was revealed in my research was that public parks, as fairly universal and ubiquitous urban spaces, are composed of a complex interaction of physical features, dominant representations and everyday uses and experiences that all combined to 'define' them as social spaces with the network of spaces and spatial arrangements that constituted the social landscape of the city. This complexity required a comprehensive understanding and analysis of existing social theories of space and spatial social theory to provide a theoretical framework for the empirical analysis of their origins and development within the historical, social, economic, political and spatial

ix

growth of the city in modernity. What became evident was that although social theoretical analyses of space exist in a number of disciplines, particularly within social and cultural geography, there is within sociology no coherent body of works that analysed space as a fundamental factor in the critical social analysis of modernity.

What was required and achieved in my own work was an investigation of various theoretical approaches and perspectives on space that led to an increasing recognition of why space is or should be important for sociological analysis. This then was the genesis of this book. Its aim is to attempt to address this omission by providing an introduction and overview of key social theories of space and spatial theories that emphasise the spatial dimension of the structure, organisation, regulation and experience of social relations and interactions. This emphasis on space is or should be considered as fundamental for sociological analysis and research as well as for other social and cultural disciplines. In this it may be a new horizon and direction for contemporary sociology but, I hope to demonstrate, one that has been present in an implicit if not explicit form in sociological theory from its inception through to more recent times.

This book is intended not just to be of interest and value to undergraduates in sociology, but also to those in other social sciences such as human geography, urban studies, politics, anthropology, economic and social history, as well as to those in architecture, design, planning and to social policy practitioners. It is also proposed as an introduction to theoretical perspectives on space for post-graduate researchers, academics and professionals engaged in teaching and research in which the spatial element of social interaction, conflict, exclusion, migration, work, etc. can be understood and applied. Consideration of the importance of space and of the applicability of spatial analyses that are grounded in a theoretical framework will be shown not only to offer essential insights into the development of contemporary social relations, formations and practices but also to provide valuable conceptual and analytical frameworks for future research. Space then can no longer be overlooked or ignored.

The social world of relations and interactions is one which increasingly is being considered or understood as global, whether networked or not. In a world increasingly represented, expressed and understood as a global network of social, economic, leisure and political links and relations the conquest of space and time is a fundamental feature of this discourse. Knowledge of the social production of space is therefore increasingly fundamental for understanding not only the how of the social relations of contemporary existence but to ask questions of how this came to be, and why they exist in such forms and arrangements as they do. But to paraphrase some objections, we must be aware that to 'think global and act local' is to consider how social relationships and interactions take place in and over the space we inhabit, occupy and use in our everyday lives. We need knowledge of the global connections of modern life as well as understanding the space(s) which we experience, and potentially shape. The questions asked of space can inform us of the development of structures and organisations, institutions and practices, behaviours and experiences, power and politics that have moulded and been characteristic of modernity. It is such a challenge that the social theory of space poses.

However, this is not the preserve of a single disciplinary perspective or fiefdom. What is apparent is the relevance and significance of space and spatial analysis for understanding and investigating the totality of the complexity of social life. It is with this re-prioritisation of space that the genesis of this book arose. If social theory had seemingly given scant notice and consideration to space until the mid- to late 20th century, would it be possible to conduct a partial archaeology of those classical theorists whose legacy for the social sciences and specifically sociology is still acknowledged as influential to the development of the discipline.

Whilst space cannot be said to be entirely absent from our experience or understanding or from the imagination of the modern era it can be said to be viewed from two distinct perspectives. The first may be said to be that of a somewhat 'out of this world', 'somewhere up there' phenomena in which the advent of technological extra-planetary expeditions and investigations has focused attention on space as a popularised 'final frontier' of humanity's and specifically scientific knowledge. The development of increasingly sophisticated and powerful telescopes has increased the scope and range of astronomy's exploration and understanding of the space of the cosmos. In a similar and related technological advance the first tentative steps of extra-planetary travel have begun the journey of the conquest of vaster distances, worlds and territories. Whilst the 'space junk' of satellite communication and surveillance systems has created a new zone of competition and enterprise, most of which is focused downwards on the monitoring, communication and transposition of information and communication flows in an increasingly coordinated global economic system. This outward space has also been colonised by the imagination of science fiction and fantasy which has provided a very broad canvas on which has been painted, written and projected numerous realms of possibilities and prophecies for the future development and experience of the species. We can call this grand macro-cosmic awareness and exploration of space a natural extension of the scientific and technological conquest of the physical space of the earth taken beyond the limited confines of narrow territorial and earthly global experience. The triumph of science whilst not complete has turned its attention to outer space.

In distinction but not necessarily in opposition to outer space is the view of space as an inner-wordly realm of religious, spiritual or individualistic knowledge, and self-awareness. This is the territory of self-actualising techniques, of developmental and faith-based systems of meaning, promised enlightenment and the expansions of the minds' horizons beyond the limits of the corporeal or physical world of existence. The realm of the soul or the spirit is an inner space of visions and the accumulation or achievement of a possible wisdom of the meaning of existence, of life, the universe and everything. An attempt to impose some order and glean some meaning in an increasingly meaningless world of consumption and vicarious experience and sensory stimulation has led to a focus on the inner space of the mind, spirit and soul. This has led to the development of numerous promissory gurus, cults, therapies and techniques that have colonised the traditional spiritual landscape of the soul of the established faiths and religions with one of an increasingly individualistic emphasis.

Whether micro-cosmic or macro-cosmic, inner or outer, space is taken to be a fertile ground for exploration and knowledge building. However, the space we inhabit, make use of, and imagine in our everyday lives is one that is inherently social. As such it is subject to the forces and processes to which all of social life has been subject. As collectivities and societies the space that is associated with and which is fashioned to represent and to perpetuate that culture and that society's values, goals and ideologies is not only historically contingent but also socially produced. The social world then is one which makes its own space, whether spaces of production, consumption, circulation, representation, of leisure and pleasure, or of play and imagination. Space is created to enact, to embody and to symbolise the dreams, aspirations and achievements of society in each stage of development. What kinds of space are produced and created has consequences for the quantity and quality of social relations. The kinds of activities that are allowed, encouraged, prohibited, etc. is influenced by the design, shape, size, organisation and ultimately control over delimited and functionalised space. Places for production and for manufacturing for example, are made to permit the maximum and most efficient processes of production. Hence the craft workshops inhabited by single skilled workers have developed to huge edifices in which thousands of workers are organised in space (as well as in time) in a variety of inter-related processes to manufacture an end product. Similarly, different spaces of play, of leisure or of consumption are created, produced or designed for particular purposes. One space does not fit all. How space is organised, designed and represented has consequences for how it can and may be used. This is the space of the social and it matters. What kinds of spaces are made, by whom, for whom, where, when and why instructs us in the kinds of social worlds we have created and the kinds or types of activities that categorise or reflect our priorities and our interests.

To know space is to understand the social world and ultimately to understand ourselves. The kinds of social space that are made and that we use and inhabit structures not only our social experiences and interactions as social beings and collectivities but also our ability to know ourselves, as individuals and as social actors and as agents of change. However, the business of space is not a one-way street. As space delimits, influences or determines our activities and actions, so the meanings attached to space and the priorities that are reflected in them can be contested and changed by the kinds of uses and practices to which we put them and which challenge the designed intentions of those who seek to functionalise space and to control our access and use of it. Space then is not just the world of plans, logic and science. It is not just the world of ideology and power. It is also the world we live in, inhabit, negotiate and make use of in our own ways. It is the stuff in which, through which and around which we as social beings attempt to make our lives and in which we dream. Space then is inherently social and needs to be critically analysed as such.

This book then is intended as a short introduction to social theory and space. As a bland and somewhat overly simplistic starting point it is nevertheless appropriate to stress that simply put 'social relations must take place somewhere' and that somewhere is always in a social space that is not neutral, not just there, a void waiting to be filled by human actions. Space is shaped by human relations, but conversely human relations are also shaped by space. This will be at the core of those theorists that will be addressed in the following chapters. How space is perceived, conceived, represented, imagined and used has been crucial to how the contemporary world has come to be. Knowledge of the history of space, as Lefebvre argues, is crucial for understanding the space of the present. To paraphrase Marx on history, without knowledge of space one cannot fully comprehend the context and factors that shape the world we inhabit and we are doomed to repeat the mistake that the landscapes of our minds and of our existence are simply insignificant by-products of other processes. We need, therefore to address the meanings of the social construction of space the better to understand it and ourselves. The following theorists address the complex interaction between human action and interaction with their environment, whether natural or human-made, and the consequences this has for social organisation and of power. In this there is an orientation and convergence on the urban as *a* if not *the* dominant spatial form of capitalism.

CHAPTER 1: KARL MARX: THE IMPLICIT SPATIALITY OF HISTORICAL MATERIALISM

The first chapter presents a critical analysis of the implicit spatial dimension of Marx's historical materialism and critique of capitalism. It will address space as both a means and force of production under capitalism in which this dual characteristic of space as both a product and a means of production will necessarily consider its abstraction as an increasingly fetishised commodity. The ownership and control of space will then be considered as a factor in the organisation and perpetuation of increasingly urban capitalism within which the alienation of the proletariat is understood as being in part from their deracination from 'nature' as well as the products of their labour. Marx's insistence on the importance of the separation of town and country as the greatest division of material and mental labour will explore this perspective as well as introduce the urban as a form of produced space. The spatial dimension to the social division of labour reflects aspects of Marx's analysis of definitive characteristics of modern urban capitalism and is concerned not only with the spaces of production, but also those of the reproduction of labour. Finally, the consideration of spatiality inherent in Marx's identification of the expansion of capitalism to encompass a world market informs an understanding of imperialism and contemporary globalisation.

CHAPTER 2: GEORG SIMMEL: THE SPACE OF FORMAL SOCIOLOGY

Simmel's recently translated essay is an early sociological contribution to the consideration of space as an important area for understanding the form and content of social interaction. Whilst Simmel does not present a theory of space as such his identification and accentuation of various 'aspects' of space illuminates both Simmel's work as a whole as well as the importance of understanding space in social theory. These aspects of space (exclusivity, boundedness, fixity, mobility in space, proximity and distance) will be presented and considered as containing profound insights into the spatial orientation of social relations. They also provide an early foundation for the exploration of other social theories on space that follow as well as conceptual characterisations that are useful for contemporary spatial analysis and investigation.

CHAPTER 3: HENRI LEFEBVRE: THE PRODUCTION OF SPACE

Lefebvre's contribution to the analysis of space is fundamental for the recent resurgence of social scientific interest in space. His complex theory of the production of space is presented as a triad of interlinked and necessary elements to develop 'true knowledge' of space. Lefebvre's theoretical contribution provides a structural framework for social analysis and introduces the importance and complex interaction of consideration of a multiplicity of elements. This chapter will provide a brief summary of Lefebvre's intellectual biography that lead to his theory of *The Production of Space* and will consider in detail the salient features and implication of his triadic elements, that of practice, representation and use.

CHAPTER 4: DAVID HARVEY: THE POLITICAL ECONOMY OF SPACE

Harvey's consideration of the development of spatial forms and structures indicative of and conducive to the growth and prioritisation of urban capitalism as the primary locus for production, consumption and circulation in modernity is heavily influenced by Lefebvre's spatial analysis. Harvey's analysis of the organisation and control of the form and structure of the space of the urban is a vital analysis of the perpetuation of processes of capital accumulation. The location of inter-related features in the space of the city reflects attempts at the efficient organisation of processes of production and reproduction of labour. Harvey's historical–geographical spatial analysis requires that factories, transport links for raw materials and finished products, a labour supply, and associated support services are concentrated and organised in an increasingly ordered and hierarchical urbanised mode of production.

CHAPTER 5: MICHEL FOUCAULT: SPACE, KNOWLEDGE AND POWER

Whilst Foucault did not produce a theory of space he did make a number of contributions that are important for understanding how the development of disciplinary knowledge of space achieved important interventions in the social and physical landscape of the city. The intervention of 'disciplinary' knowledge is explored through analyses of medical knowledge and discourses of the space(s) of the urban through the creation and perpetuation of dominant representations necessary for the application of power over the regulation and instruction of populations, areas, spaces, behaviours, etc. For example, the development of sanitary inspectors of public health and the municipal provision of a host of services represent the direct application of knowledge of space being pursued and applied by the power of the local state. Similar examples of disciplinary knowledge and discourses of space will be provided through examples of institutional spaces such as prisons, schools, work places as well as leisure spaces such as public parks and tourist resorts.

CHAPTER 6: LEGACIES AND PROSPECTS: SPATIALISING CONTEMPORARY MODERNITY

The final chapter explores the legacies and influences of those perspectives and theories considered previously. The implicit spatiality of Marx's analysis of capitalism will be assessed as providing the basis for other theories of space and for contemporary explanations of the practice and perpetuation of capitalism as well as aspects of the development of globalisation. Lefebvre and Harvey will likewise be shown to have made important contributions to the understanding of the importance of space whether in the urban or as a means and a mode by which capitalism has survived and prospered. They have also both had a profound influence on the development of new analyses of the spatiality of contemporary social life. Simmel's legacy and influence is perhaps less easy to assess but nonetheless it is possible to identify, whether acknowledged or not, examples of his 'aspects of space' being used and emphasised in the work of other investigators of space. Finally, Foucault's various contributions to social theory of space especially that of disciplinary discourses have enabled numerous investigations of how the spatial practices and representations of power have been effected and contested.

In summary it is hoped that this introduction to these social theories of space will inform the reader of the importance of an understanding of space for social scientific and especially sociological enquiry. The importance of spatial social theory for empirical and substantive studies of macro and micro social relations in which the delimitation, organisation and regulation of space in general and particular forms of space in particular are major factors in the structuring of experience of society. The social construction of space is both historically and socially contingent and dependent on the operation of relations and processes of power and knowledge. It is thus also subject to contestation and change. The space of the future of social reality is not set, it is still to be imagined and constructed but this can only be done if it is understood.

acknowledgements

Thanks to all those few who have provided assistance and encouragement, especially through all the 'dark days' of perpetual teaching on short-term, part-time contracts. Special mention to David Frisby for all the advice and expert knowledge, to Trisha McCafferty for being and remaining 'a buddy', for Mags McCarthy for 'being there' and to Bridget Fowler for the initial encouragement to submit the proposal.

Thanks are also due to Chris Rojek and Mila Steele at Sage for your patience and understanding and to the anonymous reviewer whose positive feedback and comments helped shape the final work.

I would also like to thank the following for permission to use selected text:

From POWER/KNOWLEDGE by Michel Foucault, edited by Colin Gordon, copyright © 1972, 1975, 1976, 1977 by Michel Foucault, Preface and Afterward © by Colin Gordon. Bibliography © by Colin Gordon. This collection © 1980 by the Harvester Press. Used by permission of Pantheon Books, a division of Random House, Inc.

THE SOCIOLOGY OF SPACE © Mark Ritter and David Frisby, 1997, Sage Publications

Henri Lefebvre, THE PRODUCTION OF SPACE, 1991, Blackwell Publishing
Henri Lefebvre, WRITING ON CITIES, 1996, Blackwell Publishing
David Harvey, 1985, THE URBANISATION OF CAPITAL, Blackwell Publishing

Last but not least thanks to Audrey, Rowan and Kasia: you inhabited my family space even if I wasn't always there to share it with you.

one

Karl Marx: the implicit spatiality of historical materialism

As in so much of sociology and the social sciences the obvious place to begin any consideration of social theory is with the contributions of those generally held to be the 'founding fathers' [*sic*] of classical social theory: namely, the works of Karl Marx, Emile Durkheim and Max Weber. However, with regard to a reflection on space and social theory this is not as straightforward as it appears. Whilst Marx, Weber and Durkheim all produced large bodies of work that have been and continue to be the essential foundation for the development of social and sociological theory, and which covers an enormous range of areas, factors, issues and methodologies, their relative silence on the significance of space is, to say the least, remarkable. Whilst time may have been given a relative prominence by all of them,[1] the space of modern capitalism was also transformed distinguishing it from that of previous eras. However, what received less attention was the new structural arrangements of, and in, space, those new forms, organisations and designs demanded by its delineation and functionalisation. It was as much in and through space as in time that industrial capitalism took form, flourished and was perpetuated. Indeed, space, as well as time it may be said, was the canvas against which Marx, Weber and Durkheim formulated their analyses and critical perspectives of capitalism, modernity and society. However, whilst space is an ever-present backdrop in their work, neither Marx, Weber nor Durkheim provided any clear and sustained analytical consideration of the significance of space as an essential element or concept through and upon which their social, political and economic analyses were founded. That is, the consideration, or lack of it, of space and spatial relations in classical social theory is a ghost at the feast of classical theory's considerable contribution to the development of our understanding of contemporary capitalism.

A recurrent theme in the works of Marx, Durkheim and Weber is their attempts to make sense of the new social and physical landscapes of modernity and industrial capitalism. Whilst there are noted differences in their approaches, methodologies, epistemological and ontological perspectives, conceptual devices and explanations as well as in their aims and motivations, there are also well-known similarities. This includes a concern with investigating the consequences – both negative and positive – of the new social, political and economic structures and relations that were becoming apparent as the transition from feudalism to capitalism became more developed in the mid- to late nineteenth century. To describe and analyse what characterises this 'new world' of predominantly urban capitalism, how it differed from what went before, what its institutional arrangements are, what constitutes its social relations, how they are experienced, etc., requires a need to address those features, factors and elements that relate directly to how modern capitalism organises space as well as the spatiality (how they are produced, structured, limited, experienced, etc. in and through space) of such features and relations.

And yet, despite this, modern capitalism is often portrayed in their works as a new epoch, an era distinct from what went before. However, such 'new times'[2] also incurred the radical transformation of the material, physical and social landscape in which and through which the forces, institutions, processes, social forms and divisions etc. that characterise modern capitalism came to be expressed. Such diverse phenomena as the development of the territoriality as well as the functions of the modern nation state; the rapid expansion and importance of towns and cities as the locus for government, art, culture, leisure, education, etc. as well as the site for new forms, modes, means and places of production and consumption; the expansion of the most developed division of labour in industry and in society; the separation of the public and private spheres; the alienation of labour, not only from the product of their labour, their circulation and consumption, but also from nature, etc. all imply a radical transformation of the organisation, conception and use of space.

Although it may be the case that the space of modern capitalism is fundamental for its development and perpetuation, there is an apparent neglect in their works of a detailed consideration of the importance or significance of space as a systematic and developed analysis. This is not to say that there is no spatial element in their analysis only that it is not given the degree of consideration that is accorded to other aspects of the development of modern, urban, industrial capitalism that was for all of them the focus of their analyses. Thus whilst space is implicit it is not explicitly addressed or considered in the detail or depth in which other concepts, forces, elements or factors are addressed.

The aim of this chapter however is somewhat limited. It is not possible here to explore in detail the way in which space and spatial relations are considered, however negligently, in the works of Weber and Durkheim. Durkheim could be said to have recognised that whilst different societies produce different conceptions of space and time there is only a limited reflection of this in regard to his distinctions between mechanical and organic societies (see *The Elementary Forms of Religious Life*). He does deal somewhat cursorarily with aspects of space in his consideration of material and moral densities as characteristics and causal elements in the development and experience of pathological forms in modern society. Weber may be said to have based his analysis of the development of a *Protestant Ethic and the Spirit of Capitalism* in the urban as the dominant spatial arena. Similarly, his consideration of *The City* as an early contribution to urban historical sociology is one that considers various ideal types of the city as having potentially significant spatial and social forms. Likewise, there are elements of space in his understanding of the development of private and public spheres and of the rational organisation and operation of bureaucracies and the modern nation state. However, in both Durkheim and Weber this spatiality is relatively undeveloped and has not been significantly influential in the development of theories of space that will be considered here.

The intention here will be to investigate not the explicit theorising of space and spatial relations as analysed by Marx, but to focus on the implicit spatiality of various relatively familiar aspects and concepts of Marx's historical materialist approach. It will address the importance of space both for the understanding of Marx's social theory and also as a foundation for the development of later, more rigorous, theories of space and social theories of space. It thus serves as a foundation for the subsequent chapters and ensuing analyses. It is a preliminary excavation, an archaeology of the role of space and spatial relations in sociological theory that highlights and reflects the implicit if not explicit spatiality in the theoretical and analytical perspectives developed by Marx. It also reflects the importance of returning to the foundations of social theory to cast a new light or hold up a spatial lens to those insights and conceptions that have formed the basis for much of the development of contemporary attempts at understanding the origins, development, structure, meaning and experience of the modern social world. That is, knowledge of space informs not only our understanding of classical social theory and its subsequent development, but also how and why space and spatial relations are an essential element in foundational analyses of capitalism and modernity, and what they can tell us about the development of subsequent theories of space and spatial theories.

MARX AND SPACE

Marx's analysis of the origins, development, character and consequences of modern capitalism is complex and multifaceted involving a detailed consideration of the processes and changes that differentiated modern capitalism from previous epochs. This analysis was the basis for his claim that, amongst other things, the processes by which capitalism had originated and developed was only a necessary stage to a more just, fair and egalitarian future under communism. Whereas some have argued that developments in society and in social theory in the twentieth century means that we have reached the stage where it is time 'to consign Marx to the dustbin of history', it is clear that whilst capitalism has evolved considerably and in ways that Marx did not envisage it is unarguably still *the* mode of production to which the whole world is increasingly subjected and dominated. Now as before, sociology and social theory remain in need of a 'dialogue with the ghost of Marx' to ensure that our understanding of the organisation of the means of production and the social relations of production under global capitalism recognises the similarities as well as the differences between our 'now' and his 'then' Thus new way of reading Marx – such as that proposed here of an interpretation of the space and spatial relations of Marx's analysis of capitalism – provides a means to reassess and reapply Marx's insights and analysis in the new millennium, particularly in the current paradigm of the globalisation of capitalism.

There is no question that Marx has had a direct and profound influence on the development of more explicit spatial theories and theories of space that are perhaps more familiar contributions to the development of a contemporary social theory of space. However, in returning to the beginning, it is important to illustrate the ways in which Marx conceptualised the characteristics of and transition to capitalism as the modern mode of production. Through this an appreciation of how space may be viewed as an essential conceptual element for understanding not only Marx's analysis of the origins and operation of capitalism originated but also how it has developed, perpetuated and survived.

In Marx's analysis of the mode of production and in the social relations of capitalism, there are a number of concepts in which space and spatial relations are implicitly assumed if not explicitly given a detailed consideration. Thus it is possible to identify space and spatial relations in Marx's analysis of capitalism through an emphasis on the role of space in a number of key areas that inform his overall critique of capitalism. The following are intended as illustrations of a reevaluation of Marx using spatiality as a heuristic device, to aid and enhance our understanding of the continuing importance of Marx's analyses for both the development of social theories of space as well as a more comprehensive understanding of the origins, characteristics and promulgation of capitalism.

SPACE AS A FORCE OF PRODUCTION

Marx's analysis of capitalism as a historically specific mode of production is a central focus of his work as a whole. Much of his analysis in *Capital*, for example, is a detailed exposition of what constitutes the mode of production, how it operates and what consequences there are for its increasing domination over all aspects of life and of our humanity. Marx's analysis of capitalism as a mode of production contends that the economic basis of capitalist society is composed of two interrelated elements. The first is that of the forces of production: what is required to make and do things. The second, the social relations of production relates to the ways in which social forms are organised to achieve those productive ends. The spatiality of the social relations of production will be considered later, but for the present, an understanding of the ownership and subsequent control of the forces of production is required, in that Marx's analysis of class under capitalism is, at least at a simplistic level, predicated on the dichotomy of ownership, or not, of the means of production as a characteristic feature of modern capitalism.

5

Marx's analysis of what constitutes the forces of production as the combination of raw materials, the organisation (or division) of labour, the instruments of labour (buildings, machinery, technology), energy, knowledge, skill and labour that are required for the production of goods and services allows for the inclusion of space. Space is important because if ownership of the means of production and the organisation of the social relations of production constitute the mode of production then who owns space concomitantly has the power to attempt to organise and control what activities can and should occur within it. Cohen makes the point that there is a need to consider the role of space as a force of production and as such as a fundamental element in how capitalism operates.

> Space deserves membership in the set of productive forces. Ownership of space certainly confers a position in the economic structure. Even when a piece of space is contentless, its control may generate economic power, because it can be filled with something productive or because it may need to be traversed by producers. He who owns a hole, even exclusive of its material envelope, is a man to reckon with if you must reach the far side of the hole, and cannot feasibly tunnel beneath it, fly above it, or make your way round it. (Cohen, 1978: 51)

Thus space, its ownership, organisation, control and manipulation become a force in the organisation and operation of capitalism. That space can be conceived or perceived as owned has implications for who has the means, the power, to organise, structure and functionalise the actions and activities that *can* occur within specific delineated and delimited spaces. Thus an initial analysis of Marx's critique and analysis of capitalism requires an acknowledgement of space as a fundamental force in and characteristic feature of the mode of production of society and also how it affects or has a causal relationship to the social relations of that mode of production and of the society that is constituted by it. It is important then at this point to distinguish what Marx means by society to elicit some understanding of the spatiality of capitalist society both for its organisation of the structural conditions of commodity production, circulation and consumption, not only for the social relations of production and the reproduction of labour power, but also for the spatialisation of labour and class.

SPATIALISING MARX'S CONCEPTIONS OF SOCIETY

6

It is possible to identify in Marx's work a number of dimensions of society that are given different emphases in his various writings and that he applies to the analysis of the development of capitalism as distinct from previous modes of production.[3] In these various conceptions there is an innate spatial element. First, society can be understood as a set of relations in which Marx rejects the notion of the idea of an abstract individual and with it the distinction between that of society versus the individual. The starting point for Marx is always with social individuals. Marx rejects any idea of the individual as an isolated, fundamental or singular entity who exists or can be considered independently of social and historical contexts. Individuals are always, everywhere, fundamentally social, but social within the context of the relations of production that structure existence and experience. Thus as Marx puts it:

> In the social production of their existence, men inevitably enter into definite relations, which are independent of their will, namely relations of production appropriate to a given stage in the development of their material forces of production. The totality of these relations of production constitutes the economic structure of society, the real foundation, on which arises a legal and political superstructure and to which correspond definite forms of social consciousness. The mode of production of material life conditions the general process of social, political and intellectual life. It is not the consciousness of men that determines their existence, but their social existence that determines their consciousness. (Marx, 1859, Preface to the *Critique of Political Economy*)

Society as a 'subject' or 'object' is similarly rejected as a reification that cannot exist over and apart from interacting individuals. Society is then for Marx the product of human reciprocal action, but this does not mean that society cannot be experienced as something external to its participants. Thus whilst it is a simplistic truism to say that such reciprocal actions that Marx constitutes as society must take place in space, the various types of actions that can take place are predicated to some extent on the forms of social action that space allows, permits or encourages. That is, the kind of society that is produced by the actions of a relatively dispersed and small population is different qualitatively and quantitatively from that of a dense and relatively highly populated one. Social relations organised on the basis of a predominantly rural agrarian mode of production in which experience and interaction are limited by and through kinship, fealty to an over-lord, the relative paucity of potential social interactions, etc. versus the numerous possible experiences of those living in populous towns and cities constantly surrounded by relative strangers. Knowledge and consciousness of the possibility as well as the experience of reciprocal actions form a basis from which society as the relations between individuals may appear as both external and alien. New communications and transportation technologies that conquer space and time allow not only new possibilities and opportunities for reciprocal actions, but also the kinds of reciprocity made available are increasingly anonymous. As such, society as reciprocity needs an understanding of the possibilities and consequences that that society's space secretes. That is, whether space is more or less experienced and emphasised as a barrier or a limit to reciprocity reflects an understanding of Marx's view of society as a set of relationships that link individuals.

Second, Marx views society as a material intercourse in which some social relations are essential to material life and its continuation. These social relations are definite or specific relations between human beings and nature and between human beings. Such examples would be the need to cooperate or enter into some form of relationship to carry out tasks or activities that require some collective or collaborative labour to ensure that human needs are fulfilled. This reflects Marx's emphasis in historical materialism on the need to consider the historical development of the social relations of production. Under feudalism, for example, the mode of production was based on agricultural production in which limited machinery and technology was employed to till the land and extract sustenance and raw materials. Humanity not only had a closer relationship to nature as the source of life, but also such a relationship at times required that collective endeavours be organised to maximise the potential possibilities that nature could be made to provide. For example, the common herding and grazing of sheep and cattle; the ploughing and harvesting of crops; the organisation of collective security from outside, whether natural or human, threats and dangers, etc. all required some collaborative effort, and also all have an implicit spatial element to understanding their role in the determination of how material social relations are organised and expressed. This underpins not only feudal or traditional societies but also how social relations are expressed in the organisation of the material life of all societies.

Marx's materialist theory thus postulates that any notion or theorising about society has to be understood in terms of the historical and social contexts. In particular they reflect the specific social relations brought about by bourgeois society under the capitalist mode of production. For Marx then such reifications of concepts such as society reflect the real alienation of social relations from the constituent elements and characteristics of bourgeois society. Individuals are irreducibly social and cannot be described or analysed independently of their social and historical context. This would necessarily also include an analysis of the transformation of human nature through labour. Society then for Marx becomes

8

> the product of human reciprocal action. Are men free to choose this or that form of society? By no means. Assume a particular state of development in the productive faculties of man and you will get a particular form of commerce and consumption. Assume particular stages of development in production, commerce and consumption and you will have a corresponding social constitution, a corresponding organisation of the family, of order or of class, in a word a corresponding civil society. Assume a particular civil society and you will get particular political conditions which are only the official expression of civil society. (Marx, Letter of 28 December 1848 in Tucker, 1978, 136–7)

Forms of production, commerce and consumption in different societies and in different times have spatial as well as social characteristics and features in that space are used and experienced in different ways. Society is then for Marx that set of relationships that links individuals, and the fundamental and primary relations are those that compose people's materialistic connections. This aspect of the spatial materialism of industrial capitalism will be considered later in respect of Marx's analysis of production and circulation under capitalism.

Third, Marx sees society as a historical process in which society is not merely a determining object but is itself a changing dynamic entity. It has a history that can appear both timeless (natural and universal) and authorless. However, Marx's analysis seeks to demonstrate the historical specificity and transitory nature of social formations. Society therefore is the product of social relations that are specific to and allied with the specific needs and requirements of each epoch. In these spatial forms are the product of societal needs that may change their function or be destroyed entirely, as social relations require new spatial and structural arrangements that befit new priorities and requirements. This third aspect of Marx's concept of society is related to the previous two in that it considers how production differentiates people from all other species in that how humanity can produce the means of their own existence. But as Marx famously points out only in the specific context in which they find themselves:

> men make their own history, but not of their own free will; not under circumstances they themselves have chosen but under the given and inherited circumstances with which they are confronted. (Marx, The 18th Brumaire (1852) Chapter 1)

As part of the process of making history in contexts not of our own choosing, the way in which space is organised and experienced is a factor in the inherited circumstances that are necessarily confronted. We as social individuals must act within the context by which the mode of production is organised. All those spaces of production, consumption, circulation and reproduction that manifest themselves not only as relations in space but also as spatially delimited forms, opportunities and experiences is part of the spatial as well as the social context. We confront our history through how our social relations and our activities are organised in particular places as well as in particular times. The experience of work is one such example. The social relations and the space of the peasant or artisan under feudalism are different from that of the urban industrial working class under capitalism.

Finally, Marx views society as a mirage. Society is a historical process that does not appear as a mirage to its participants, it appears as a concrete and structured reality. For Marx then the analysis of society requires a critique of common sense conceptions of the social world and a critique of ideology where ideology is not merely generated in forms of (political) domination but also in the mechanisms of capitalist society itself.[4] Thus the forms, structures, possibilities, etc. that develop as manifestations of society (such as the seeming concreteness of national boundaries and concomitant national identities) are also taken for granted and assume spatiality. Similarly, as new demands necessitate the destruction of previous forms and organisations of space (for production, consumption, etc.) so new forms take their place and become accepted. An example of this in Marx's writing refers to the demise of common lands through the various Enclosure Acts and their replacement with landed estates in which ownership is no longer in common, but in the hands of an individual. What was once perceived and understood as a shared or collective interest in land, common and necessary to all, became the preserve of individuals to apportion, delineate, buy and sell according to their own interests, and not necessarily those of the community or society at large. What was once considered, understood and utilised through collective guardianship became the preserve of an individual's will. This 'privatisation' of land provides an example of how the seeming concreteness of society's spatial arrangements and relations in space are also illusions that can be shattered and replaced by new ones.

Marx's conceptualisation of society then raises questions concerning his claims to a revolutionary emancipation from capitalist forms, structures and relations. How can knowledge and understanding of the structure, the reciprocity of human interactions, the social relations and hidden reality of society lead to the means to overthrow the oppressive manifestation of capitalist society. If our actions in space are organised, structured, manipulated and controlled to ensure the perpetuation of the means of production (by the bourgeoisie under industrial capitalism) how does the possibility of its overthrow arise? Does class-consciousness develop through confrontation, conflict and contestation of the meanings, values, norms, ideologies and practices of capitalism that are inscribed in space and experienced in part as spatial forms and arrangements? Social divisions and conflicts take place in and over space as well as being reflected in the spatial divisions of society that both constitute and characterise the mode of production and the reproduction of the relations of production. New spaces, of production, consumption, circulation, etc. that are necessary to allow the expansion and perpetuation of capitalism also provide new opportunities for conflict over the organisation of the social relations of production and over the means by which the reproduction of labour power is organised and provided. Thus the development of an urban industrial self-conscious proletariat was/is possible only through their concentration in space as a requirement of capitalism which in itself provides the means by which such space may be appropriated and returned to collective, social ownership.

This preliminary account of Marx's various dimensions of society provides a brief introduction to the development of a spatial reading of Marx. To distinguish capitalism as a new mode of production and to identify its characteristics allows for a comparative analysis of and exploration of the spatiality of capitalism. To understand the role of space in the social relations of production as well as the means of production of capitalism requires further analysis of the spatiality of other aspects of Marx's analysis.

THE VARIOUS STAGES IN THE DIVISION OF LABOUR: THE TRANSITION FROM FEUDALISM TO CAPITALISM

A key element of Marx's analysis of capitalism as an epoch with a distinct mode of production concerns his consideration of the importance of the division of labour. It is possible to apply a spatial perspective to these various stages. In *The German Ideology* Marx identifies the various stages in the development of the division of labour through different historical periods. He writes of the first stage as *tribal ownership* that is the undeveloped stage of production where people live by hunting, fishing, husbandry and agriculture. The division of labour is rudimentary and is viewed by Marx as an extension of the natural division of labour in the family. The social structure is therefore limited to an extension of the family in that there are patriarchal family chieftains, below which are members of the tribe, with slaves at the bottom, etc. Thus the spatiality of this division of labour is fairly limited by the non-specialisation of tasks, social relations based on kith and kin in an identifiable area of known territoriality based on the home, farmstead, tribal area, etc.

The second stage, that of *Ancient Communal City-States* Marx reasoned, was achieved by the amalgamation of several tribes into a city-state either by agreement or by conquest but which is still accompanied by slavery. The development of private property occurs at this stage but is still secondary to communal ownership. The whole structure of society is based on communal ownership and with it the power of the people. However, as private property evolves, this communal 'power' is prone to diminish in importance. This is also the period that marks the beginning of the transformation of peasants into wageworkers. Whilst the city becomes the central focus or hub of religion, politics, administration, etc. productive land still remains the basis of the mode of production and of power. The spatial orientation of such formations becomes focused on the city but not dependent on it despite the development of wider trade links and a more specialised division of labour.

The third stage, that of *feudalism*, is where nobility dominated the peasants by their possession of landed property. In the towns, small-scale production is carried on by guilds. Thus the chief form of property during the feudal epoch is on the one hand landed property and on the other the labour of the individual who with a small amount of capital can command the labour of other workers. These stages of the division of labour are marked by a gradual increase in the significance of private property and its effect on communal life and the intensification of class conflicts. The spatiality of feudal society was one in which social relations

11

were organised around and through the material needs of survival of that societal structure. The organisation of the relations of production and of reproduction necessitated a closer relationship to nature as the source for survival and of power. As such the spatiality of feudalism was one that was built on farm, estate, county and kingdom and assumed a structured relationship to knowledge and experience of one's place in the world and in heaven. The pyramidal hierarchy, of sovereign, lord, free man and peasant, was not only a reflection of the cosmic order on earth but was also supported by a material base in which the organisation of social relations had an inherently spatial determinism that restricted both physical and social mobility. However, this process of social and historical change is best exemplified by Marx and Engels' account of the transition from feudalism to the fourth form of the division of labour, that of *capitalism*. The essence of which is the dominance of private property in the production process and of society as a whole.

If as Marx contends, society is, in part, the product of human reciprocal action, then the transition from feudalism to modern urban industrial capitalism represents a change in human's relationship not only with each other, but also with nature. The feudal mode of production was one that required a close connection, interaction and relationship with the land and the products of nature. Under feudalism the health, wealth and well-being of individuals and of society was closely related to an intimate knowledge of and interaction with the rhythms and routines of Nature as the source of material sustenance and the raw materials. People lived in small communities bound by intimate connections with each other and with their livestock, their cultivated crops and their pastoral lands that provided their material and social needs. Feudalism as an agrarian-based economic and social system was reflected in the types of organisation, institutional and hierarchical arrangements and also in a relatively undifferentiated division of labour. Any small-scale industrial production and specialist skills that were developed occurred primarily in small workshops under the auspices of the guild system that protected its members' interests. Whilst there were traders and merchants who traversed space to deal in surpluses and luxuries, the majority of the population were peasants who worked the land, and like artisans were intimately connected and dependent on the limited space of their immediate environment.

In his description of primitive accumulation, Marx seeks to uncover the underlying mechanisms of capital social relations whereby the means of production became the private property of one class which 'caused' the increasing 'pauperisation' of the direct producer. This is inextricably related to the development of 'formally free labour' separated from

12

the means of production and constituted as the seller of labour power. This occurs by the expropriation of the agricultural labourer from the land by forcible eviction and enclosure which was followed by the legal transfer of what had been 'communal' feudal land into the hands of private individuals. Marx argues that

> as soon as capitalist production stands on its feet, it not only maintains this separation between the worker and the means of production but reproduces it on a constantly extending scale. The process which creates capitalist relations can be nothing other than the process which divorces workers from the ownership over the conditions of their own labour...It is a process which operates two transformations, whereby the social means of subsistence are turned into capital and the immediate producers are turned into wage labourers. [Thus,] primitive accumulation is nothing else than the historical process of divorcing the producer from the means of production. It appears as primitive because it forms the pre-history of capital and the mode of production corresponding to capitalism. (Marx, *Capital*, vol. 1: 874–5)

For Marx there were two phases in this process both of which have a discernible spatial element to them. The first was the expropriation of the agricultural labourer from the land by foreclosure, eviction and enclosure. One can find numerous references to this phase in Marx's work including a description of the Highland Clearances (Ch. 27, *Capital*, vol. 1) and in his articles for the *New York Daily Tribune* in February 1853 in which land is increasingly viewed as more or less productive space to be apportioned, delimited and functionalised. The second stage of primitive accumulation, formally called by Marx the 'proletarianisation of the feudal peasant class', was marked by the legal transfer of feudal lands into private hands. By the middle of the nineteenth century, this had created the industrial worker, the free labourer of capitalism, free in the sense of being relieved of a direct connection to the land and free to sell their labour on the market to whoever would buy it and for what remuneration could be achieved. This stage of societal development sees sweeping demographic shifts in the population of nations as the push factor of enclosure forced agricultural labour to migrate to towns and cities, whilst simultaneously being pulled by the prospect of work in new and expanding industries. E. P. Thompson in his *Making of the English Working Class* (1963) elegantly provides a detailed and illuminating description of this process of the transition from a predominantly rural and agrarian-based society to one organised through the private ownership of the means of production, of land and the concomitant development of a labour market. Whilst this process, as Thompson argues, was not without resistance and conflict, and was formative for the development of working-class consciousness, the

13

transition from feudalism to industrial capitalism was in part concerned with the creation of new spaces of production (factories, mills, etc.) as well as the transformation of social relationships and the division of labour.

In this context of those forces and processes of social transformation that characterise the transition from one mode of production and epoch to another, the increasing complexity of the division of labour figures prominently. There is in this an inherent spatial as well as social understanding of the historical development of the division of labour and the organisation of the means of production. Marx identifies the division between town and country, the rural and the urban as a key element or factor fundamental for the development of the division of labour as characterised under capitalism. This is emphasised in *The German Ideology* where Marx argues that the

> greatest division of material and mental labour is the separation of town and country. The antagonism between town and country begins with the transition from barbarism to civilisation, from tribe to State, from locality to nation, and run through the whole history of civilisation to the present day...The existence of the town implies, at the same time, the necessity of administration, police, taxes, etc.: in short, of the municipality, and thus of politics in general. Here first became manifest the division of the population into two great classes, which is directly based on the division of labour and on instruments of production. The town is already in actual fact the concentration of the population, of the instruments of production, of capital, of pleasures, of needs, while the country demonstrates just the opposite fact, isolation and separation. The antagonism between town and country can only exist within the framework of private property...It is the most crass expression of the subjection of the individual under the division of labour, under a definite activity forced upon him – a subjection which makes one man into restricted town-animal, the other into a restricted country-animal, and daily creates anew the conflict between their interests. Labour is here again the chief thing, power over individuals, and as long as the latter exists, private property must exist. The abolition of the antagonism between town and country is one of the first conditions of communal life, a condition which again depends on a mass of material premises and which cannot be fulfilled by the mere will, as anyone can see at the first glance...The separation of town and country can also be understood as the separation of capital and landed property, as the beginning of the existence and development of capital independent of landed property – the beginning of property having its basis only in labour and exchange. (Marx, *The German Ideology*, 1964: 64–5)

Similarly, Marx makes the same point in *Capital*:

> The foundation of every division of labour which has attained a certain degree of development, and has been brought about by the exchange of commodities, is the separation of town from country. (Marx, *Capital*, vol. 1, 1976: 472)

14

For Marx the historical development of the division of labour can be understood at a spatial level in that there is not only a concentration of populations forming larger tribes/nations/societies that both inhabit and control larger areas of land, but also an increasing concentration of populations in towns and cities. Thus his identification of the separation of town and country as a fundamental division of labour reflects an implicit awareness of space as a key element in understanding the development of capitalism. With the transition to industrial capitalism, humanity became and still is increasingly and predominantly concentrated in towns and cities and the urban became the key site for the mode of production of capitalism. The concentration of labour, of the means and mode of production, circulation and consumption made the urban the new and predominant spatial form. The urban became the hub in which, through which and from which modern capitalism originated and was perpetuated. The urban became the central point at which were concentrated the means and forces of production and from which was disseminated the products of production, as well as being the centre of government, learning, the arts, finance and commerce. The reliance on land as the basis for material wealth as existed under feudalism shifted to the urban as the locus for wealth generation. This separation of town and country creates a new spatial orientation for society and which transforms not only social relations of production and reproduction but also its spatial organisation.

15

The city as *the* spatial form of capitalism required its structural transformation from the old medieval towns and city structures of narrow streets centred on the church or cathedral. Thus urban capitalism required not only a new and expanded spatial form but also demanded new spaces, for production, for consumption, for the circulation and communication of commodities, services and knowledge. It also needed to create an infrastructure, however rudimentary to ensure that the reproduction of a healthy and able, available and malleable workforce could be accommodated. What was required of the city was a need to accommodate not only the rapid growth in population, but also its consolidation status as the locus for production, consumption as well as the social relations of production.

This is a process that can still be witnessed in the developing world today. As developing nations play 'catch-up' with the Western model of free market neoliberal economics there is a movement away from agriculture-based production and labour to the concentration of populations and economic activities in the urban with the concomitant rise of the urban poor. What Marx describes in the nineteenth century as the development of a more detailed division of labour in society has a spatial context that remains pertinent in contemporary analyses of population movements and international migration trends.

THE SPATIALITY OF THE DETAILED DIVISION OF LABOUR

Marx's complex analysis of the origins of capitalism includes an understanding of fundamental changes in the mode of production in which the consequences of the organisation of the means of production not only creates new social relations of production, but also necessarily generates the destruction of all opposing tendencies or practices that oppose or inhibit its development and perpetuation. Thus in *The Communist Manifesto* he writes of the constant revolutionising of the means of production by the bourgeoisie as changing forever the nature and experience of humanity:

> All fixed, fast-frozen relations, with their train of ancient and venerable prejudices and opinions are swept away, all new-formed ones become antiquate, before they can ossify. All that is solid melts into air, all that is holy is profaned, and man is at last compelled to face with sober sense his real conditions of life and his relations with his kind. (Marx and Engels, *The Communist Party Manifesto*, 1848/1971: 39)

16

In this Marx views the separation of town and country as a key and fundamental division of labour that becomes expressed in and characteristic of modern capitalism. It is in the urban that those new spaces of production, reproduction and consumption came to be concentrated. The re-fashioning, the re-making and re-design of the space of towns and cities and their inevitable expansion into new social forms and relations in urban space required that existing and traditional social relations had to be swept away as well as the spaces and places in which they occurred.

It is possible to identify in Marx's writings two general forms of the division of labour. First, Marx is concerned with the division of labour in society. Whilst this is commonly acknowledged as being concerned with the organisation of exchange on the basis of open free competition it is also related to the number and density of population. This has an obvious spatiality in that size and density are concerned with identifying and calculating numbers within given and recognisable areas, whether that be national populations or those of towns, cities, regions, nations, etc. The second form is the division of labour in manufacture. This refers to production and the greater control of the labour force and labour process as employed wage labour. Marx states that the two are inter-related and there cannot be a division of labour in manufacture without first a division of labour in society. As Marx writes:

> Just as a certain number of simultaneously employed workers is the material pre-condition for the division of labour within manufacture, so the number and density of the population, which here corresponds to the collection of workers together in one workshop, is a pre-condition for the division of labour in society...Since the production and the circulation of commodities are the general prerequisites of the capitalist mode of production, division of labour in manufacture requires that a division of labour within society should have already attained a certain degree of development. Inversely, the division of labour in manufacture reacts back upon that in society, developing and multiplying it further. (Marx, *Capital*, vol. 1, 1867/1976: 473)

It is possible to further distinguish in Marx's writings different types of the division of labour. These include the division of labour in general (e.g. agriculture/industry); in particular (branches of trade); in detail (division of labour in the workshop) and the division of social labour or the separation of capitals (industrial, commercial, financial, etc.). Marx writes that the

> division of labour within a nation brings about, in the first place, the separation of industrial and commercial from agricultural labour, and hence the separation of town and country and the opposition of their interests. Its further development leads to the separation of commercial from industrial labour. At the same time, through the division of labour, various new groups are developed, within these various branches, among the individuals cooperating in distinct kinds of work. The relative position of these groups is determined by the methods employed in agriculture, industry and commerce (patriarchialism, slavery, estates, classes). (Marx, *The German Ideology*, 1846/1964: 11)

It is clear that Marx recognises that groups are separated into different occupations, interests and types of activity. It is not a hypothetical, a theoretical or an administrative separation but one that can be understood to occur or be realised in space as well as in the organisation of those social relations necessary for production and exchange to occur. What is possible is the identification of such labour in the space of modern nation states, as well as particularly in the urban as the locus for the new mode of production of capitalism. Thus, the developing urban landscape became one in which different areas are given over to different economic or social functions, for example areas of commerce, finance, industry, transportation, etc. There is in both these general forms (of the division of labour in society and industry) an implied spatial as well as social division of labour. To investigate this spatiality it is necessary to explore a little further the meanings of both the general forms that Marx identified.

17

the division of labour in society

In *The German Ideology* Marx considers the origins of the division of labour as based on a quasi-natural and spontaneous development of an understanding of human consciousness as a social product in which in the beginning of self-consciousness, there was only a limited awareness of Nature, the environment and of other individuals. This he termed an 'animal-like' awareness of living in society that was merely a *'herd-consciousness'*.[5] As the division of labour appears and becomes more complex, the separation of specific activities and spheres leads to the development of, amongst other things, a hierarchy of specialisation of the means of existence that increasingly divorces people from their potentials and from nature. As Marx puts it

> as soon as the division of labour begins, each man has a particular, exclusive sphere of activity, which is forced upon him and from which he cannot escape. He is a hunter, a fisherman, a shepherd, or a critical critic, and must remain so if he does not want to lose his means of livelihood; whereas in communist society, where nobody has one exclusive sphere of activity but each can become accomplished in any branch he wishes, production as a whole is regulated by society, thus making it possible for me to do one thing today and another tomorrow, to hunt in the morning, fish in the afternoon, rear cattle in the evening, criticise after dinner, in accordance with my inclination, without ever becoming a hunter, fisherman, shepherd or critic. (Marx, *The German Ideology*, 1846/1964: 22)

This then is the point in history when some become predominantly workers, farmers, hunters, shepherds and the like, and others become predominantly rulers, priests and overseers. Marx argues that the division of labour in capitalist society not only becomes associated with the specialisation of particular kinds of labour, but also that that labour is necessarily tied to particular places and spaces. Under communism such de-humanising limitations will no longer exist. In *Capital*, Marx goes further in analysing the particularities of the division of labour as consequently and fundamentally associated with those spaces that tie the worker to their labour. The division of labour then into 'particular and exclusive spheres of activity' results in the bondage of labour to those particular spaces in which such labour takes place. Whilst some spheres of activity may provide more 'freedom of movement' others are more explicitly tied to locations and spaces where labour must occur. As we shall see later this is ever more the case with the development of the factory system of mass manufacture. This increasing division and specialisation of labour is also connected to the rise of towns and the division of the population into town-dwellers and country dwellers.

18

Marx views the division of labour in society arising as part of a complex that includes private property, exchange and class divisions, so that to speak of an individual doing only one kind of work is already to assume a society where people's activity and their products are not their own.[6] It is for Marx the end of primitive communism and of a clan-dominated society. Marx also considers the division of labour in society as general social labour which like the workshop is increasingly organised and, it may be argued, controlled in space.

> Society as a whole, like a workshop, has its division of labour. If the division of labour within a modern workshop were taken as a model to be applied to a whole society, the society best organised for the production of wealth would, without question, be that which has only a single entrepreneur in charge, apportioning the work to the various members of the community in accordance with a predetermined rule. But things are not at all like this. Whereas, in a modern workshop, the division of labour is regulated in detail by the authority of the entrepreneur, modern society has no other rule, and no other authority for apportioning work, than free competition. (Marx, *The Poverty of Philosophy*, 1847: 198)

In his analysis of the division of labour in society, Marx is alerting us not only to the development of specialist labour that requires increasing concentration into those areas of production which create the best and most efficient means for extracting surplus value from labour (the concentration of labour increasingly in towns and cities, the separation of spheres of activity, of labour, of capital, etc.), but also that such labour is forced to compete in the labour market that increasingly organises the spaces and times of industrial production. Thus as a concomitant of the division of labour, as the apportioning of tasks and work, labour is increasingly forced to move to find work, whilst at the same time, there is an increasing restriction on both movement in, to and from work spaces and in the organisation of those spaces of work.

19

the division of labour in industry

In Marx's analysis of the development of capitalism as a mode of production, he identifies how social relations are changed, affected and manipulated in space as well as more popularly acknowledged, in time. In *Capital* and elsewhere he describes in detail the development of the factory system of large-scale industry, the extraction of surplus value as well as the fundamental description of the rise and rise of the commodity, its fetishisation and its role in the concomitant alienation of labour. In this the understanding of the role of time, its manipulation, its codification and use in measuring and valuing labour power, its standardisation and the conquest of traditional ways of producing is well known. However, what is less acknowledged or given as much consideration are the spaces of this new mode of production. Marx spent a considerable time focusing on the development of industrial manufacturing and the creation of the factory system as the centre of capitalist production. For Marx the impact of industrial manufacturing on the worker takes place along three broad planes of activity and change. Each involves substantial shifts in the way labour was carried out and can be discussed under three broad categories: (i) cooperation and large-scale industry, (ii) division of labour and manufacture and (iii) machinery and large-scale industry. In each of these, the organisation and control of activities in space as well as space itself are important factors in how they operate under industrial capitalism.

cooperation and large scale industry

The starting place for the division of labour in large-scale industry was for Marx the assembly of large number of workers in factories brought together for the purposes of production. This presupposes the decline of the trade guilds that had restricted the unification of crafts and trades under one roof. Capitalist production therefore unifies many workers and many trades under the command of one capitalist in one place that has consequences for the organisation of the relations of production. According to Marx, the process of the division of labour which developed throughout the period of the nineteenth century with the progress of manufacturing and industry led to a 'particular sort of co-operation' which he named complex co-operation. The distinction between simple and complex co-operation is based on the difference between an individual worker or craftsman making the entire commodity from beginning to end or when each individual performs operations which are disconnected and separated from one another and carried out side-by-side. Each operation is assigned a craftsman and the commodity is produced by the combined action of a number of co-operators, but no individual produces the commodity in its entirety.[7] Thus the commodity has gone from being the product of the individual craftsman to being the social product of the union of craftsmen, each of whom performs only one operation.[8] What Marx is describing is the development of a highly functionalised and socially divisive division of labour that becomes evident and most expressed in the division of labour in manufacture and which has a spatial element as well as a social one. As well as concentrating labour in one place (the spaces of industry) the restriction of movement, of being tied to a single work station/area/place in large-scale factory production is in part about fixing the worker in the space organised for their labour by someone else for someone else. The individual worker then becomes one small cog in an industrial process that requires their labour to be fixed in space as well as time to ensure that co-operation occurs.

division of labour and manufacture

For Marx then the specialisation of tasks of industrial workers becomes set and regulated by individual capitalists in the organised space of the factory.

> The division of labour within manufacture presupposes a concentration of the means of production in the hands of one capitalist; the division of labour within society presupposes a dispersal of those means among many independent producers of commodities. (*Capital*, vol. 1: 477)

Marx identifies that the specialised worker in manufacture no longer produces commodities as an individual skilled worker. They are involved in partial and specialised tasks and functions that contribute to the production of the whole commodity which in turns 'belongs' to the capitalist. In manufacture it is only the common product of all the specialised workers that become a commodity. In this specialisation of tasks what develops is the organisation of production into separate but co-ordinated and inter-related areas of production. Separate production units are constituted and organised in which the production of individual elements of the whole commodity takes place. Thus the worker no longer organises and plans their own labour and the control of the processes of production is in the hands of the capitalist.

21

> In manufacture, as well as in simple co-operation, the collective working organism is a form of existence of capital. The social mechanism of production, which is made up of numerous individual specialised workers, belongs to the capitalist. Hence, the productive power which results from the combination of various kinds of labour appears as the productive power of capital. Manufacture proper not only subjects the previously independent worker to the discipline and command of capital, but creates in addition a hierarchical structure amongst the workers themselves. (*Capital*, vol. 1: 481)

This command and control aspect of capitalism subjects the worker not only to time-discipline but to the discipline of the spaces of production. Whilst under the capitalist or their managers' control the worker must ensure that they obey the rules of production. The worker must remain at their post for the duration of their shift and only some workers have the privilege of moving between different production zones. The hierarchy of limited freedom of movement ensures that knowledge of the entirety of the production process remains with the very few and trusted. The process of manufacture in which all the means of production including labour and raw materials become concentrated and organised in space requires an overarching control and understanding of the co-ordination and inter-relation of multiple operations and activities. What eventually results is the organised workplace of conveyor-belt and assembly-line production. It also has relevance for understanding the organisation of labour in new workplaces such as call-centres and in the organisation of spaces of consumption such as shopping centres and supermarkets. Thus space, knowledge and power are inter-connected in the operation of division of labour in manufacture and in consumption.

machinery and large-scale industry

As a result of new technological innovation, machine production increasingly dominates the work place in large-scale industry. For Marx, this results in workers becoming de-skilled in that they are reduced to the role of being machine minders or to put it in Marx's terminology: living labour (the worker) is confronted by dead labour (machines). As a consequence of the invention and application of machinery in the factory, the worker is not only increasingly alienated from the product of their labour but also from the process of labour. Thus Marx talks of the 'factory system' as a production centre in which machinery, raw materials and labour are brought together to extract the maximum surplus value from the processes of commodity production. Thus production is concentrated in a space which is increasingly organised, functionalised and delimited by the needs of capital to ensure the most efficient operation of machine production at the expense of the needs of the worker. Marx describes how such operations are organised in the factory.

> In so far as the division of labour re-appears in the factory, it takes the form primarily of a distribution of workers among the specialised machines, and of quantities of workers, who do not however form organised groups, among the various departments of the factory, in each of which they work at a number of machines placed together; only simple cooperation therefore takes place between them... The essential division is that between workers who are actually employed on the machines (among whom are included a few who look after the engine) and those who merely attend them (almost exclusively children). More or less all the 'feeders' who supply the machines with the material which is to be worked up are counted as attendants. In addition to these two principal classes, there is a numerically unimportant group whose occupation it is to look

22

after the whole of the machinery and repair it from time to time, composed of engineers, mechanics, joiners etc. This is a superior class of workers, in part scientifically educated, in part trained in handicraft, they stand outside the realm of the factory workers, and are added to them only to make up an aggregate. (Marx, *Capital*, vol. 1: 546)

Most workers then are fixed in space by having to attend to or mind the machines whilst others are required to move around the factory to repair them to ensure the efficient operation of independent but inter-related processes and activities. The factory then is an organised space of production in which machinery is prioritised over labour and yet where labour is increasingly concentrated and fixed in space and forced to suffer the consequences. These consequences are described by Marx and refer explicitly to his understanding of space as a necessity of life which is undermined or assaulted by the conditions of labour in the factory. As Marx puts it:

Here we shall merely allude to the material conditions under which factory labour is performed. Every sense organ is injured by the artificially high temperatures, by the dust-laden atmosphere, by the deafening noise, not to mention the danger to life and limb among machines which are so closely crowded together, a danger which, with the regularity of the seasons, produces its list of those killed and wounded in the industrial battle. The economical use of the social means of production, matured and forced as in a hothouse by the factory system, is turned in the hands of capital into systematic robbery of what is necessary for the life of the worker, i.e. space, light, air and protection against the dangers of the unhealthy concomitants of the production process, not to mention the theft of appliances for the comfort of the worker. Was Fourier wrong when he called factories 'mitigated jails'? (*Capital*, vol. 1: 553)

This allusion to factories as prisons is one in which not only is liberty denied but also space as a necessity of life. It also reflects aspects of Marx's analysis of the alienation of labour from the products of their labour as well as the labour process in that the workplace is the arena through and in which alienation becomes enacted and experienced as a consequence of methods of production. Space is, according to Marx, a necessity of life that can be measured, quantified and apportioned,[9] albeit in an increasingly controlled and instrumental way by the needs of capital. The factory system then is a spatial system that concentrates activities, labour, processes, etc. and which organises such activities and processes in an enforced complex co-operation that necessarily requires that space is increasingly organised in such a way that it is stolen from the worker as a necessity of life. The negative consequences of the production process for the spatial needs of labour in the workplace is, as we shall see in the following section, mirrored in the organisation and

23

experience of the city and the urban as the space for the reproduction of labour power.

THE SPACE OF THE REPRODUCTION OF LABOUR

Whilst Marx analyses how capitalism extracts surplus value from labour and leads to a division of labour in industry and manufacture that creates new spaces of production, there is also a spatial element in the organisation of the reproduction of the social relations of society. As class relations come to the fore and are fundamental to Marx's critique of capitalism, it is possible to identify a socio-spatial analysis of the distribution of classes in society, particularly the new urban society of the nineteenth century. Marx in *Capital* refers specifically to Engels' famous study of *The Condition of the Working Class* to indicate the consequences of industrialisation and urbanisation for the living conditions of the working class. What is evident in Engels' study, and echoed by other commentators on the 'problem of cities' in the nineteenth century, is a description of the socio-spatial division of modern, urban, industrial society. The following quote provides an indication of this socio-spatial division of the urban and also reminds us of Marx's persistent warning to look for the hidden truth behind the surface or façade that is all too often taken for granted. Engels gives us a potent description of how that façade is experienced and structured into the built environment of the urban landscape. It is instructive in providing an understanding of the way in which space is increasingly understood and organised to reflect and perpetuate class divisions and is fundamental for understanding the consequences of capitalism. Engels describes Manchester as

24

peculiarly built, so that a person may live in it for years and go in and out daily without coming into contact with a working-people's quarter or even with workers, that is, so long as he confines himself to his business or to pleasure walks. This arises chiefly from the fact, that by unconscious tacit agreement, as well as with out-spoken conscious determination, the working people's quarters are sharply separated from the sections of the city reserved for the middle class; or if this does not succeed, they are concealed with the cloak of charity. Manchester contains, at its heart, a rather extended commercial district, perhaps half a mile long and about as broad, and consisting almost wholly of offices and warehouses. Nearly the whole district is abandoned by dwellers, and is lonely and deserted at night; only watchmen and policemen traverse its narrow lanes with their dark lanterns. This district is cut through by certain main thoroughfares upon which the vast traffic concentrates, and in which the ground level is lined with brilliant shops. In these streets the upper floors are occupied, here and there, and there is a good deal of life upon them until late at night. (Engels, 1882/1986: 79)

What Engels describes here is the structuring of space to reflect not only its role in particular functions (finance, commerce, production, residential, etc.) that require its de facto zoning, but also an associated aestheticisation that encourages the socio-spatial divisions to be exercised and accommodated in the spatial organisation of the classes. Thus segregation is not only enacted in space, but it is partitioned to ensure that it does not offend the eye. What is also interesting in Engels' account is how the temporal rhythms of night and day reflect not only the organisation of activities in the space of the commercial district, but also its relative abandonment. This is a feature noted in many contemporary cities in which after office hours the 'business' of town and city centres is that of pleasure and the pursuit of excess. In addition, Engels identifies how the socio-spatial segregation of the classes is effected through the organisation and structuring of residential neighbourhoods and the production of networks of streets and thoroughfares to accommodate the circulation of the moneyed classes so that they can efficiently move through the city without having to address the living conditions of the working classes. As Engels writes:

25

With the exception of this commercial district, all Manchester proper, all Salford and Hulme, a great part of Pendleton and Chorlton, two thirds of Cheetham Hill and Broughton are all unmixed working-peoples quarters, stretching like a girdle, averaging a mile and a half in breadth, around the commercial district. Outside, beyond this girdle, lives the upper and middle bourgeoisie, the middle bourgeoisie in regularly laid out streets in the vicinity of the corking quarters, especially in Chorlton and the lower lying portions of Cheetham Hill; the upper bourgeoisie in remoter villas with gardens in Chorlton and Alnwick, or on the breezy heights of Chetham Hill, Broughton and Pendleton, in free, wholesome country air, in fine, comfortable homes, passed once every half or quarter hour by omnibuses going into the city. And the finest part of the arrangement is this, that the members of this money aristocracy can take the shortest road through the middle of all the labouring districts to their places of business, without ever seeing that they are in the midst of the grimy misery that lurks to the right and the left. For the thoroughfares leading from the Exchange in all directions out of the city are lined, on both sides, with an almost unbroken series of shops, and are so kept in the hands of the middle and lower bourgeoisie, which out of self-interest cares for the decent and cleanly, external appearance and can care for it. True these shops bear some relation to the district behind them, and are more elegant in the commercial and residential quarters than when they hide grimy working working-mens quarters; but they suffice to conceal from the eyes of the wealthy men and women of strong stomachs and weal nerves the misery and grime which form the complement of their wealth. (Engels, 1882/1986: 80)

What Engels describes then is the 'sorting out' or structuring of the urban environment, the development of a hierarchy of preferred locations associated with class. This then forms the basis for a rudimentary marketisation of urban land as real estate in that some locations/areas are associated with higher monetary values because of their use and delimitation as markers of social status as well as land valued for its functional utility (for commerce, industry, transport, etc.). Thus the reproduction of the social relations of capitalism involves not only the design and organisation of urban spaces of production such as factories and workshops but also the spatial organisation and differentiation of the space of the city. What Engels describes, and which is mirrored in many accounts of the nineteenth-century city, is how the social distancing of the classes was effected in the residential patterns and inhabitations. Thus new bourgeois suburbs were created as a means, for some, to escape the increasing squalor, pollution and deprivation found in the central areas. Other investments in urban infrastructure such as public parks provided not only spaces for rational recreation but also such delineated green-space-afforded views that impacted on the value of adjacent properties. Eventually, the inevitable pressure of such potentially revolutionary conditions would lead to the wholesale redesign and rebuilding of most cities in an attempt to ameliorate the worst consequences of rapid industrialisation and urbanisation. However, the advent of planned zoning of different areas of the city organised by function merely reflects the aspects of socio-spatial segregation identified by Engels in Manchester and which is extant in the twenty-first century. One can see this clearly in the peripheral housing schemes, high-rise flats and owner-occupied suburban estates that feature in most towns and cities, as well as inner-city gentrification and town house refurbishment.

SPACE AND CIRCULATION

A further spatial element in Marx's analysis of capitalism is that of the circulation of commodities. For Marx, commodities under capitalist production take on a fetishised form as exchange value comes to dominate or sublimate use value. Relations between commodities appear to take on the appearance of relations between people as they enter into a world of exchange and circulation. The production of commodities for exchange requires not only a means for their display and sale but also an infrastructure that ensures their movement: circulation from centres of production to centres of exchange and consumption. At the root of Marx's analysis of the commodity as the 'cell form of capitalism' is the assumption of the requirement of their movement through space. Thus the spatial organisation of production and consumption requires mastery over space to ensure the most efficient organisation of production and consumption. Hence the movement and concentration of labour in the factory, the movement of raw materials, the distribution of commodities produced, etc. requires that space is conquered, fashioned and made to ensure the most efficient extraction of surplus value from their exchange. The need to minimise circulation costs promotes the concentration of production within a few large urban centres which become, in effect, the workshops of capitalist production. Therefore the concentration of the 'rational' location of all activities associated with the production of particular commodities minimises the costs of movement (of labour, of materials, of commodities, etc.) Marx is then aware of how space is a fundamental factor in the development of capitalism as the creation of commodities for exchange. He writes:

> The more production comes to rest on exchange value, hence on exchange, the more important do the physical conditions of exchange – the means of communication and transport – become for the costs of circulation. Capital by its nature drives beyond every spatial barrier. Thus the creation of the physical conditions of exchange – of the means of communication and transport – the annihilation of space by time – becomes an extraordinary necessity for it...Thus, while capital must on the one side strive to tear down every spatial barrier to intercourse, i.e. to exchange, and conquer the whole earth for its market, it strives on the other side to annihilate this space with time, i.e. to reduce to a minimum the time spent in motion from one place to another. The more developed the capital, therefore, the more extensive the market over which it circulates, which forms the spatial orbit of its circulation, the more does it strive simultaneously for an ever greater extension of the market and for the greater annihilation of space by time...There appears here the universalising tendency of capital, which distinguishes it from all previous stage of production. (Marx, *The Grundrisse*, 1973: 539–40)

What is required then is the creation of physical landscapes and transportation techniques that ensure the most efficient means of overcoming the barriers that space creates to the production and circulation of commodities. Thus as Marx identifies, capital comes to invest in the creation of built environment of the towns and cities to ensure that the production and circulation of commodities can be most efficiently expedited. This provides a partial analysis for the development of particular forms and patterns of arrangement of the industrial cities of the nineteenth century that Marx was concerned with. The creation of built environments in the service of capitalism then means, according to Marx,

> a growth of that portion of social wealth which, instead of serving as direct means of production, is invested in means of transportation and communication and in the fixed and circulating capital required for their operation. (*Capital*, vol. 2: 251)

27

However, there is the apparent contradiction that whilst capital creates the space it requires for accumulation these very same spaces may in the future serve as barriers to further expansion. That is, concentration in space of the means of production necessitated the creation of particular spatial structures and arrangements as centres of production and as circulation nodes that may, with the development of new technologies, products, markets, etc. serve as a barrier to further capital expansion. This provides some explanation for the periodic redevelopment and regeneration of the urban to meet the changing needs and requirements of capital. For Marx circulation is an essential element of the capitalism as a mode of production. It necessitates the creation of forms and structures of and in space, as cities, as factories, as roads, railways, canals, etc. to facilitate the production, circulation and consumption of commodities. This requirement to overcome space and to mould or shape it to serve the needs of capital is a feature of Marx's analysis that is developed and expanded by later theorists (see Lefebvre, Harvey, Massey, etc.) and reflects an important element in many analyses of globalisation.

CAPITALISM AS A WORLD SYSTEM

28   Marx's analysis of the development of capitalism as a world system, a world market is the final feature of spatiality to be addressed here. Marx viewed capitalism as a necessarily expansionary mode of production in which space as distance and as a barrier to development had to be overcome to establish both new markets for commodities and as sources of raw material and labour. Marx in *the Communist Party Manifesto* writes that

> Modern industry has established the world market, for which the discovery of America paved the way. This market has given an immense development to commerce, to navigation, to communication by land... The need of a constantly expanding market for its products chases the bourgeoisie over the whole surface of the globe. It must nestle everywhere, settle everywhere, establish connections everywhere. (Marx and Engels, *Communist Party Manifesto*)

The development of capitalism then as a world market as a global sphere for the extraction of raw materials, for labour and for commodity production and exchange required that new means and methods of communication and transportation be developed to overcome the spatial barrier of distances on a grand scale. As Marx writes:

> The transformation of the mode of production in one sphere of industry necessitates a similar transformation in other spheres... the revolution in the

modes of production of industry and agriculture made necessary a revolution in the general conditions of production, i.e. in the means of communication and transport. In a society whose pivot...was small scale agriculture, with its subsidiary domestic industries and urban handicrafts, the means of communication and transport were so utterly inadequate to the needs of production in the period of manufacture, with its extended division of social labour, its concentration of instruments of labour and workers and its colonial markets, that they in fact became revolutionised...the means of communication gradually adapted themselves to the mode of production of large scale industry by means of a system of river steamers, railways, ocean steamers and telegraphs. (Marx, *Capital*, vol. 1: 506–7)

Thus what Marx describes is the need for a means in which the conquest of space, the distances between sites of the extraction of raw materials, of sites of industry, of production, of markets, of sites of consumption, etc. not becoming a burden or brake on the expansion of large-scale industry. Thus, for the perpetuation and expansion of the mode of production under capitalism there required the revolutionising not only of the spaces of production of the factory system but also a need to overcome the limits previously imposed by distance. Thus in the processes involved in the production of commodities there also required the development and application of new technologies for the conquest of space. In this then how space is understood and put to use as well as how it can be overcome to link markets, consumers, producers, etc. spawned not only new industries and occupations (the transport industry) but also new conceptions of the world as a less inhibiting geographical obstacle to economic growth.

Marx's analysis of imperialism in India discusses amongst other things the effect of British rule as the application of science and technology that disrupts the native traditional union of agriculture and manufacturing industry and with it the village system that supported it. In this Marx is clear that imperialism is primarily concerned with the expansion and imposition of capitalism to those colonies brought under the sway of the world market:

England had to fulfil a double mission in India: one destructive the other regenerating – the annihilation of old Asiatic society and the laying of the material foundations of Western society in Asia...They destroyed it by breaking up the native communities, by uprooting the native industry, and by levelling all that was great and elevated in native society...The political unity of India was the first condition of its regeneration. That unity imposed by the British sword, will now be strengthened and perpetuated by the electric telegraph...Steam has brought India into regular and rapid communication with Europe, has connected its chief ports with those of the whole south-eastern ocean, and has re-vindicated it from the isolated position which was the prime law of its stagnation. The day is not far distant when, by a combination of railways and steam vessels, the distance between England and India will be shortened to eight days, and when that once fabulous country will thus be actually annexed to the Western world. (Marx, 1853)

It is clear that the application of new communications technologies opened the globe to expansion by what Marx in relation to India calls the 'English millocracy'. Science and technology was to revolutionise the means and mode of production of colonised peoples to ensure the expansion of capitalism. Marx's paradigm of capitalist production then is one that fundamentally recognises space as an element to be overcome or conquered if capitalism is to survive and expand into all spheres of activity and into all corners of the globe. Whilst political and military subjection was a prime means by which this was to be achieved, imperialism was concerned primarily with the expansion of capitalist means and methods. Engels provides a description of the process of the expansion of the modern industry and the world market that has a remarkable prescience of many contemporary descriptions of neo-liberal globalisation.

> The great geographical discoveries and the colonisation following upon them
> multiplied markets and quickened the transformation of handicraft into
> manufacture. The war did not simply break out between the individual
> producers of particular localities. The local struggles begot in their turn national
> conflicts, the commercial wars of the seventeenth and eighteenth centuries.
> Finally, modern industry and the opening up of the world market made the
> struggle universal, and at the same time gave it an unheard of virulence.
> Advantages in natural or scientific conditions of production now decide the
> existence or non-existence of individual capitalists, as well as whole industries
> and countries. He that fails is remorselessly cast aside. (Engels, Utopian and
> Scientific in Tucker, 1978: 706)

30

CONCLUSION

What this chapter has sought to provide is an all too brief overview of the spatiality inherent in Marx's analysis of capitalism. Whilst there is evidence of Marx's awareness of the spatial dimensions of capitalism as a new mode of production it is relatively undeveloped and lacking in the detailed consideration and description that was applied to other factors, forces, elements processes, etc. in his analysis of the origins, development and experience of capitalism. Thus he acknowledges that capitalism required the creation and organisation of new spatial structures and forms for the production, circulation and consumption of commodities, and the consequences this had for the organisation of space for the division of labour in the workplace and for the spaces of reproduction in which labour was forced to live he provides only a limited description and analysis. He does not address or analyse space directly. Similarly, Marx recognises capitalism as developing a world market in which spatial limits needs must be overcome. In this, then what is provided is the basis for the development of more sophisticated and detailed critiques of the space of capitalism and the way in which space has been a fundamental factor for its expansion and perpetuation.

NOTES

1 Indeed it is clear that time is given a particular emphasis by all of these early and influential theorists not only by its increasing codification and standardisation but also by the way in which it is fundamentally implicated in the transformation of the social relations of production and consumption, and of the experience of life in modern, predominantly urban, capitalism. Marx pays particular attention to the way in which time is organised and structured in the factory system and used to analyse the way in which surplus value is extracted (see for example Marx's comments on 'socially necessary labour time'). Weber also emphasises that in the development of an ethical orientation to the world in which the best usage of time in all matters of business, personal and spiritual affairs is paramount. Durkheim in his consideration of the consequences of the social concentration of new social and structural arrangements that resulted from the transition from mechanical to organic society alludes to the effects of time in the division of labour.

2 Classical theory may be said to have been preoccupied with historical or temporal transformations. Marx was concerned with explaining the transition to a capitalist socio-economic formation and by extension to a potentially more equitable communistic one; Durkheim sought to explore and detail the transition from a mechanical to an organic division of labour that constituted characteristic differences in historical epochs and societies; finally, Weber provided an analysis of the emergence of modern Western rational capitalism and key differences and similarities with both previous epochs, societies and cultures.

3 For a detailed exposition of Marx's various definitions and uses of 'society' see Frisby and Sayer (1986).

4 Compare this with Marx's analysis of commodity forms and commodity fetishism as a way in which labour power is hidden by the process of the exchange of commodities which appear to have a life of their own.

5 Marx describes this as follows:

This sheep-like or herd consciousness receives its further development and extension through increased productivity, the multiplication of needs, and what underlies both of these, the increase of population. Along with these changes there is the development of the division of labour which was at first nothing but the division of labour in the sexual act, and then the division of labour which emerges spontaneously or 'naturally' by virtue of natural abilities (e.g. physical strength), needs, accidents, etc. (*The German Ideology*, 1846/1964: 21)

31

6 Marx maintains that

> The division of labour implies form the outset the division of the conditions of labour, of tools and materials, and thus the splitting up of accumulated capital among different owners, and thus, also, the division between capital and labour, and different forms of property itself. (*Capital*, vol. 1: 384)

7 Marx famously uses the example of the carriage maker. Under simple co-operation the production of carriages involved various handicrafts and skills: coach work and enamel work, upholstery and wheelwrights, etc. Before capitalism each of these operations specialised trades regulated by guilds in order to maintain their separation from each other. Soon after the division of labour, the carriage maker becomes 'exclusively occupied with making carriages'. As a consequence, individual trades immediately lose their specialised skills and this concentrates their combined activity exclusively in making carriages. As Marx wrote:

> at first the manufacture of carriages appears as a combination of various independent handicrafts and trades. But it gradually began to involve the splitting up of carriage production into various and detailed operations and each single operation crystallised into the exclusive function of a particular worker, the manufacture as a whole being performed by these partial workers in conjunction. (*Capital*, vol. 1: 455–6)

8 As Marx writes the development of the division of labour presides over the breakdown of handicraft skills and "the decomposition of handicrafts into different and partial operations' in which labour is transformed into a life long partial function" (*Capital*, vol. 1: 458).

9 Elsewhere in *Capital* Marx talks of space as a right or as a necessity that is denied or stolen from the worker as a consequence of the development of new methods and means of production.

> It has been repeatedly noted that the English doctors are unanimous in declaring that where the work is continuous 500 cubic feet is the very smallest space that should be allowed for each person... The health officers, the industrial inquiry commissioners, the factory inspectors all repeat, over and over again, that it is both necessary for the workers to have these 500 cubic feet, and impossible to impose this rule on capital. They are in reality, declaring that consumption and the other pulmonary diseases of the workers are conditions necessary to the existence of capital. (*Capital*, vol. 1: 612)

Marx notes that these conditions are to be found expressed in an even more deleterious form in the domestic industries as a consequence of competition with the factory system of production because workers not being concentrated together cannot organise resistance to their labouring conditions.

> In the so-called domestic industries this exploitation is still more shameless than in modern manufacture, because the workers' power of resistance declines with their dispersal, because a whole series of plundering parasites insinuate themselves

between the actual employer and the worker he employs; because a domestic industry has always to compete with the factory system, or with manufacturing in the same branch of production; because poverty robs the worker of the conditions most essential to his labour, of space, light and ventilation; because employment becomes more and more irregular; and finally, because in these last places of refuge for the masses made 'redundant' by large-scale industry and agriculture, competition for work necessarily attains its maximum. (Marx, *Capital*, vol. 1: 591)

two

Georg Simmel: the space of formal sociology

The previous chapter sought to extricate the spatial dimension in Marx's historical materialist analysis of capitalism. It was possible to recognise an implicit if not explicit and formal consideration of the spatiality of capitalism as a mode of production, of space as a force of production, of the spatial division of labour, of the socio-spatial division of the urban and the reproduction of labour, and the global expansion of capitalist space through imperialism. Similarly, whilst both Weber and Durkheim failed to produce a systematic and detailed consideration of space either for interpretive sociology as the meaningful understanding of social actors or for the functional characteristics of the social organisation of social relations, spheres, etc. there are implicit aspect of spatiality in their analyses. However, the recent publication of the first English translation of Georg Simmel's 'The sociology of space'[1] provides the opportunity to consider what may be called the first sociological account of the importance of space for social relations. As Frisby, states in the introduction to the texts:

> [a]long with time, quantity and mass, all of which receive varied treatment by Simmel during various stages of his career, it is the study of space which constitutes one of the most extensive chapters of his major sociological work *Soziologie*... The study of social space as a crucial dimension of social interaction and also of cultural formations constitutes one of those projects in which it can be said that Simmel, in many respects, was a pioneer. (Frisby and Featherstone, 1997: 10–11)

'The sociology of space' contains an examination of what Simmel identified as five 'aspects of space' and provides a somewhat abstract and formalised treatment of the significance of space for understanding social interaction. For Simmel, space is a crucial and fundamental element in human experience because social activities and interactions are and must be spatially contextualised. That is, the form in which social interactions are experienced and manifest are operative in delimited, delineated and prescribed space. Space then is both a determining aspect of interactions, but which is also simultaneously socially constructed by such interactions.

If 'The sociology of space' is appraised alongside other works it provides the opportunity for a reconsideration of Simmel's sociology as a whole from a spatial perspective, one that makes a significant and early contribution to the social theory of space. Therefore, for Simmel, unlike other early theorists there is a need to critically theorise and incorporate a spatial awareness in his investigations of modernity. In this, Simmel prefigures other work on the importance of space in social relations and deserves acknowledgement as the only 'founding father' [*sic*] that sought a critical social analysis and appreciation of the crucial significance of space.

Simmel's contribution to the social theory of space may also be considered as significant in that his treatment raises aspects, elements and issues that are identified and developed elsewhere by later, perhaps better-known, theorists of space.[2] In much the same way that Simmel's work on culture can be said to have been relatively neglected until recently, so has Simmel's contribution to the social theory of space. Jurgen Habermas comments that the 'disappearance' of Simmel's 1911 collection of essays *Philosophische Kultur* (first published in 1911, 3rd edition, 1923) for over 60 years indicates that "Simmel as a critic of culture is in a peculiar way both near to, and far away, from us" (Habermas, 1996: 403).[3] The intention here is to acknowledge this early sociological contribution by Simmel and to propose that Simmel's 'aspects of space' as well as the way in which space is examined in a number of diverse ways in his other works demonstrate an inherent spatial analysis that provide insights that are important for our more comprehensive investigation of social reality. Some elucidation of this spatial awareness and its significance for specific forms of sociation as well as the investigation of specific social spaces, whether they are for production or consumption, the circulation of goods, people, services, etc. or for leisure, recreation and culture as well as the experience and consequences of the space of modernity is a necessary correlate of this perspective. However, this is not the place for a detailed exegesis of how Simmel's conceptualisation of space was woven into his analyses of specific forms of sociation in modernity. A more comprehensive and detailed investigation remains for another day. What will be provided is a detailed consideration of Simmel's conceptualisation of his 'aspects of space' and the elucidation of their application in a number of other, perhaps better-known works. This will include highlighting the diverse ways in which Simmel examined space, the configuration and transformation of social space in modernity, the formation and expression of cultural forms and social interaction as mediated by, in and through space. It will be argued that Simmel's conceptualisations and consideration of space is significant in the context of his better-known contributions to the investigation of modernity, and more specifically the sociology of the city. This is rooted in his analytical perspective on the importance of everyday, however seemingly inconsequential, 'forms of sociation' that are expressed, experienced and determined in the everyday life and spaces of the mature money economy of urban modernity. It is pertinent however to begin with a brief introduction to his sociological project as a whole in which it will be argued the significance of space is crucial.

SPACE IN THE CONTEXT OF SIMMEL'S PROJECT

Simmel's overall project can be described as concerned with establishing the object of sociology as the "investigation of the forces, forms and development of sociation, of the co-operation, association and co-existence of individuals" (Simmel, in Frisby, 1992: 12). Simmel asserted that the study of society as a whole, 'real' object, was a reification and needed to be abandoned in favour of a perspective that was less anti-individualist. As Frisby puts it:

36

> In contrast to Durkheim, who viewed society as a 'system of active forces' operating *upon* individuals, Simmel here sees society as constituted by interactional 'forces' *between* individuals. (Frisby, 1992: 14. Italics in Original)

The influence of a variety of intellectual trends, collectively termed 'neo-Kantianism', at the end of the nineteenth century had a profound influence on Simmel's thought and his conceptualisation of what should be the foundation of sociology. In his essay 'How is society possible?'[4] Simmel discusses the influence of Kant's philosophy on his understanding of society and sociology, in particular, Kant's argument that it is our minds that structure our sensual experience of the world. As such, a distinction between the objective phenomenal world, as studied by the natural sciences and the social realm of action and values was emphasised. For Simmel, Kant's principle of the active mind participating in the understanding of the world was of central importance to the development of his understanding of sociology. Knowledge of the social world was not to be viewed or understood only as a collection of facts, but alternatively also as a construction made by selection and interpretation. As Simmel puts it:

> Society is 'my representation' – something dependent on the activity of consciousness – in quite a different sense from that which the external world is.

> For the other individual has for me the same reality which I have myself, and this reality is very different from that of a material thing. (Simmel, 'How is society possible?' in Wolff, 1958: 339)

Sociology then for Simmel should be the study not of societal facts but of those conscious interactions or associations. This constitutes one of Simmel's conceptions of society; as grounded in the everyday experience of its participants, and emphasises Simmel's argument against positivism. However, Simmel's sociology includes four conceptions of society: society as a totality (*Gesellschaft*), as a process of interactions or sociation (*Vergesellschaftung*), as an aesthetic object and as grounded in the everyday experience and knowledge of its participants.[5] All of Simmel's conceptions of society share a common theme in that, "they are either directly grounded in or presuppose the concept of interaction or reciprocal effect (*Wechselwirkung*)" (Frisby, 1992: 6). For Simmel, everything in the world interacts with everything else and this is also true of the social world. Therefore, the inter-relatedness and interaction of the most diverse phenomena is at the core of Simmel's analysis of the individual and of society and his concern with the relations between phenomena is one of the reciprocal effect of the interaction of phenomena with one another. That is:

37

> Society appears as a cosmos whose complex nature and direction are unlimited, but in which every single point can be fixed and can develop only in a particular way because otherwise the structure of the whole would change. (Simmel, 'How is society possible?' in Wolff 1959: 352)

From 1890 onwards, Simmel defines sociology as the study of 'forms of interaction' and by 1894 in 'The problem of sociology',[6] sociology is still defined as such but becomes expressed more specifically as the 'forms of sociation' (Vergesellschaftung), that is the processes by which we engage in or are members of society. Sociology for Simmel should then be concerned primarily with the forms rather than the contents of social interaction and sociation, because other social sciences already deal with these contents. Form is abstracted from content, whilst recognising that the two exist together in empirical reality. For Simmel, sociology is defined not in terms of its subject matter, that is society, but in terms of its method. Sociology is therefore to be the investigation of the forces, forms and development of sociation, of the co-operation, association and co-existence of individuals. That is for Simmel "society exists where a number of individuals enter into interaction" (Simmel, 'The problem of sociology' in Wolff, 1959: 314) and is the only science which really seeks to know only society 'sensu strictissimo'. If sociology is the study of forms of social interaction, then for Simmel sociology can and should examine any form of sociation, however insignificant (mealtimes, the rendezvous, flirtation, sociability, fashion, etc. are all forms that Simmel considered). Simmel therefore is interested in the minutiae of everyday life, the small-scale interactions and relations that form the basis of human existence. Simmel's sociology may be said to prioritise or reflect an interest in the micro-processes and relations of everyday existence that are expressed or identified as typifications or forms regardless of their specific contents. As such, these forms may be studied historically and comparatively in order to discover their general features (and also the study of the same form with different contents). For example, Simmel considers conflict as a general or pure form of interaction that may be found in both a political and an economic context and may be expressed in different ways, that is having different contents.

Simmel's contribution to the social theory of space may be placed within his overall corpus of work in which the investigation of forms of social interaction, their basis and the processes of reciprocal interaction by which we come to be members of society, were the foundation of his analysis. The investigation of apparently mundane, everyday, interactions and the subjective experience of them was, a fundamental part of Simmel's approach to sociology and his conception(s) of society as a 'web of interactions'. As Frisby contends, "[p]robably unique among his sociological contemporaries, Simmel explored time and time again the world of everyday social interactions and their cultural manifestations" (Frisby, 1997: 8–9). For Simmel social interactions have a spatial dimension – even the fact that he defines his sociology as the study of forms of sociation or social interaction suggests a spatial dimension. He also occasionally explicitly expresses this spatial approach to sociology as when he talks of the 'geometry of social relations'. Simmel writes:

> Only if we follow the conception here outlined can we grasp what in 'society' really *is* society. Similarly, it is only geometry that determines what the spatiality of things in space really is. Sociology, the discipline that deals with the purely social aspects of man (who, of course, can be an object of scientific inquiry in innumerable other respects), is related to the other special sciences of man as geometry is related to the physico-chemical sciences. Geometry studies the forms through which any material becomes an empirical body, and these forms as such exist, of course, in abstraction only, precisely like the forms of sociation. Both geometry and sociology leave to other sciences the investigation of the contents realised in the forms, that is, the total phenomena whose forms they explore. (Simmel, 'The problem of sociology' in Wolff, 1958: 320)

It is possible then to identify in Simmel's work a variety of ways in which he examined a diversity of elements of space that have a reciprocal effect/impact/influence on the character and expression of social interactions. For example, whether things, objects are fixed or mobile in space, whether they are near or far, how space can be open or closed, how it can separate or connect, make things/people insiders or outsiders, etc. It is these qualities that Simmel seeks to address in the somewhat formal study of 'aspects of space' in 'The sociology of space' which will be addressed. These in turn will be shown to have relevance for Simmel's understanding and investigation of other socio-spatial processes that he explores at different levels in other perhaps better-known works.

SIMMEL'S SOCIOLOGY OF SPACE – 'ASPECTS OF SPACE'

Simmel's sociology of space is a complex and somewhat abstract and formal attempt at identifying how and in what ways space is important in understanding social relations. Lechner suggests that Simmel's chapter on space can be interpreted in three ways. First, the abstracted possibility of individuals being together is reinterpreted in 'The sociology of space' so that, for Lechner, Simmel "emphasises...that interaction between individuals is usually experienced as the filling of space: the being together of individuals means that they share space" (Lechner, 1991: 196). Second, by investigating the spatial form of various social relations the project of Simmel's formal sociology is expanded. Third, the chapter on space must be viewed as part of Simmel's analysis of modernity in which the investigation of social forms in space illuminates how modern social structures are spatialised and how space itself comes to be modernised through reciprocal interaction with social formations.

39

The importance of the spatial element in social interaction is, for Simmel, a quality of space itself which, when combined with the dynamics and creative potential of human interactions, carries meaning and significance both for activities in space and of space itself. Therefore, space may said to be a 'necessary though not sufficient' condition of sociation. It is these spatial conditions that Simmel sought to define in his identification and definition of his 'five aspects of space'. Simmel's analysis of space is thus rooted in his analysis of forms of sociation in space.[7] There is in Simmel's conception of space a familiar neo-Kantian assertion of the active mind participating in understanding the world, that is, knowledge of the social world is viewed not as a collection of facts but a construction made by selection and interpretation. He writes:

Space always remains the actually ineffectual form, in whose modifications real energies are manifested, but only in the way that language expresses thought processes, which occur *in* words but not *through* words...space in general is only an activity of the mind, only the human way of connecting sensory impulses that are unrelated in themselves into uniform interpretations...Kant defines space at one point as the possibility of being together; sociation has brought about quite different possibilities of being together – in the intellectual sense – among the different types of interactions of individuals; not many of these are realised in such a way that the spatial form in which this happens, as it does in all of them, justifies special emphasis. Thus in the interest of ascertaining the forms of sociation we enquire into the significance that the spatial conditions of a sociation possess sociologically for their other determinants and developments. (Simmel, SoS: 137, 138)

However, the possibility of 'being together' in space can be realised beyond an abstract level of intellectual thought. This makes the spatial form of sociation and of such socio-spatial formations have a significance that needs to be considered.[8] The relevance of Simmel's 'aspects of space' then lies in his attempt to give some detailed consideration to the way in which space has a significance for how and where and why particular social formations and interactions are possible and are framed and shaped by their spatiality. That is, Simmel's 'aspects of space' provide an early sociological analysis of space as an important element for the substantive analysis of social spaces, whether these are those of production, consumption, circulation, distraction or display.

40

exclusivity

The first aspect that Simmel considers in 'The sociology of space' is that of 'exclusivity'. For Simmel, every portion of space is unique. That is, no two objects, states, municipalities, houses, etc. can occupy the same portion of space simultaneously. For Simmel:

This uniqueness of space communicates itself to objects, so long as they can be conceived of merely as occupying space, and this becomes particularly important in practice for those whose spatial significance we tend to emphasise and put to spatial use. This applies especially to land, which is the condition for fulfilling and fructifying the three-dimensional quality of space for our purposes. To the extent to which a social formation is amalgamated with or is, as it were, united with a specific extension of land, then it possesses a character of uniqueness or exclusivity that is not similarly attainable in other ways. (Simmel, SoS: 138–9)[9]

This implies that sociological forms such as, for example, the state, the city, or the municipality exist in an exclusive space that forms and is formed by the particular associations within its territory that preclude the existence of another form, within that space. As Simmel writes:

The type of association among individuals which the state creates, or which creates it, is so much connected to the territory that the concept of a second state on the same territory cannot be sustained at all. (Simmel, SoS: 139)

Spatial exclusivity thus confers on some forms of association a unique and, potentially, dominant existence. Within the spatial association that is the state, for example, all other associations come to be dominated. It is impossible to conceive of two states occupying the same space. The state then is dependent on the exclusivity of its territoriality for its legitimate domination of activities that occur within it. Thus the power that resides within the space of the nation state is formed within and active over the space within and through which it has exclusive control. The nation state then as a political entity is impossible without a claim to the exclusiveness of its spatial domain.

In contra-distinction to this spatial exclusivity, Simmel posits the example of religion, notably the Catholic Church (although the extra-territoriality of Islam would serve equally well), to claim, in principle, that there is the possibility of a non-spatial and thus universal structure to some forms of association. Although individuals are localised in congregations that have a spatial exclusivity akin to the state they are part of a whole that is not spatially constricted to an exclusive space. Each congregation or diocese is orientated to Rome as the central authority through and in which the web of the church acts universally over the whole of its earthly domain. Thus as Lechner concludes, "social configurations vary in the extent to which they require exclusive occupation of 'their' space" (Lechner, 1991: 197). Exclusivity then becomes a fundamental aspect of consideration when investigating or analysing particular social formations. That is, to what extent is the exclusiveness of a specific spatial domain a requirement for a particular form of association to assume dominance. This then relates, in part, to questions of power.

41

boundaries of space

The second aspect of space that Simmel considers and one that has considerable significance for Simmel's understanding of the spatiality of forms of sociation is that of boundaries.[10] Simmel states:

> A further quality of space, which has a fundamental effect on social interactions, lies in the fact that our practical use of space is divided into pieces which are considered units and are framed by boundaries – both as a cause and an effect of the division. (Simmel, SoS: 139)

The boundary in Simmel's analysis infers that space itself is not solely a physical or material fact, but instead a social construction that frames relationships between individuals and between groups. This social construction of space also acts by delimiting it to structure the spatial relatedness of objects, features and social relations within it (its contents) and also the human interactions that can be manifest (forms of sociation). This distinction between forms and contents is a crucial aspect of Simmel's sociology as a whole. By delineating its form and spatial arrangement the boundary serves a dual purpose. Objects and actions can be ordered and regulated under the aegis of a plan or functional prerequisites based upon some overarching value, principle or purpose whilst at the same time it also structures the inter-relatedness of its contents. Thus the social construction of space sets real and potential limits on that space and its contents. The boundary acts to structure the spatial and social relations that can occur between objects and human actions. This for Simmel is a fundamental point in the analysis of the importance of a space for social interactions. The extent to which space, as land for example, can be framed or bounded is significant as a fundamental aspect of space, in that not only does it close the space from an 'outside' giving it a more 'real' and concretised spatial character, it also constructs an inner cohesiveness that is subject to its own, localised regulations. This is a point emphasised by Simmel:

> Similarly, a society is characterised as inwardly homogeneous because its sphere of existence is enclosed in acutely conscious boundaries; and conversely, the reciprocal unity and functional relationship of every element to every other one gains its spatial expression in the enclosing boundary...Once it has been laid down, the physical border's existing absolute precision illustrates well the formative power of the social context and its inwardly motivated necessity in this very lack of prejudice by natural space. (Simmel, SoS: 141)

42

This boundedness of space thus represents a crucial aspect of Simmel's sociology: that of considerations of inside and outside.[11] Lechner demonstrates that the quality of space that Simmel conceived of as boundedness has ramifications for who, how, why, when and where space is delimited in an increasingly urban society, in which ownership and use of land as a relatively scarce commodity signifies the creation of a space economy.[12] The partitioning of space thus prioritises and creates the potential for social hierarchies to be created and maintained by the spatial structuring of the landscape. The spatial framework that an individual or a group occupies has consequences for order and for control in and of space that feeds back into the social relations and actions of groups. This reciprocal effect, a dominant theme in Simmel's sociology, of the social construction of space being a determining factor or condition for social interaction has important implications for movement, circulation and control in the city of modernity. Thus Simmel emphasises that

> through the structuring of its surface, space often receives divisions which colour the relationships of the inhabitants to each other and to third parties in

a unique fashion...The boundary is not a spatial fact with sociological consequences, but a sociological fact that forms itself spatially. The idealist principle that space is our conception, or more precisely, that it comes into being through our synthetic activity with which we give form to sensory material, is specified here in such a way that the formation of space which we call the boundary is a sociological function. (Simmel, SoS: 142, 143)

This aspect of the boundedness of space contains elements that reflect later concerns with the development of disciplinary discourses that sought to 'know' space in order to control what occurred within it. Boundedness also reflects the potential for conflict and contestation over the meanings, values and uses of delimited and delineated space in that everyday activities have the potential for re-appropriating space by undermining its ordered and prescribed regularity. Who sets, maintains and polices the boundary is a key concern for those involved in the analysis of movement and migration, of the creation and maintenance of cultural, ethnic or social identities. Without some means of sustaining 'us' there can be no way of excluding or identifying the 'other'.

fixity of social forms in space

Simmel's third significant aspect is the capacity for social forms to become fixed by space. For Simmel, "whether a group or certain of its elements or essential objects of its interest are completely fixed or remain spatially indeterminate must obviously affect their structure" (Simmel, SoS: 146). The fixedness of objects and social relationships in space had, for Simmel, obvious repercussions for economic arrangements and relationships. He uses the mortgage and insurance policies on ships as an example of how formal and structural relationships are dependent on whether an object is fixed or mobile in space.

By making such unstable objects that existed only in mere interactions between people, once more the object of economic interactions would have led to even more unstable and precarious conditions if all these rights and relationships had not had the distinctive feature of *being immovably fixed at the place where they were exercised*. This was the stabilising factor which gave so much solidity to their purely dynamic and relativistic nature that it was possible to group additional economic interactions around them. Their spatial determinacy was not like that of a substantive object, which one would always find at the same place, but akin to the abstract stability of a pivotal point, which keeps a system of elements in a specific distance, interaction and interdependence...The significance of fixed spatiality as a pivotal point for social relationships emerges whenever the contract or union of otherwise independent elements can only occur at one particular place. (Simmel, SoS: 147)

The ship is not fixed in space but it can be considered and acknowledged as a pivot around which financial and social relationships can accrue and cohere. This aspect of the fixity of objects in space can in contra-distinction be applied to objects that are not mobile but instead are fixed in space. The market for land and real estate acts in accordance to that fixity in which land and objects in space can be considered as immovable. This may have economic as well as social consequences both for the objects themselves or for surrounding areas.

This fixing of activities in space is for Simmel a crucial aspect of the development of forms and structures of social relations. He thus considers the fixity of space as a defining characteristic of social forms, and it may be said, of epochs. He writes of the distinctions that can be made between those forms of activities that are fixed around a point or are more fluid.

> The typical contrast between forms of social dynamism is whether they merely signify a striving beyond that which exists socially and objectively, like the cycle of alternating pastures of pastoral peoples, or, on the other hand, whether they move around fixed points. Only in the latter case are they actually formed and only there do they gain a crystallisation point for the commencement of lasting values, even if these only exist in the persisting form of relations and movements. (Simmel, SoS: 148)

44

Thus it is possible to begin to identify objects in space or fixed spatial entities that may be said to have acted, at least at times in the past if not at present, as urban 'crystallisation points', around and through which, social interactions, values and functions are structured, coalesce or revolve.

A further aspect of the fixity of space is revealed when Simmel characteristically, returns to seemingly mundane, everyday interactions to postulate space as of fundamental significance both for sociology and for human actors in his presentation of the *rendezvous*. Simmel considers the spatial element to be of fundamental importance both to the event and to its survival as a sentimental memory. Indeed, Simmel argues that space rather than time is paramount for memory. For him, the nostalgic biography is written and remembered through the association of those spaces and places of important, pleasurable or eventful encounters. That is, space is invested with meaning and emotional attachment. For Simmel,

> the rendezvous as a specifically sociological form, whose spatial determinacy is characterised linguistically through the ambiguity of the word: it signifies both the encounter and its location...Because it is more vivid to the sense, place generally exhibits a greater associative effect for recollection than time...the

place remains the focal point around which the remembrance weaves individuals into the web of interactions that have now become idealised. (Simmel, SoS: 148, 149)

This fixedness quality of space reflects considerations explored by later theorists of space concerned with establishing a historical–geographical materialistic analysis of the political economy of (particularly) urban space and the production of the socio-spatial organisation of urban capitalism. Fixing social forms in space allows for the organisation and management of urban social relations and for the development of both exchange values for land as well as use values associated with specific functions. The zoning of urban areas into leisure, residential, industrial, commercial, etc. is an attempt to fix portions of urban space into patterns of use.

spatial proximity and distance

Simmel's fourth aspect of proximity and distance is concerned with highlighting distinctions or possibilities between different forms of interactions as a condition of their relatedness to nearness and farness. Simmel writes:

45

A fourth type of external circumstances, which translate themselves into the liveliness of sociological interactions, is offered by space through which the sensory proximity or distance between people who stand in some relationship or other to one another. (Simmel, SoS: 149)

Whether interactions take place at a distance or in close proximity has a qualitative and perhaps quantitative aspect to them. If face to face interactions are limited because of the distance between actors, or actors and objects, spaces, etc., then the quality as well as quantity of social relations may be affected. If particular spaces have an exclusivity in terms of their being demarcated as sanctioned places for certain social interactions, activities and formations to occur then proximity and distance is clearly a factor in accessing potential opportunities for inter- actions. As Werlen writes, "[h]is [Simmel's] analysis could possibly be adapted to the relationship of agents to immobile objects and artefacts relevant to action" (Werlen, 1993: 170).

This idea of proximity and distance and its conditioning of interactions raise questions and issues concerning communications and social relations that are dependent on technology to cover distances. The invention of the telegraph had revolutionary consequences for the devel- opment of social and economic relations across space and time that is mirrored in the claims made for the effects and possibilities of the virtual realities and networks associated with the internet and more modern information and communication technologies. The analysis of the location of objects, features and the socio-spatial organisation of the infrastructure of the city supports the assertion that proximity and distance are significant when considering access to and use of amenities as well as for the circulation costs of economic production. The development of urban features such as out-of-town shopping, recreation and sports centres mitigates against those who lack mobility or accessible and affordable transport.

mobility in space

Mobility in space is a related aspect to that of fixity. If an object or cultural institution, such as a museum, art gallery, recreation or educational facility, etc., is immobile in space then social actors must have to travel to it to use it or access its resources. They are fixed in location therefore, social interactions must necessarily occur in, around and through them in that they exist (in and of themselves) in an exclusive location that requires mobility on the part of the population to access its potentiality as a site of interaction, framed and fixed for this purpose. Whether a material object is mobile or immobile offers the possibility for explaining how social and cultural activities and formations can be given stability by their permanent location in a physical world that contextualises these relations through their interdependent arrangement and structure.

> The immobility of a material object relevant to action thus obliges agents to go to it if they wish to utilise it in achieving a goal. This means that certain social relationships must be ordered around immobile material objects. The spatially defined location of the immobile material object thus becomes a socially important pivot of human interactions. Such a pivot may be represented by a single building or a whole town, according to the observational scale used. At all events it is clear that this fixed spot in the physical world becomes a 'pivot for the relationship and the social context' for all agents integrating this immobile material object into their actions. (Werlen, 1993: 169)

Thus, a spatial pivot may acquire real and symbolic contents and meanings, which acts as a unifying force for social cohesion in an increasingly competitive, fragmented and transitory existence. That is, they may in a secular sense, "awaken a consciousness of belonging among members of the denomination whose religious consciousness has long lain dormant in their isolation" (Simmel, SoS: 147). In other words, the mobility or not of individuals to access arenas or fora where national, civic, class or communal solidarities can be displayed, expressed or promulgated in public is a factor in one's inclusion or exclusion from the social life of the collective. For Simmel

> Modern life is able to bring about the consciousness of social unity, first, by means of those objective regularities and the knowledge of the common points of contact; second, through the institutions which are permanently fixed; and third, through written communication. (Simmel, SoS: 165)

This mobility on the part of populations raises questions as to the inclusion or exclusion to 'common points of contact' whether for social, economic, cultural, educational or leisure purposes, are located near or far populations that may be dispersed on the outskirts of cities in peripheral housing schemes or who may live in rural areas, and for whom access to transport may make mobility difficult. If populations are prohibited through lack of mobility then access to key areas of social life then disenfranchise them from participation.

SIMMEL'S ANALYSIS OF SOCIO-SPATIAL PROCESSES EXPLORED

47

In Simmel's somewhat formal consideration of those 'aspects of space' that he identified as significant for understanding the forms of interaction/ sociation, it is clear that his awareness of space as a crucial element was also applied in his roles as a philosopher of culture and sociologist of modernity. Simmel's analysis of the spatial dimension of forms of sociation is a key operating principle in his varied analyses of the 'particularly abstract existence' that was, for him, the everyday life of the city and which constituted the basis of society where "Society exists where several individuals enter into interaction" (Simmel, 'How is society possible?' in Wolff, 1958: 314). What follows is a brief examination of those 'fundamental qualities' in Simmel's various investigations and analyses of the social spaces and experiences of modernity.

the city as space of modernity

The city was for Simmel *a* if not *the* key 'site of modernity' and provided a rich source of material for investigating the everyday 'web of interactions' that for him constituted society. Simmel's sociology of the city provides a well-known example of how his approach both to sociology and to space is applied in his analyses. In 'The metropolis and mental life' Simmel provides a social–psychological analysis of the consequences, of the increasing transitory and fragmented tempo of urban experience and social relations in modernity. That is, the consequences and effects for the individual of the rapid growth and intensification of modern city living is rooted in his analytical perspective of the importance of everyday, however seemingly inconsequential, forms of sociation that take place in the spaces of the city and lead to the concomitant creation of a self-preserving blasé, urban personality.

> The psychological basis of the metropolitan type of individuality consists in the intensification of nervous stimulation which results from the swift and uninterrupted change of outer and inner stimuli ... With each crossing of the street, with the tempo and multiplicity of economic, occupational and social life, the city sets up a deep contrast with small town and rural life with reference to the sensory foundation of psychic life. The metropolis exacts from man as a discriminating creature a different amount of consciousness than does rural life. Here the rhythm of life and sensory mental imagery flows more slowly, more habitually, and more evenly. Precisely in this connection the sophisticated character of metropolitan psychic life becomes understandable – as over against small town life which rests more upon deeply felt and emotional relationships. (Simmel, 'The metropolis and mental life' in Frisby and Featherstone (eds), 1997: 175)

48

The development of the blasé personality thus had, fundamentally, a spatial context. It is through this concentration in space that the city exerts these influences on the modern psyche. The city is the spatial form of modernity in and through which modern life is experienced and characterised. Simmel emphasises the speed, variety, quality and quantity of sensory and social experiences and interaction of urban living which marks the dichotomy between town and country life. In Simmel's analyses of the city he stressed the high levels of nervous stimulation, psychological bombardment of stimuli and the need to develop a social and psychological distancing. As Frisby puts it:

> The sphere of consumption and the circulation of individuals as customers or as commodities is also concentrated in the metropolis ... Not surprisingly, the impact of this reified world of the metropolis and the money economy upon individuals is all the greater because human subjects are themselves compelled to respond to their 'particularly abstract existence' only by attempting to distance themselves from it. Above all they must respond to the shock of 'the rapid and unbroken change in external and internal stimuli' that is experienced 'with every crossing of the street, with the speed and diversity of economic, professional, and social life', as 'the rapid crowding of changing images, the sharp discontinuity in the grasp of a single glance, and the unexpectedness of onrushing impressions'. (Frisby, in Rojek (ed.), 1989: 80)

There is an obvious resonance in Simmel's analysis of the city as the site of increased experience and activity with Töennies' (1955) classification of human relationships in which the distinction between *Gemeinshaft* and *Gessellschaft* has been represented as illustrating the rural/urban, pre-modern/modern qualities of social relations that Simmel recognised.[13] For Simmel social relationships in urban modernity came to be increasingly impersonal, fleeting, fragmented and superficial. They took place within a large network of social circles that held no exclusive or undivided commitment and were based on specific roles rather than the qualities of the individuals themselves. In Simmel's study of 'The philosophy of money' he documents the increasing reification of social relationships through the medium of money and the concomitant decline of subjective culture at the expense of an increasingly objective culture dominated by monetary transactions. This concern with the distinctive qualities that made the modern city a new phenomenon with consequences for the individual and for the organisation, maintenance and regulation of modern society provided Simmel with the raw material for his analyses and investigations of the forms of sociation and was influential for later analyses of the city.[14]

figures in space

In 'The metropolis and mental life' Simmel identified the creation of a self-preserving blasé, urban personality. Also associated with the modern metropolis is perhaps the most celebrated and most studied of urban pedestrians, the *flaneur*. The *flaneur*, that self-conscious secret spectator, the 'undiscoverable, hidden man' of the crowd, the objective observer, who perambulates the streets, the spaces and places of the city in search of new sensations and experiences reflects and characterises aspects of Simmel's awareness of the spatiality of social relations in the city.[15] Walter Benjamin's contribution to the analysis of the ambiguous figure of the flaneur as the sometime dandy and bohemian "urban stroller, observer, even idler" (Frisby, 1994: 86) is set within an analysis of the mundane experiences of the urban population, that is, the everyday life of the city which is influenced by Simmel. As Benjamin observes: "an intoxication comes over those who wander through the streets for a long time without any particular goal. The activity of walking itself grows in power with each step taken" (Benjamin, cited in Gilloch, 1996: 152). The streets and the movements and activities that occur there take on a new meaning and perspective through the creative eye of the flaneur. They become representative of the masses' private as well as public sphere. As Benjamin writes in the *Arcades Project*:

> Streets are the dwelling place of the collective. The collective is an eternally unquiet, eternally agitated being that – in the space between the building

fronts – experiences, learns, understands, and invents as much as individuals do within the privacy of their own four walls. For this collective, glossy enamelled shop signs are wall decorations as good as, if not better than, an oil painting in the drawing room of a bourgeois; walls with their 'Post No Bills' are its writing desk. Newspaper stands its libraries, mailboxes its bronze busts, benches its bedroom furniture, and the café terrace is the balcony from which it looks down on its household. The section of railing where road workers hang their jackets is the vestibule, and the gateway which leads from the row of courtyards into the open is the long corridor that daunts the bourgeois, being for the courtyards the entry to the chambers of the city. Among these latter, the arcade was the drawing room. More than anywhere else, the street reveals itself in the arcade as the furnished and familiar interior of the masses." (Benjamin, 1999: 423)

Both the flaneur and the blasé personality can be said to reflect aspects of social distancing whilst they observe or seek to preserve their individuality in the face of the tumult of modern urban existence. Indeed distance is a central concept for Simmel and in his varied analyses of forms of sociation it is evident that he was well aware that spatial relations are determining conditions as well as symbolic of social inter- actions. He writes of the ambiguities as well as the dynamism involved in socio-spatial interactions:

50

At the moment two persons begin to interact, the space between them appears to be filled and inhabited. This appearance of course rests only on the ambiguity of the concept 'between': that a relation between two elements which actually consists only of a certain movement or modification within the one and the other takes place between them in the sense of a spatial interposition. Although the ambiguity in question may give rise to errors, it represents a matter of quite profound sociological significance. The '[i]n-between' as a purely functional reciprocity, whose contents stay within each of the parties to a transaction, also takes the form of a claim on the space which exists between these parties, actually manifesting itself in all cases between two spatial locations at which each party has a specifically designated place, one to be occupied by himself alone. (Simmel, in Levine et al., 1976a: 840)

Simmel explicitly identifies 'the stranger' as a figure that epitomises this in-between-ness and reflects aspects of his spatial analysis, that of nearness and remoteness, of fixity and mobility, inside/outside, etc. In the opening passage of 'The Stranger' Simmel writes that:

If wandering is the liberation from every given point in space, and thus the conceptional opposite to fixation at such a point, the sociological form of the 'stranger' presents the unity, as it were, of these two characteristics. This phenomenon too, however, reveals that spatial relations are only the condition, on the one hand, and the symbol on the other, of human relations. (Simmel, 'The Stranger' in Wolff, 1950: 402)

In identifying and analysing figures in space Simmel applies a spatial analysis that reflects his 'aspects of space' to characterise social forms that he viewed as indicative of modernity. For Simmel, what was also fundamental and indicative of modernity was the creation and experience of the mature money economy.

money

For Simmel, the city was not only the site of the concentration of stimuli and the magnification of possible social relationships and interactions it was also the locus for the expression of the mature money economy where money was the medium of exchange relations. In 'The philosophy of money' Simmel attempted to identify in the processes of exchange a means to clarify and deepen his conception of society. Simmel explicitly points to the relevance of exchange for society. Society is:

> a structure that transcends the individual, but that is not abstract. Historical life thus escapes the alternative of taking place either in individuals or in abstract generalities. Society is the universal which, at the same time, is concretely alive. From this arises the unique significance that exchange, as the economic-historical realisation of the relativity of things, has for society; exchange raises the specific object and its significance for the individual above its singularity, not into the sphere of abstraction, but into that of lively interaction. (Simmel, *The Philosophy of Money*: 136)

In exchange relations then, Simmel found a constellation of interactions that embodied what he intended by the notion of sociation. Not only is it the case that 'the interaction between individuals is the starting point of all social formations' but the exchange of possessions is:

> obviously one of the purest and most primitive forms of human sociation; not in the sense that 'society' already existed and then brought about acts of exchange but, on the contrary, that exchange is one of the functions that creates an inner bond between human beings – a society in place of a mere collection of individuals. (Simmel, *The Philosophy of Money*: 165)

If for Simmel society is the synthesis of specific interactions and is composed of these interactions then exchange is not merely 'a form of sociation'; it is also 'the purest sociological occurrence, the most complete form of interaction'. This sociological occurrence is epitomised in money, because money:

> represents pure interaction in its purest form; it makes comprehensible the most abstract concept; it is an individual thing whose essential significance is to reach beyond individualities. (Simmel, *The Philosophy of Money*: 168)

51

In the developed economy the function of exchange as a direct interaction between individuals then becomes 'crystallised in the form of money as an independent structure' that appears to exist over and above the individual but, for Simmel, money embodies the network of interrelationships that constitutes society. Frisby writes that for Simmel:

> The social relationships that constitute society not only exist in space as a web, labyrinth or network. They also exist in time as fleeting relationships, as permanent relationships, as a constellation of relationships in flux. Money embodies this social reality that is in 'constant motion'. There exists, for Simmel, 'no more striking symbol of the completely dynamic character of the world than money... the vehicle for a movement in which everything else that is not in motion is completely extinguished. It is, as it were, an *actus purus*.' It is the spider that spins society's web. (Frisby, 1984/2002: 100)

It is in this sense of money as a spider spinning webs of reciprocal interactions that we can discern a spatial aspect in his analysis of the mature money economy of modernity. Money not only serves to connect it also adds to their distantiation across both space and time. Debts, possessions, shares, mortgages, leased property, etc. need not be materialised but can be managed by the capacity of money to be transferred. It is the aspect of social and spatial distance that Simmel again identifies as a key characteristic of money and of the experience of modernity. He writes that

> The power of money to bridge distances enables the owner and his possessions to exist so far apart that each of them may follow their own precepts to a greater extent than in the period when the owner and his possessions still stood in direct and mutual a relationship, when every economic engagement was also a personal one and when every change in economic direction or position meant at the same time, a corresponding change in economic interests. (Simmel, *The Philosophy of Money*: 333)

It could be argued that in this twenty-first century era of instantaneous electronic banking and financial transactions that this time–space distantiation is even more pertinent. Simmel also identified spaces of circulation and exchange as increasingly characteristic of the mature money economy of modernity. Whether in the new spaces created for consumption such as the department store or the increasingly fleeting and fragmented relationships that occurred in everyday transactions, money was the medium through and in which the means by which the increasing movement and circulation of people, goods and services was accomplished.

52

escape into space and spaces of escape

Simmel's exploration of micro-sociological phenomena, the forms of sociation, takes place within the everyday life and spaces of the city of modernity as well as the sometimes negative consequences for the human condition of their concentration, circulation and exchange. The spatial dimension of forms of sociation in modernity suggests there is also a need for spaces and places where the rapid circulatory system of the city operates at a slower tempo, allowing a temporary withdrawal from the pressure and strains of 'work' time and the domination of experiences mediated by money. It involves a consideration of the spatial dimension of human interactions in which Simmel also explores, as a necessary correlate and extension, the need sometimes to escape from this overwhelming intensification of interactions and sensory stimulation of increasingly objectified culture. Thus Simmel writes of the need to find new experiences and new places outside of the run-of-the-mill demands of the day in the development of modern forms of leisure and tourism. For example, in 'The Alpine journey', he explores how as a consequence of the conquest of distance the mountains become an accessible escape for the masses of the city.

53

> A process which has been in the making for decades in the Swiss transport system has recently been completed. It has something more than an economic analogy to call it the wholesale opening-up and enjoyment of nature. Destinations that were previously only accessible by remote walks can now be reached by railways, which are appearing at an ever-increasing rate...Now there is the lure of the open road, and the concentration and convergence of the masses – colourful but therefore as a whole colourless – suggesting to us an average sensibility. (Simmel, The Alpine journey, in Frisby and Featherstone, 1997: 219)

Whilst Simmel accepts this 'socialistic wholesale opening-up of the Alps' as more a less a good thing, the effects of a temporary escape from the mundane routine is nevertheless only a temporary respite.

> The uplift which a view of the high Alps gives is followed very quickly by the return to the mood of the mundane. (Simmel, The Alpine journey, in Frisby and Featherstone, 1997: 220)

Whilst the ability to afford a 'break' was and is still a necessary condition for travel outwith ones routine existence, those spaces and places conditioned by the need to exchange one's labour for money or familial obligation – tourism – then as now, involves a return. As more and more places become colonised by affordable and accessible travel the possibility of escape seems to Simmel less worthwhile. However, he does identify that there is still, potentially, opportunities for enriching the psyche or the soul.

> More precisely, the most general form of adventure is its dropping out of the continuity of life. 'Wholeness of life', after all, refers to the fact that a constant process runs through the individual components of life, however crassly and irreconcilably distinct they may be. What we call an adventure stands in contrast to that inter-locking of life-links, to that feeling that those counter-currents, turnings, and knots still, after all, spin forth a continuous thread. An adventure is certainly a part of our existence, directly contiguous with other parts which precede and follow it; at the same time, however, in its deeper meaning, it occurs outside the usual continuity of this life. (Simmel, The adventure, Frisby and Featherstone, 1997: 222)

The adventure then involves risk-taking and stepping out of ordinariness, and for that time and those places associated with it, a journey begins and ends. Simmel uses spatial metaphors to describe how the boundaries and limits of 'normal' social life are suspended in 'the island' of adventure. As Simmel writes:

54
> The adventure lacks that reciprocal interpenetration with adjacent parts of life which constitute life-as-a[-]whole. It is like an island in life which determines its beginning and end according to its own formative powers and not – like the part of a continent – also according to those of adjacent territories. This factor of decisive boundedness, which lifts an adventure out of the regular course of human destiny, is not mechanical but organic: just as the organism determines its spatial shape not simply by adjusting to obstacles confining it from right and left but by the propelling force of life forming from inside out, so does the adventure not end because something else begins; instead, its temporal form, its radical being-ended, is the precise expression of its inner sense. (Simmel, The adventure, Frisby and Featherstone, 1997: 223)

There is a further example of the spatiality of Simmel's micro-sociological analysis "of finding in each of life's details the totality of its meaning" (Simmel, The philosophy of money: 55) that supports the examination of the fragments of everyday life and activity, within space, as a means of theorising the uses and popular practices to be found in modernity. The essay 'The Berlin trade exhibition' may be considered as the expression of the modern idea of consumption as an escape or compensation from "modern-man's one-sided and monotonous role in the division of labour" (Simmel, in Frisby and Featherstone, 1997: 257). Simmel, in his consideration of 'The Berlin trade exhibition' of 1896, demonstrated that the simultaneity of the assault on the senses of such a number and variety of products, collected, displayed and presented in such a concentrated experience, was crystallised into an almost inevitable experience of entertainment and amusement:

> In the face of the richness and diversity of what is offered, the only unifying and colourful factor is that of amusement. The way in which the most heterogeneous industrial products are crowded together in close proximity paralyses the senses – a veritable hypnosis where only one message gets through to one's consciousness: the idea that one is here to amuse oneself... It is on the architectural side that this exhibition reaches its acme, demonstrating the aesthetic output of the exhibition principle. From another point of view its productivity is at least as high: and here I refer to what could be termed the shop-window quality of things, a characteristic which the exhibition accentuates. The production of goods under the regime of free competition and the normal predominance of supply over demand leads to goods having to show a tempting exterior as well as utility. Mere competition no longer operates in matters of usefulness and intrinsic properties, the interest of the buyer has to be aroused by the external stimulus of the object, even the manner of its presentation. It is at the point where material interests have reached their highest level and the pressure of competition is at an extreme that the aesthetic ideal is employed. The striving to make the merely useful visually stimulating – something that was completely natural for the Orientals and Romans – for us comes from the struggle to render the graceless graceful for consumers. The exhibition with its emphasis on amusement attempts a new synthesis between the principles of external stimulus and the practical functions of objects, and thereby takes this aesthetic superadditum to its highest level. The banal attempt to put things in their best light, as in the cries of the street trader, is transformed in the interesting attempt to confer a new aesthetic significance from displaying objects together – something already happening in the relationship between advertising and poster art. (Simmel, 'The Berlin trade exhibition' in Frisby and Featherstone, 1997: 255, 257)[16]

55

Similarly, Benjamin after Simmel, in his analyses and interpretation of the Paris exhibitions emphasised the fetishisation of the commodities on display in the fantastical spectacle of the exhibition as acting as a training ground through which the masses could be educated and entertained by the seeming limitlessness of technological innovation and production, the aestheticisation of consumption, and the celebration of civic, national and/or imperial power and status, amid the vicarious experience of the pleasure park. In these 'folk fairs of capitalism' the seeming distraction of the amusement park and the entertainments were an inherent component of the propaganda role of the exhibitions:

> World exhibitions are places of pilgrimage to the commodity fetish... It arises from the wish "to entertain the working classes", and it becomes for them a festival of emancipation. The worker occupies the foreground, as customer. The framework of the entertainment industry has not yet taken shape; the popular festival provides this... World exhibitions glorify the exchange value of the commodity. They create a framework in which its use value becomes secondary.

They are a school in which the masses, forcibly excluded from consumption, are imbued with the exchange value of commodities to the point of identifying with it: "Do not touch the items on display!" World exhibitions thus provide access to a phantasmagoria which a person enters in order to be distracted. Within these *divertissements*, to which the individual abandons himself in the framework of the entertainment industry, he remains always an element of a compact mass. This mass delight in amusement parks with their roller coasters, their "twisters" their "caterpillars" in an attitude that is pure reaction. It is thus led to that state of subjection which propaganda, industrial as well as political, relies on. (Benjamin, 1999: 7, 18)

The World Fairs and Great Exhibitions then may be said to have been a showcase for production and consumption but become a place of pleasure and vicarious entertainment. They like the modern 'temples of consumption and consumerism', the shopping centres, malls and galleries become spaces of albeit temporary, distraction and escape.

a phenomenology of space

A final example of Simmel's exploration of the fundamental role of space in understanding everyday experiences and interactions comes through the reciprocity inherent in the social construction of space and the unique capacity of humans to shape, mould, connect and separate space. He uses the example of road building as an achievement that freezes "movement into a solid structure that commences from it and in which it terminates" (Simmel, 'Bridge and door' in Frisby and Featherstone, 1997: 171). For Simmel, this 'miracle' of achievement

> reaches its zenith in the construction of a bridge. Here the human will to connection seems to be confronted not only by the passive resistance of spatial separation but also the active resistance of a special configuration. By over-coming this obstacle, the bridge symbolises the extension of our volitional sphere over space. Only for us are the banks of a river not just apart but 'separated': if we did not first connect them in our practical thoughts, in our needs and in our fantasy, then the concept of separation would have no meaning. (Simmel, 'Bridge and door': 171)

Thus Simmel sees the ability to overcome obstacles by separating them in our minds and imagining the conquest of space by the fantastic construction of human artefacts that transcend nature and yet at the same time aesthetically add a picturesque element. The practicality of spatial forms that accommodate and translate the acts of mobility, of unity and separateness, of distance and nearness is accomplished by road-making and bridge-building and yet their very materiality symbolises our desire for command and conquest of space. The phenomenon of the human capacity to conquer space is similarly evident in Simmel's discussion of the door.

> The human being who first erects a hut, like the first road builder, revealed the specifically human capacity over against nature, in so far as he or she cut a portion out of space out of the continuity and infinity of space and arranged this into a particular unity in accordance with a single *meaning*. A piece of space was thereby brought together and separated from the whole remaining world. By virtue of the fact that the door forms, as it were, a linkage between the space of human beings and everything that remains outside it, it transcends the separation between the inner and the outer. Precisely because it can also be opened, its closure provides the feeling of a stronger isolation against everything outside this space than the mere unstructured wall. The latter is mute, but the door speaks. It is absolutely essential for humanity that it set itself a boundary, but with freedom, that is, in such a way that it can also remove this boundary again, that it can place itself outside it. (Simmel, 'Bridge and door': 172)

Simmel thus shows again a clear and analytical approach to the phenomenology of socio-spatial processes that may be taken for granted and overlooked in everyday structures and forms yet which is fundamental for our investigation and understanding of them.

GEORG SIMMEL: THE FIRST SOCIOLOGIST OF SPACE

Simmel's sociology of space is an important beginning for a social theory of space. In seeking to address in a somewhat formal way through the identification and consideration of key 'aspects of space' he demonstrates an awareness of the need to provide an analysis of the significance of space for social relations. It reflects his conceptualisation of society as reciprocal interaction between individuals and his project of establishing sociology as the study of forms, not contents of sociation. Simmel's treatment of the significance of space as socially constructed but which also limits, or feeds into the social formations and interactions that can occur within it. This dynamic relationship, a symbiosis between social construction and environmental, that is, geographical determinism is illustrated in other more familiar work. It is possible to identify how Simmel's awareness of space was applied in his investigations of the consequences for subjective experience of modernity. As Lechner states, Simmel, "emphasises that in principle space is one of the most 'concrete' features of social life, one that helps to make social life 'real' in terms of human experience" (Lechner, 1991: 200). For Simmel, then, there are many forms of sociation that cannot be understood fully without taking into account both their spatial context and their use of space. In this it can be said that Simmel is the first sociologist of space and his early work raises issues and themes that are examined, extended and expanded by later theorists of space.

NOTES

1 'The sociology of space' appeared in the 1908 German publication of Simmel's major work *Socziologie* although it had been published in earlier form in 1903. The first English translation appears in Frisby, D. and Featherstone, M., 1997, *Simmel on Culture*, London, Sage. Hereafter 'The sociology of space' will be referred to as SoS and the page numbers refer to Frisby and Featherstone's translation.

2 The contrast and similarities between Simmel's symbiosis of spatial determinism and social construction and Lefebvre's three inter-linked elements for the production of space will I hope become evident later (see Chapter 3).

3 See for example Foucault's emphasis on the importance of boundaries as well as power/knowledge of and over space (Chapter 5).

4 'How is society possible?' in Wolff, K. 1958, *Essays on Sociology*, Ohio State University Press, Columbus, Ohio.

5 See Frisby (1992) and Frisby and Sayer (1986) for a detailed discussion of Simmel's various conceptualisations and uses of 'society'.

6 In Wolff (1958).

7 As Lechner puts it, although sociation 'fills in space' "[t]he spatial embeddedness of social configurations should not be confused with the actual causes of social processes. And yet, while he shows how space is in some ways socially formed, he does not treat space as simply a social construct. It retains a reality of its own. Simmel's overall position, then, lies somewhere between spatial determinism and social constructionism" (Lechner, 1991: 196).

8 Urry puts it thus: "Social life involves spending *time* with other people, and it involves crossing *space* to be in their company. Time and space are thus two central aspects by which 'nature' constrains social activity" (Urry, 1987: 215–16).

9 As Werlen states this exclusivity of space "means that if an object is considered only from the point of view of its location on the earth's surface, and all its other characteristic dimensions are ignored, it is always unique: at any given time only one object can occupy a particular position" (Werlen, 1993, 168).

10 Other later theorists of space also consider the boundary as a fundamental aspect or condition of space. See Foucault on 'Heterotopias and disciplinary spaces of learning, punishment, health, etc.' (Chapter 5) and Harvey on the political economy of space (Chapter 4) and Lefebvre on the planners and urban designers for the importance of the boundary for delimiting space for developing markets in land and for the design of cities and of particular spaces of leisure, culture, everyday life, etc. (Chapter 3).

11 This aspect of being able to open and close a space is also one of Foucault's six fold categorisations of Heterotopias giving the impression of isolation/exclusion but with a specified, and thus controllable, means of access. See Foucault, 1984 and Chapter 5 for a more thorough analysis.

12 Lechner considers that "[e]ven more important from a social point of view is the partitioning of space, since boundaries contribute to the integration, or 'centripetality', of a society. Bounded space makes any social order more concrete

and intensely experienced. But spatial ordering not only reinforces social order, it also lends greater clarity to conflictual relations. Partitioning thus influences relations within and across boundaries (which can be drawn more or less narrowly)" (Lechner, 1991: 197).

13 Tonnies posits *Gemeinschaft* as a perfect unity of human wills characterised by 'real', organic life and representing community, family, and private relations and Gesellschaft representing public life and society, characterised by the co-existence of independent people.

14 In particular, Simmel's influence on American Sociology and the development of the Chicago School in particular is well documented. (See Levine et al., 1976a and b.) Louis Wirth's theory of the industrial city aimed to present the analysis and findings of their major premise is what distinguishes the city from the country through the three interrelated concepts of size, heterogeneity and density. (See Wirth, 1938: 1–24.) For the Chicago School these were viewed as the key features of the city in their biologically based metaphor of the human ecology model of urban development and competition.

15 For an account of the Flaneur see Tester, K., 1994, *The Flaneur*, London, Routledge in particular Frisby, D. 'The Flaneur in social theory'.

16 For a fuller examination of Simmel's treatment of Exhibitions see Frisby, D., 2001, *Cityscapes of Modernity*, Polity Press, Cambridge. For a consideration of World Fairs see Allwood, J., 1977, *The Great Exhibitions*, London, Studio Vista.

59

three

Henri Lefebvre: the production of space

Henri Lefebvre's project, culminating in *The Production of Space*, was the result of a long process in which his analyses of various aspects of modernity resulted in his reprioritisation of space as fundamental for understanding capitalism. His analysis of space is complex and challenging and, it will be argued, significant for the theoretical and substantive analysis of space in contemporary social theory. Indeed Lefebvre's role as the key figure in the development of contemporary interest and concern with space provides explanation for the weight given to his work here. Lefebvre's analysis of space will be presented in the context of his work on nature, the city, the urban, and everyday life. Lefebvre's ultimate aim was to demonstrate that space was political. The assertion that "[a]uthentic knowledge of space must address the question of its production" (Lefebvre, 1991: 111) locates his analysis as concerned with the fundamental importance of social relations in historically specific epochs and societies. For Lefebvre, this is an important point: space and time are inextricably linked in processes subsumed under modes of production.[1]

> Space is nothing but the inscription of time in the world; spaces are the realisations, inscriptions in the simultaneity of the external world of a series of times, the rhythms of the city, the rhythms of the urban population. (Lefebvre, 1970, cited in Kofman and Lebas, 1996: 17)

Lefebvre's theory understands the production of space as emphasising the need to consider space as both a product (a thing) and a determinant (a process) of social relations and actions. This application of dialectics to space and the triad of necessary and inter-linked elements (spatial practices, representations of space and spaces of representation) in understanding space will be considered in detail. Similarly, the centrality of everyday social attitudes to and practices in space will be explored in relation to the importance of the spatial in the social organisation of Lefebvre's conception of the development of the city and the urban.

Space, as Lefebvre makes clear, is also the product of ideological, economic, and political forces (the domain of power) that seek to delimit, regulate and control the activities that occur within and through it. Lefebvre offers an account of space that demonstrates the complexity of a plurality of meanings that can be applied to the investigation of particular social spaces. The intention here, given that Lefebvre developed his analysis over a period of years and in various contexts, is to present an analysis of his theory of 'the production of space' which takes into account a number of aspects which were essential to its formulation.

What follows will be a consideration of Lefebvre's dialectical approach to the analysis of the production of space. The definition of his triadic elements will be clarified by linking spatial practices and socio-spatial organisation to an analysis of planning as an example of the operation of power and ideology in creating representations of space and by the consideration of everyday life as intrinsic in the conceptualisation of spaces of representations. However, a consideration of Lefebvre's analysis of space as a process of development will begin with his work on the rural and the urban. As Lefebvre was well aware, the historical context must be considered as fundamental in any analysis of the development and production of space:

61

> In space, what came earlier continues to underpin what follows. The preconditions of social space have their own particular way of enduring and remaining actual within that space...The task of architectonics [*as Lefebvre described his project*] is to describe, analyse and explain this persistence, which is often invoked in the metaphorical shorthand of strata, sedimentary layers and so on. (Lefebvre, 1991: 228)

LEFEBVRE'S HISTORY OF SPACE: THE COUNTRY AND THE CITY

For Lefebvre, space is at the centre of a continuing social and historical process, involving conflict and struggle over meanings and values. His analysis, his 'history of space', may be understood as a process, in which different modes of production produce their own space. Lefebvre writes:

> What we are concerned with, then, is the long history of space, even though space is neither a 'subject' nor an 'object' but rather a social reality – that is to say a set of relations and forms. This history is to be distinguished from an inventory of things in space...as also from ideas and discourses about space.

It must account for both representational spaces and representations of space, but above all for their interrelationships and their links with social practice. The history of space thus has its place between anthropology and political economy. (Lefebvre, 1991: 116)

Many of the essential concepts that Lefebvre uses in his understanding of the development of the city, the urban and space show indebtedness to the work of Marx. For example, Lefebvre's use of the concept of production as applied to space is an extrapolation of Marx's concept to encompass all of human activity and historical development under capitalism based upon the divisions between town and country, one that Marx saw as the basis of every division of labour. Lefebvre argues

> For Marx, the dissolution of the feudal mode of production and the transition to capitalism is attached to a subject, the town. The town breaks up the medieval system (feudalism) while transcending itself...the town is a 'subject' and a coherent force, a partial system which attacks the global system and which simultaneously shows the existence of this system and destroys it. (Lefebvre, 1972, cited in Shields, 2000: 21)

Lefebvre's analysis of the town and the country divide identified by Marx (See chapter 1) makes manifest the distinctions between old and new orders, modes of production, ways of life, etc. They are represented as having symbolic resonance both with the romanticisation of nature as a lost idyll and of the idea of the city as a model of enlightened, rational progress. As Lefebvre puts it:

> The countryside, both practical and reality and representation, will carry images of nature, of being, of the innate. The city will carry images of effort, of will, of subjectivity, of contemplation, without these representations becoming disjointed from real activities. (Lefebvre, 1996: 87–8)

Nevertheless, the distinction between town and country, for Lefebvre, becomes increasingly erroneous for understanding the produced space and experience of modernity, that is, the space of the capitalist mode of production, whose locus is the city. The city, as *the* site of modernity, is where urbanisation and industrialisation have the fullest effect on the production of space under capitalism but it would not be limited to the city. That is, for Lefebvre:

> The inevitable urbanisation of society would not take place at the expense of whole sectors, nor would it exacerbate unevenness in growth or development; it would successfully transcend the opposition between town and country instead of degrading both by turning them into an undifferentiated mass. (Lefebvre, 1991: 55)

However, a consequence of modernity, the 'progress' of scientific rationalism, was not to be viewed as an altogether welcome and positive development:

> It is impossible to escape the notion that nature is being murdered by 'anti-nature' – by abstraction, by signs and image, by discourse, as also by labour and its products. Along with God, nature is dying. 'Humanity' is killing both of them – and perhaps committing suicide into the bargain. (Lefebvre, 1991: 71)

Thus, our alienation from nature is, for Lefebvre, evident in our ambivalent understanding of ourselves and our relationship with the environment in which we live. Modern society is created out of our needs, desires and ability to conquer and use 'Nature'. Yet, the 'need' to understand our place in the world involves an appreciation of the 'natural', which we are destroying.

> On the one hand it points to the 'human being', the 'human nature' which will emerge and is already emerging from history, which will never be able to separate itself completely from nature as a given. The human being is forced to dwell with anti-nature (abstraction) painfully and long, and is already trying to return to nature, to put down roots, to find meaning in it, and peace of mind. On the other hand, nature designates the origin, what history has emerged from, something which both transforms and reveals itself in the succession of forms taken by action, by abstraction, by the signs that underpin and facilitate action, and by human power. (Lefebvre, 1995: 134)

63

This understanding is reminiscent of Weber's argument concerning the consequences of the dominance of formal means–end rationality leading to disenchantment. There is also evidence of a distinctly Nietzschean tone in Lefebvre's warning of the destruction and denial of nature. The domination of nature by narratives of science and humanism is viewed as a necessary element in understanding the progress of rational capitalism in the industrial world. However, this new 'common sense' hides the 'will to power' that limits opportunities and possibilities for human practices within a rationalist objectifying ethic. Nature is 'understood', exploited and 'used' as a consequence of this project of rationalism.[2] Lefebvre investigates the apparent contradictions that exist in relations between nature and culture. The first is that,

> In culture and civilisation, there is an initial 'given' – profound, primordial and yet ungraspable as such, obscure, fertile – from which nothing can emerge without being transformed by praxis, which in truth remains part of it. The 'given' we call nature; human power constantly reinvests the abstract forms it has extracted and the structure it has erected from it. ... Labour, technology,

knowledge, concepts – these do not cut the human off from nature, except perhaps when, consciously or not, thought copies understanding and makes the separation analytically. On the contrary, it is through praxis – that is, in everyday life – that particularities and differences which have emerged in art, in symbols, and images, in cultures, in physical fulfilment via the transformation of needs into desires, become explicit. (Lefebvre, 1995: 144)

The second is that, despite this apparent negation of the cycles of the 'natural' and our understanding of our place in the 'grand scheme of things' beyond our making, there are times and events which persist or survive the process of modernisation. An example Lefebvre uses is the perpetuation of a philosophy of nature that dates back to an ancient conception of nature as a fundamental power that operates in cycles of time or partial cycles, which have an importance in the everyday lives and activities of people throughout the ages. Lefebvre uses the survival of Dionysian springtime into modern cultures and cities. In a passage reminiscent of Gurevitch's and Bahktin's analysis of the Carnival as 'world-upside-down', Lefebvre describes the survival of the month of May as significant in festivals and fairs to argue that the ancient connection "in which the spring festival disrupts the human order of praxis, joining forces with nature to act out a game, a serious game, *repeating* the initial gestures of basic needs (eating, lovemaking) *reanimating* the divine and the cosmic which the logos of the city has lost – *identifying* with the rhythm of the cosmos" (Lefebvre, 1995: 146) is not the same in the modern city. In modernity, the re-identification with Nature is of a different order than in the past. It is constituted within and around the partial re-construction of a sanitised, malleable and useful depiction of nature.[3]

Modernisation is concentrated in the city, and the subsequent negative consequences for individuals (alienation, disenchantment, anomie, etc.) and groups (class exploitation, disease, overcrowding, etc.) inherent under capitalism are thought ameliorated by access to and enjoyment of a designed and regulated pseudo-nature. Culture and civilisation emerge as being acquired or won from nature, albeit a nature transformed by the application of knowledge, technology and labour, whilst at the same time recognising that we, as part of nature, are not totally detached from it. As Lefebvre puts it, the consequences in modernity of these contradictions and conflicts are that

> Nature, destroyed as such, has already had to be reconstructed at another level, the level of 'second nature', i.e. the town and the urban...The town, anti-nature or non-nature and yet second nature, heralds the future world, the world of the generalised urban. Nature, as the sum of particularities which are external to each other and dispersed in space, dies. It gives way to produced space, to the urban. (Lefebvre, 1991: 15)

What develops then, for Lefebvre, is a new order of being, of social reality, of space inextricably linked to the growth, development and eventual domination of the urban over all other forms of organisation of social relations. However, Lefebvre is keen not to overplay any apparent division or distinction between nature, country and the environment and the town, culture and the social within an analysis of how forms of urban domination operate within the mode of production.[4] Thus, the development of the city takes a more accelerated and central role under capitalism. The city is not only the site of political power (as it has been from antiquity) but also becomes the pivot for all economic activity, whether directly as the site of industrial production and consumption, or indirectly as the centre for the circulation and manufacture of ideas, knowledge and ultimately decisions on the conduct of life outwith the purely economic sphere. It is the city that Lefebvre views as the locus for the development and perpetuation of capitalism as a mode of production, for the social relations of production and their reproduction, for organisation and administration. Lefebvre asks what it is that constitutes the city and the urban and how it came to dominate. For Lefebvre,

> The urban is not a certain population, a geographical size or a collection of buildings. Nor is it a node, a trans-shipment point or a centre of production. It is all of these together, and thus any definition must search for the essential quality of all these aspects. The urban *is* social centrality, where the many elements and aspects of capitalism intersect in space, despite often merely being part of the place for a short time, as is the case with goods or people in transit. 'City-ness' is the simultaneous gathering and dispersing of goods, information and people... The city was the seat of intellectual development and administration – by necessity given the growing, restless population, given the wealth generated by urban trade, and given the plagues and contagions, which demanded the development, administration and enforcement of forms of quarantine and regulation. All these gave the city-based governments an advantage over those based in the rural hinterlands. From the cities, financial, ideological and governmental control spread out to regiment the countryside. (Lefebvre, 1991: 145, 148)

65

To describe and analyse the modern urban, it is essential to begin with industrialisation, as it is industrialisation that characterises modern society and by extension, modern cities. Cities have been in existence before industrialisation and modern rational capitalism. The city then for Lefebvre should not be viewed as a simple material product. It is the locus for production, for social relations and thus "production and reproduction of human beings by human beings, rather than a production of objects" (Lefebvre, 1996: 101). They contain monuments and edifices representing the production and consumption of materiality but also have spaces for entertainment, play, leisure, festivals, etc. This illustrates an important point both in Lefebvre's analysis of the city and the urban but also in his consideration of space. That is the "urban does not simply represent the transformation of space into a commodity by capitalism, but it is also the potential arena of play (festival)" (Lefebvre, 1987: 27).[5] Capitalism needs spaces for the reproduction of the relations of production as well as those for production. Designs and planning practices must not, for Lefebvre, ignore this dual quality of cities, that of the market but also a place of play, leisure and festival. To do so is to risk the consequences of a rational organisation of the city that loses its human scale and the necessary spaces for social interactions beyond those purely necessary for the accumulation of capital.[6] It also served an ideological role in the perpetuation of a hegemonic conception of appropriateness in terms of recreation and leisure time. For Lefebvre,

> The city must be a place of waste, for one wastes space and time; everything mustn't be foreseen and functional, for spending is a feast. You can't reduce this concept, either the festival disappears and becomes a simple commercial market, or it is something which goes beyond it...But for a festival, you need a rich and free society. (Lefebvre, 1987: 36)

66

In the processes of industrialisation and urbanisation, there is an apparent contradiction and conflict between what Lefebvre identifies as exchange value (growth, development and economic production) and use value (social and cultural life).[7] Lefebvre points to this crisis in the city as the result of the rise of industrial capitalism in which the city as a work of art, unique and able to take account and make space and time for play, festival and celebration, was submerged beneath the demands of capital. The 'crisis' of the nineteenth-century city as a result of industrialisation and urbanisation is a well-known phenomenon. What is interesting in Lefebvre's writing on the city, in relation to the production of space is the distinction he makes between the city as a work, as of nature or art, unique and the reproducibility of the urban form as an industrial commodity or product.

> We should perhaps introduce here a distinction between the city, a present and immediate reality, a practico-material and architectural fact, and the urban, a social reality made up of relations which are to be conceived of, constructed and reconstructed by thought...Urban life, urban society, in a word cannot go without a practico-material base, a morphology. (Lefebvre, 1996: 103)

The development of an urban system under capitalism, for Lefebvre, represents a fundamental aspect of his analysis of the city, and of space: "We now come to a basic and essential idea: capitalism is maintained by the conquest and integration of space. Space has long since ceased to be a passive geographical milieu or an empty geometrical one. It has become instrumental" (Lefebvre, 1970: 262, cited in Shields, 2000: 154–5). This instrumentality was evident in what Lefebvre saw as the development of capitalism as a system in which space itself came to be viewed as a scarce resource and was treated as a homogenous and quantifiable commodity, with an exchange value to be traded, like any other commodity on the market.

> Space, e.g. volume, is treated in such a way as to render it homogenous, its parts comparable, therefore exchangeable...The subordination of space to money and capital implies a quantification which extends from the monetary evaluation to the commercialisation of each plot of the entire space... Space now becomes one of the new 'scarcities', together with its resources, water, air and even light.' (Lefebvre, 1970: 261–2)

It is in the sense of the logic of capitalism in which ownership, control and organisation of space is achieved through concepts, plans and practices concomitantly affecting everyday life that gives space, for Lefebvre, a highly political character. The following quote bears some remarkable similarities to Simmel's analysis of the city and in his distinction between forms and contents:

67

> It is also evident that in so-called modern society, simultaneity is intensified and becomes more dense, that the capacities for encounter and assembly become strengthened. Communications speed up to quasi-instantaneity. Ascendant or descendent circuits of information flow are diffused from this *centrality*. This aspect of the 'socialisation of society' has already been emphasised (reservations having been made about the 'reformist' nature of this well-known formulation). It is evident that under the same conditions dispersion increases: the division of labour is pushed to the extreme segregation of social groups and material and spiritual separations. These dispersions can only be conceived or appreciated by reference to the form of simultaneity. Without this form, dispersion and separation are purely and simply glimpsed, accepted, confirmed as facts. Thus form enables us to designate the content, or rather, contents. Movement in its emergence reveals a hidden movement, the dialectical (conflictual) movement of content and urban form: the problematic. The form in which is inscribed this problematic asks questions which are part of it. Before whom and for whom is simultaneity established, the contents of urban life assembled? (Lefebvre, 1996: 138)

Those essential 'necessary elements' identified by Lefebvre for the production of space will be explored below after consideration of Lefebvre's analytical approach, that of the dialectics of space.

LEFEBVRE'S DIALECTICS OF SPACE

The importance of Lefebvre's conceptualisation of the production of space is that it is presented as a critical analysis of the significance of space in modern capitalist society, that is, it is not to be separated from social relations. Lefebvre's understanding and use of the term production detailed in *The Production of Space* is also expressed elsewhere and explicitly reflects his indebtedness to Marx.[8] His thesis is that space must be considered alongside raw materials, instruments of production and labour power as belonging to the set of productive forces that are the basis for the capitalist mode of production.

> What constitutes the forces of production, according to Marx and Engels? Nature, first of all, plays a part, then labour, hence the organisation (or division) of labour, and hence, also the instruments of labour, including technology, and ultimately, knowledge. (Lefebvre, 1991: 69)

Ownership or control of space confers a position in the economic structure by its ability to be used, more or less productively over time (with some shapes of space, volumes, etc. having different uses and therefore market value). Space is not considered as being used up, nor is it reproduced and may be considered as developing, for example, through the conquest of new spaces or the improved use of existing spaces. There is, therefore, a unique quality to space that must be considered in any analysis of capitalist relations of production.[9]

Lefebvre's approach was to apply the dialectical method to space. Dialectics is *both* a statement about what the world is, an ontology, as well as epistemology, a theory of knowledge, a critical study of validity, methods and range, by which one organises the world for the purpose of study and presentation. There is a fundamental dynamism in this dialectical approach as movement, interconnection and interaction of money, people, commodities, etc. occur in and through space. Therefore, how change occurs in the material and social world is fundamental to Lefebvre's project. For Lefebvre, authentic knowledge of space must address the question of its production and "...must account for both representational spaces and representations of space, but above all for their interrelationships and their links with social practice" (Lefebvre, 1991: 116). Lefebvre's spatial dialectic involves the *thesis* that space is a material thing (defined, analysed and quantified according to its fixity, that is its geographical location as defined by Cartesian co-ordinates that locate an object in space). The *antithesis* is that space is a process involving social relations between people and between people and things in space. His *synthesis* is that capitalist space is produced; it is an object, a thing, whilst simultaneously a process, a means, a tool through which and in which, social relations, and therefore change, can occur. Space then

> is not a thing among other things, nor a product among other products: rather, it subsumes things produced, and encompasses their interrelationships in their coexistence and simultaneity – their (relative) order and /or (relative) disorder. It is the outcome of a sequence and set of operations, and thus cannot be reduced to the rank of a simple object...Itself the outcome of past actions, social space is what permits fresh actions to occur, whilst suggesting others and prohibiting yet others. Among these actions, some serve production, others consumption (i.e. the enjoyment of the fruits of production). Social space implies a great diversity of knowledge. (Lefebvre, 1991: 73)

For Lefebvre, the fundamental flaw with most theories of space is that space is conceived as a receptacle or frame to be filled by contents. Thus, Lefebvre's fundamental concern in his analysis of space is to try to reconcile what he identified as two distinct and competing conceptions of space. The first was that of a mental or ideological space, the domain of intellectual disciplines, and second, the physical or natural space in which we live. Lefebvre thus develops the concept of *social space* which

69

> is revealed in its particularity to the extent that it ceases to be indistinguishable from mental space (as defined by the philosophers and mathematicians) on the one hand, and physical space (as defined by practico-sensory activity and the perception of 'nature') on the other...such social space is constituted neither by a collection of things or an aggregate of (sensory) data, nor by a void packed like a parcel with various contents, and that it is irreducible to a 'form' imposed upon phenomena, upon things, upon physical materiality...social space is produced and reproduced in connection with the forces of production (and within the relations of production). And these forces, as they develop, are not taking over a pre-existing, empty or neutral space, or a space determined solely by geography, climate, anthropology, or some other comparable consideration. There is thus no good reason for positing such a radical separation between works of art and products as to imply the work's total transcendence of the product. A social space cannot be adequately accounted for either by nature (climate, site) or by its previous history...Mediators and mediations, have to be taken into consideration: the action of groups, factors within knowledge, within ideology, or within the domain of representation. (Lefebvre, 1991: 27, 77)[10]

Lefebvre's thesis may thus be articulated as a spatialised rendition of Marx's conception of fetishism. He considers that the social relations necessary for the existence, that is the production, of space are masked or hidden by the emphasis given to space as simply existing outwith the means and mode of capitalist production. For Marx, commodity fetishism was the process by which commodities as material things mask the underlying and specific social relations that create them by the dominance of the market and the emphasis on exchange as opposed to use value. Lefebvre's emphasis on the unique qualities of space must be considered as holding the potential not only for a radical spatial reconceptualisation of the mode of production in modernity, but also for having practical and political significance in contesting dominant categorisations or representations of space. This is because:

> Space is not merely economic, in which all parts are interchangeable and have exchange value. Space is not merely a political instrument for homogenising all parts of society. On the contrary...Space remains a model, a perpetual prototype of use value resisting the generalisations of exchange value in the capitalist economy under the authority of the homogenising state. Space is a use value...[*similar to*]...time to which it is ultimately linked because time is our life, our fundamental use value. (Lefebvre, 1978, p. 291, cited in Shields, 2000: 168)

Therefore, since commodities are processes that take material form, however "unlike other commodities or products, space has both a material reality and a formal property that enables it to constrain other commodities and their social relations. It continually recreates or reproduces the social relations of production" (Shields, 2000: 159). Social relations are thus hidden in the reified world of material goods, as space itself becomes fetishised. Lefebvre seeks to make clear this application of Marx's concept to social space.

> The *ideologically* dominant tendency divides space up into parts and parcels in accordance with the division of labour. It bases its image of the forces occupying space on the idea that space is a passive receptacle. Thus, instead of uncovering the social relationships (including class relationships) that are latent in spaces, instead of concentrating our attention on the production of space and the social relationships that are inherent to it – relationships which introduce specific contradictions into production so echoing the contradiction between the private ownership and the means of production and the social character of the productive forces – we fall into the trap of treating space as space 'in itself', as such. We come to think in terms of spatiality, and so fetishise space in a way reminiscent of the old fetishism of commodities, where the trap lay in exchange, and the error was to consider 'thing' in isolation, as 'things in themselves'. (Lefebvre, 1991: 90)

Lefebvre's aim was to uncover the social relations involved in the production of space and the significance this has for a comprehensive knowledge of space, that is, the consequences for our understanding of space as fundamental for understanding modernity and the possibility or potential for liberation from the alienation inherent in modern rational capitalism.

> Once brought back into conjunction with a (spatial and signifying) social practice, the concept of space can take on its full meaning. Space thus rejoins material production: the production of goods, things, objects of exchange...It also rejoins the productive process considered at a higher level, as the result of accumulated knowledge...Lastly, it rejoins the freest creative process there is – the signifying process, which contains within itself the seeds of the 'reign of freedom'. (Lefebvre, 1991: 137)

Lefebvre's insistence on the interplay of different elements in the production of space necessarily includes social relations, activities and movement. Place is the delimited order of inter-related elements that are prescribed in a distinct location, which defines that place through these inter-relationships. A space, on the other hand, exists only when mobile elements (implying direction, velocity and time) intersect, and it is this relationship of movements that produce space. The qualification between space and place is a reminder that abstracted notions need to be grounded in the everyday world of social practices which are conceived as taking place in the material landscape as produced, localised place. These landscapes become imbued with meaning that highlights the dialectical analysis of space itself by exploring the contradictions and conflicts that exist in relation to social practices in place.[11]

71

The implications of this for the analysis of social space will be demonstrated later but will be shown to reside in the control, organisation and design of space for different functions and practices. Who owns and ultimately regulates the activities that can occur or are allowed in space is rooted in a process that enhances the contradictions and conflicts inherent in its production. There are many public spaces where such conflicts and contradictions between different conceptions and practices are focussed in specific locations. The contradictions between notions of space as neutral and objective and those that consider space to be the product of historically situated processes (including that of ideology and power) is, as Lefebvre argues, fundamental for understanding its production:

> there is no getting around the fact that the bourgeoisie still has the initiative in its struggle for (and in) space...The state and each of its constituent institutions call for spaces – but spaces which they can then organise according to their specific requirements...here we see the polyvalence of social space, its 'reality' at once formal and material. Though a product to be used, to be consumed, it is also a *means of production*; networks of exchange and flows of raw materials and energy fashion space and are determined by it. (Lefebvre, 1991: 56, 85)

Lefebvre goes even further in his criticism of perspectives on space that do not consider the role of dominant ideologies in our understanding of how space is produced and used:

> a space that is apparently 'neutral', objective', fixed, transparent, innocent or indifferent implies more than the convenient establishment of an inoperative system of knowledge, more than an error that can be avoided by evoking the 'environment', ecology, nature and anti-nature, culture and so forth. Rather, it is a whole set of errors, a complex of illusions, which can even cause us to forget completely that there is a total subject which acts continually to maintain and reproduce its own conditions of existence, namely the state (along with its foundation in specific social classes and fractions of classes). (Lefebvre, 1991: 94)

The underlying nature of Lefebvre's project, which is exposed by his emphasis on the state and concomitantly on how class struggle becomes inscribed in space, is to use his understanding of space, to provide a theoretical analysis that can contribute "to the dismantling of existing society by exposing what gnaws at it from within" (Lefebvre, 1991: 420). There is in Lefebvre's analysis the attempt to produce a theoretical analysis of space that has within it the potential for radical political action. His aim is to present an understanding of space that can then be used to subvert or challenge the authority of the hegemonic concepts and practices in space, and to propose alternatives that have practical advantages that can rescue us from the alienating consequences of capitalism. For Lefebvre, knowledge of space involves the interrelation between three spatial elements, a threefold dialectic within spatialisation. Form, structure and function individually cannot provide a comprehensive understanding or knowledge of space. The dynamic interaction between all three shows the complexity and polyvalence of the concept of social space as simultaneously a means of the social relations of production as land, property (the economic base) and as an object to be consumed, an element of social struggle in which space is a political instrument. Knowledge, of social space, that is its full meaning, for Lefebvre "must account for both representational spaces and representations of space, but above all for their interrelationships and their links with social practice" (Lefebvre, 1991: 116). It is these necessary elements for the production of space that will now be considered.

LEFEBVRE'S THREE NECESSARY ELEMENTS FOR THE PRODUCTION OF SPACE

spatial practices

Spatial practices refer to the physical and material flows (of individuals, groups or commodities), circulations, transfers and interactions that occur in and across space, structured in such a way as to assure social life is produced and reproduced. That is, specific places and spatial compositions or arrangements are necessary and appropriate to the organisation or structuring of social relations. This includes the use of particular types of buildings, the form and structure of the urban landscape and areas set-aside for specific purposes or functions: for example, sites for housing, industry, commerce, shopping or, leisure and recreation. Spatial practice for Lefebvre

> embraces production and reproduction, and the particular locations and spatial sets characteristic of each social formation. Spatial practice ensures continuity and some degree of cohesion. In terms of social space, and of each member of a given society's relationship to that space, this cohesion implies a guaranteed level of competence and a specific level of performance...The spatial practice of a society secretes that society's space; it propounds and presupposes it, in a dialectical interaction; it produces it slowly and surely as it masters and appropriates it. From the analytical standpoint, the spatial practice of a society is revealed in the deciphering of its space...It embodies a close association, within perceived space, between daily reality (daily routines) and urban reality (the routes and networks which link up the places set aside for work, 'private' life and leisure). This association is a paradoxical one, because it includes the most extreme separation between the places it links together. The specific spatial competence and performance of every society member can only be evaluated empirically...A spatial practice must have certain cohesiveness, but this does not imply that it is coherent (in the sense of intellectually worked out or logically conceived). (Lefebvre, 1991: 33, 38)

73

In other words, a person's understanding of their social reality conditions their usage of space in respect of how they interact with others in specific places for particular reasons (i.e. for work, leisure, consumption, etc). This understanding also includes how one negotiates the spaces between sites, for example areas to avoid at different times of the day or night, routes to work or favourite places, or family and friends' homes. We make sense of our daily actions by having an understanding of how things and social relations are structured in space. Spatial practice is the experience of the circulation of goods, people, money, labour power, information, etc. which associates the ownership, use and designation of land within a hierarchy of administrative and organisational divisions of space, with an intrinsic element of social control (policing and surveillance). This link between spatial practice and the cohesiveness of social organisation will be developed later. However, it is clear that Lefebvre's use of the term 'spatial practices' refers to the production of spatial forms and structures and, specifically in the urban context of spatial relations, how space is implicated in processes of habituation, of people, places and practices. As Merrifield puts it, "[s]patial practices structure daily life and a broader urban reality and, in so doing, ensures societal cohesion, continuity and a specific spatial competence" (Merrifield, 1993: 524). Therefore, for conceptual clarity in later discussions of Lefebvre's 'necessary' elements, it is perhaps more appropriate to refer to this factor/experience of space as 'production'.

representations of space

Representation de l'espace is the dominant space in society and is "tied to the relations of production and to the 'order' which those relations impose, and hence to knowledge, to signs, to codes and to 'frontal' relations" (Lefebvre, 1991: 33). It may also be thought of as discourses on space, regimes of analysis, and they are as Shields puts it, "the logic and forms of knowledge, and the ideological content of codes, theories, and the conceptual depiction of space linked to production relations" (Shields, 2000: 163). For Lefebvre representations of space are:

74

> Conceptualised space, the space of scientists, planners, urbanists, technocratic sub-dividers and social engineers, and of a certain type of artist with a scientific bent – all of whom identify what is lived and what is perceived with what is conceived ... This is the dominant space of any society (or mode of production). (Lefebvre, 1991: 38–9)

This is the realm of expert knowledge in which space is conceptualised and discursively constructed by

> professionals and technocrats such as planners, engineers, developers, architects, urbanists, geographers and those of a scientific bent. This space comprises the various arcane signs, jargon, codifications, objectified representations used and produced by these agents ... it is always a conceived and abstract space since it subsumes ideology within its practice. (Merrifield, 1993: 523).

Therefore, it is argued by Lefebvre that those who control how space is represented control how it is produced, organised and used. The development of planning as a professional discipline with an inherent ideology of space, Lefebvre views as significant in terms of control of representations of space and, concomitantly, the application of spatial practices that impinge upon everyday life. Planning, as an ideology and a practice will be explored later in relation to Lefebvre's conception of the politics of space.

spaces of representation

Espaces de la representations may be described as discourses on space in that they

> are mental inventions (codes, signs, 'spatial discourses', utopian plans, imaginary landscapes, and even material constructs such as symbolic spaces, particular built environments, paintings, museums, and the like) that imagine new meanings or possibilities for spatial practices (Harvey, 1990: 218–19).

Representational Space, as Nicholson (1991) translates it, is directly lived space, the space of everyday life in contrast to the domination of the conceived, ordered, regulated space of hegemonic force. Spaces of representation then are subject to rationalisation, codification, measurement, intervention, and usurpation. Nevertheless, they also contain the potential for challenging dominant spatial practices and perceptions by the imaginative use of space. For Lefebvre, representational space is

> Space as directly *lived* through its associations and images and symbols, and hence the space of 'inhabitants' and 'users', but also some artists and perhaps of those, such as a few writers and philosophers, who *describe* and aspire to do no more than describe. His is the dominated – and hence passively experienced – space which the imagination seeks to change and appropriate. It overlays physical space, making symbolic use of its objects. Thus representational spaces may be said, though again with certain exceptions, to tend towards more or less coherent systems of non-verbal symbols and signs. (Lefebvre, 1991: 39)

75

Spaces of representation, then, are the spaces of everyday life where a complex of dichotomous factors, mental and social interact. For example, attraction/repulsion, access/denial, fear/ desire, familiarity/unfamiliarity, open/closed and public/private. They are thus the imagined or utopian spaces produced from cultural and social forces and associated with ritual, symbol, tradition, myth, desire, dreams, etc. Everyday life is a fundamental factor, one leg of the tripod, in which Lefebvre's conception of the production of space rests. As such Lefebvre's use of everyday life will be considered below.

SPATIAL PRACTICE AND SOCIAL ORGANISATION

Lefebvre's argument is that "[a]uthentic knowledge of space must address the question of its production" (Lefebvre, 1991: 111) and therefore must take "account for both representational spaces and representations of space, but above all for their interrelationships and their links with social practice" (Lefebvre, 1991: 116). A dynamic relationship, a simultaneity, exists between material form, social function and hierarchical structures that recognises the fundamental importance of social activity or practices within space. It is recognition of the multiplicity of meanings that can exist in relation to social spaces. This inter-dependence, in which the relative dominance of one aspect over the others at any one time, has the potential for liberating, that is the appropriation of differentiated spaces by popular use and practice, or for the domination of sites by the hegemonic forces of capital. This has important implications for Lefebvre in that

> Once brought back into conjunction with a (spatial and signifying) social practice, the concept of space can take on its full meaning. Space thus rejoins material production: the production of goods, things, objects of exchange... It also rejoins the productive process considered at a higher level, as the result of accumulated knowledge... Lastly, it rejoins the freest creative process there is – the signifying process, which contains within itself the seeds of the 'reign of freedom'. (Lefebvre, 1991: 137)

This dynamic relationship of all three necessary elements in which one dominates relative to the others was for Lefebvre the means by which historically specific spatialisations were socially produced:

76

> spatial practice, representations of space and representational spaces contribute in different ways to the production of space according to their qualities and attributes, according to the society or mode of production in question, and according to the historical period. (Lefebvre, 1991: 46)

Lefebvre's project is to present space as a means as well as a medium through which different historical periods and modes of production have created spaces indicative of and necessary for their survival and expansion. Indeed, *The Production of Space* may be read as an attempt by Lefebvre to understand and explain the role of space in the perpetuation of and expansion of the capitalist mode of production. He writes

> what has happened is that capitalism has found itself able to attenuate (if not resolve) its internal contradictions for a century, and consequently, in the hundred years since the writing of *Das Capital*, it has succeeded in achieving 'growth'. We cannot calculate at what price, but we know the means: *by occupying space, by producing a space.* (Lefebvre, 1976: 21. Italics in original)

The importance of Lefebvre's analysis in relation to social space lies in the consideration of space as neither a 'subject' nor an object but is a social reality of relations and forms that include possibilities and potentials for social interaction as, "any space implies, contains and dissimulates social relationships – and this despite the fact that a space is not a thing but rather a set of relations between things (objects and products)" (Lefebvre, 1991: 82–3). Space is part of the social relations of production as well as one of the forces of production, and therefore the need to consider the spatial organisation of society is essential. Lefebvre is emphatic in this: "The main point to be noted, therefore, is the production of a social space by political power – that is by violence in the service of economic goals. A social space of this kind is generated out of a rationalised and theorised 'form' serving as an instrument for the violation of an exiting space" (Lefebvre, 1991: 151–2). There is then in Lefebvre's work the attempt to synthesise the urban and everyday life, through his conception of the production of space, as experience, conception and practice in which 'nature' has been colonised and put to use, leading to its virtual destruction.[12] Lefebvre's aim is to uncover, using his concept of social space, how this has come about, how it exists and operates in the world. Thus he writes

> What exactly is the mode of existence of social relationships? ...The study of space offers an answer according to which the social relations of production have a social existence to the extent that they have a spatial existence; they project themselves into a space, becoming inscribed there, and in the process producing that space itself. Failing this, these relations would remain in the realm of 'pure' abstraction – that is to say, in the realm of representations and hence of ideology: the realm of verbalism, verbiage and empty words. (Lefebvre, 1991: 129)

77

The spatial structure and social relations within urban industrial society must be viewed as a dynamic process in which "spatial structure is now seen not merely as an arena in which social life unfolds, but rather as a medium through which social relations are produced and reproduced" (Gregory and Urry, 1985: 3). The spatial organisation of society is for Lefebvre a fundamental social factor.[13] As argued previously, space may be considered as part of the forces of production, the means by which the mode of production functions, but it is also a commodity to be used for various functions. It can be compartmentalised and 'designed' for various planned functions, such as housing, industry, commerce or leisure. To that extent space can become a scarce resource with potential for conflict over control:

> Also threatened with destruction are the 'elements', as they were called in classical philosophy; water, air and daylight...Now, not in every country, but virtually on planetary scale, there is an abundant production of these formerly scarce goods. Nonetheless, new scarcities, such as water, air, daylight

and space, emerge and there is an intense struggle over them. (Lefebvre, 1977: 344–5)[14]

Lefebvre argues that potentially a political economy of space is possible, in which the spatial organisation of social relations represents a physical manifestation of social hierarchies through which power is displayed, oriented and organised. This is evident in the organisation and process of government:

> The state and each of its constituent institutions call for spaces – but spaces which they can then organise according to their specific requirements...here we see the polyvalence of social space, its 'reality' at once formal and material. Though a product to be used, to be consumed, it is also a *means of production*; networks of exchange and flows of raw materials and energy fashion space and are determined by it." (Lefebvre, 1991: 85)

This political element to the production and control of space is expressed in earlier writings by Lefebvre:

> Space has become for the state a political instrument of primary importance. The state uses space in such a way that it ensures its control of places, its strict hierarchy, homogeneity of the whole and the segregation of parts. It is thus an administratively controlled and even policed space." (Lefebvre, 1978: 288 cited in Gottdiener, 1985: 46)

The hegemony of capitalism then is carried out in and through space to ensure the segregation and the ordering of society by the intervention and control of the structure and design of predominantly urban spaces. Therefore, it is possible to view class and other social segregations and divisions as the operation of a dominant spatial structure and organisation. It is in this skewed relationship where abstract perceptions of space are prioritised over the practices and spaces of representations that has led to the space of the everyday becoming constrained, regulated, framed, ordered and thus dominated by the economy and the authority and power of the state. This then becomes normalised and elite representations of space function as technologies of control, discipline and power.

It is in the realm of the body that Lefebvre considers this exercise of the power of spatial technologies and conceptions to operate in the everyday life of the inhabitants of the modern urban world. Lefebvre, it may be said, prioritises the body in his analysis of how power is effected in the spatial organisation of society: not only economic and political power creating, ordering and using space, but also the dominance of male power in space.[15] Such a perspective posits a reading of space as part of a political and geographical project in which the interaction between each element in his triad of perceived – conceived – lived is emphasised and illustrated.

> Dominated space and appropriated space may in principle be combined – and ideally at least, they ought to be combined. But history – that is to say the history of accumulation – is also the history of their separation and mutual antagonism. The winner in this contest, moreover, has been domination. ... [and] ... the reappropriation of the body, in association with the reappropriation of space ... [is] a non-negotiable part of its agenda. (Lefebvre, 1991: 167, 168)

The dominance of abstract conceived space, in which capital, money, commodities and phallocentricity are the fundamental forces, over the social space of everyday lived experience denies or subjugates the sensual experience and traditions of play. Therefore, Lefebvre sees class and social struggle as central to this domination of homogenising abstract space. The emphasis returns to Lefebvre's political analysis and project of viewing space as the medium and means for social struggle:

> As for the class struggle, its role in the production of space is a cardinal one in that this production is performed solely by classes, fractions of classes and groups representative of classes. Today, more than ever, the class struggle is inscribed in space. Indeed, it is that struggle alone which prevents abstract space from taking over the whole planet and papering over all differences. (Lefebvre, 1991: 55)

79

For Lefebvre, the body is "at the very heart of space and of the discourse of power is irreducible and subversive. It is the body which is the point of return" (Lefebvre, 1991: 89). Spatial practices function as technologies of power, as disciplinary technologies for producing useful and docile bodies. A discussion of Foucault's conception of disciplinary spaces will follow later (see Chapter 5), but the intention here is to highlight the similarities with Lefebvre's perspective on the production of space within socio-historical processes and regimes of power. The everyday lived experience in social space is thus replete with the operation and representation of technologies power, in and though space. Thus, "[l]iving bodies, the bodies of 'users' are caught up not only in the toils of parcelised space, but also in the web of images, signs and symbols. These bodies are transported out of themselves, transferred and emptied out, as it were, via the eyes" (Lefebvre, 1991: 98). Space may thus be viewed as produced or created, organised and regulated to facilitate the needs and demands of capitalism: the good, moral ordering of the city and society for the benefit of accumulation of surplus value. Thus, spatial practices derive their effect from social life only through how the structure and organisation of the social operates. That is, they take on their meanings under specific social relations (of class, gender, community, ethnicity, or race, etc.) that are historically specific.

In relation to much of urban public and social space in the contemporary landscape of the city as both a relic of the nineteenth century and as newly produced space, it may be said they were produced according to the 'habitus', that set of 'classificatory practices' and 'ultimate values' belonging to the dominant political and social order of the day, namely the political, mercantile, financial and administrative elite.[16] There is within these dominant spatial practices an inherent exercise of power through the operation of procedures that seek to limit, regulate and control movements, choices, behaviours, etc. through their design and ornamentation. The aim was and is to imbue the landscape of city with symbols of power so that those who use it come to internalise the civilising bourgeois values of those who designed them. Thus the flow and circulation of people through the streets is not only about efficient transportation or circulation, it is also concerned with controlling movement along allowed routes replete with symbols of power. The interconnectedness of spatial and social practices and the potential for the former to destroy the latter are for Lefebvre part of the inter-relatedness of the three elements:

80

> For everything (the 'whole') weighs down on the lower or 'micro-level, on the local and the localisable – in short, on the sphere of everyday life. Everything (the 'whole') also depends on this level: exploitation and domination, protection and – inseparably – repression. The basis and foundation of the 'whole' is dissociation and separation, maintained as such by the will above; such dissociation and separation are inevitable in that they are the outcome of a history, of the history of accumulation, but they are fatal as soon as they are maintained in this way, because they keep the moments and elements of social practice away from one another. A spatial practice destroys social practice; social practice destroys itself by means of spatial practice. (Lefebvre, 1991: 366)

The attempt here is to link Lefebvre's first element of his triad to the relationship between spatial practice and social organisation. The relevance of this concept is obvious both for an appreciation of Lefebvre's dialectics of space but also for understanding how Lefebvre's dialectic of space has provided a starting point for other theorists of space. The following will similarly seek to draw out Lefebvre's second element, representations of space, by an examination of planning as an ideology.

THE POLITICS AND POWER OF SPACE

There is in Lefebvre's work a clear understanding of the historicity of the development of concepts of the city, and his criticisms of other urban theories bemoan their lack of acknowledgement of the ideological element in these concepts. For example, he stresses that "[a]ny representation is ideological if it contributes either immediately or 'mediately' to the reproduction of the relations of production. Ideology is therefore inseparable from practice" (Lefebvre, 1976: 29). Thus ideologies have the practical effect of maintaining the dominance of particular class interests: "It is the role of ideologies to secure the assent of the oppressed and exploited" (Lefebvre, 1968: 76). Thus, hegemony is a dynamic relationship in which the 'dominant' must continually strive to maintain their position in the face of opposition and alternatives.[17] Hegemony is therefore not simply outright domination or coercion but involves an element of leadership in attempting to inculcate or educate those values, meanings and 'norms' that are considered important to the reproduction of relations of capital. It is in this sense that Lefebvre describes planning as part of the hegemonic practice of power and the politics of, in and over space.

For Lefebvre, the ideology of planning became expressed in the development of practices that conceived urban space as a means by which it could be represented, homogenised, divided up for sale as a commodity, and parcelled out for specific functions. Lefebvre views concepts of the city as

81

> made up of facts, representations and images borrowed from the ancient pre-industrial and pre-capitalist city, but in a process of transformation and new elaboration. In practice, the urban core (an essential part of the image and the concept of the city) splits open and yet maintains itself: overrun, often deteriorated, sometimes rotting, the urban core does not disappear...Until now we have shown how the city has been attacked by industrialisation...The ruling classes or fractions of the ruling classes intervene actively and voluntarily in this process, possessing capital (the means of production) and managing not only the economic use of capital and productive investments, but also the whole society, using part of the wealth produced in 'culture', art, knowledge, ideology. Beside, or rather in opposition to, dominant social groups (classes and class fractions), there is the working class: the proletariat, itself divided into strata, partial groups, various tendencies, according to industrial sectors and local and national traditions. (Lefebvre, 1996: 7)

Lefebvre views the development of planning as an ideology, and as particular practices, as originating at a specific time in history that is, in the late nineteenth and early twentieth century. It is important to clarify the point that Lefebvre is here concerned with planning as an organised and instituted discipline. Clearly, planning as designed interventions in the physical, social and spatial infrastructure of the urban sphere has a longer history than that to which Lefebvre refers. This he views as the result of a process, the progress of an instrumental rationality (Zweckrational to use Weber's term) into urban organisation as it had into all other spheres of society. However, Lefebvre concedes that

> there is in fact no single or unitary approach in planning thought, but several tendencies identifiable according to this operational rationalism...It begins from a most detailed methodical analysis of elements – productive operation, social and economic organisation, structure and function. It then subordinates these elements to a finality...Finality is an object of decision. It is a strategy, more or less justified by an ideology. Rationalism that purports to extract from its own analyses the aim pursued by these analyses is itself an ideology...The city as chaotic confusion in which organisational rationalism seeks to solve. This is not a normal disorder. How can it be established as norm and normality? This is inconceivable. This disorder is unhealthy. The physician of modern society sees himself as the physician of sick social space. Finality? The cure? It is coherence. (Lefebvre, 1996: 81, 82)

Lefebvre considered town planning to be subsumed by an implicit but rarely expressed ideology that was composed of three elements. Town planning approximated to (a) a consistent activity with a scientific and technical approach that, (b) engaged in a methodical examination of the discipline with the aim of establishing an epistemology for it that (c) could use this body of knowledge, to claim to be a science of space involved at the micro or macro level of social activity. The development of planning as ideology developed more and more precise definitions:

82

> To study the circulation, of the conveying of orders and information in the great modern city, leads to real knowledge and to technical applications. To claim that the city is defined as a network of circulation and communication, as a centre of information and decision-making, is an absolute ideology...This ideology has two independent aspects, mental and social. Mentally, it implies a theory of rationality and organisation whose expression date from around 1910, a transformation in contemporary society...It is then that socially the notion of space comes to the fore, relegating into shadow time and becoming. Planning as ideology formulates all the problems of society into questions of space and transposes all that comes from history and consciousness into spatial terms. It is an ideology which immediately divides up. Since society does not function in a satisfactory manner, could there not be a pathology of space? Within this perspective, the virtually official recognition of the priority of space over time is not conceived of as an indication of social pathology, as symptom among others of a reality which engenders social disease. On the contrary, what are represented are healthy and diseased spaces. The planned should be able to distinguish between sick spaces and spaces linked to mental and social health which are generators of this health. As physician of space, he should have the capacity to conceive of an harmonious social space, normal and normalising. Its function would then be to grant to this space (perhaps identical to geometrical space, that of abstract topologies) pre-existing social realities." (Lefebvre, 1996: 98–9)

For Lefebvre the object 'par excellence' of this science was space not time and the hidden understanding behind its ideology was that

> planned space was objective and 'pure'; it was a scientific object and hence had a neutral character. Space, in this sense, passes as being innocent or, in other words, apolitical...Indeed, if this science is the science of formal space, of spatial form, it implies a rigid process and this science would consist of nothing more than the sum total of the physical constraints placed in the living environment of the affected population. (Lefebvre 1997: 340)

In a sense Lefebvre's critique appears directed at the element of environmental determinism he identifies in the ideology of planning as a discipline and of concepts of the city. The lack of engagement with or acknowledgement of ideology denies the politics inherent in space. This is a central argument in his understanding of the production of space. Space cannot be thought of or understood as a passive, neutral, objective object. It does not exist in a vacuum but is part of the history of society in which processes and interactions exist between various spheres. Thus, the social, the economic and the political act on, in and through space and vice versa. For Lefebvre, what is necessary is to place the political element of space, what the ideology of planning sublimated or denied, at the core of his understanding of the production of space. Space as both a product and a process means that Lefebvre emphasises his critique of apolitical theories of space, such as those of the planning profession, as recognition that spatial forms are politically created and serve political functions:

83

> Space is not a scientific object removed from ideology or politics; it has always been political and strategic. If space has an air of neutrality and indifference with regard to its contents and thus seems to be 'purely' formal, the epitome of rational abstraction, it is precisely because it has already been occupied and used, and has already been the focus of past processes whose traces are not always evident in the landscape. Space has been shaped and moulded from historical and natural elements, but this has been a political process. Space is political and ideological. It is a product literally filled with ideologies. There is an ideology of space. Why? Because space, which seems homogeneous, which seems to be completely objective in its pure form, such as we can ascertain it, is a social product. The production of space can be likened to the production of any given particular type of merchandise. (Lefebvre, 1977: 341)

Planning therefore represents a profession in which ideologies are acted out, explicitly or implicitly, in representations of space. How a space is perceived, subjected to logic, codes, theories, etc. is the realm of expert knowledge in which it is abstracted and put to use. Space needs to be considered as political because how a space is represented has implications for how it is to be used: for what purposes, by whom, when and why. Gregory thus refers to representations of space as "constellations of power, knowledge, and spatiality – in which the dominant social order is materially inscribed (and, by implication, legitimised)" (Gregory, 1994: 403). This has implications therefore for the control and domination of one group by another by limiting contact or interactions by segregation or isolation. The potential for conflict over control of representations of space is thus in the arena of potential conflict between social classes or class fractions. Mitchell, in his analysis of the conflict over different understandings of what constitutes public space, is clear in his assessment of the ideological element of representations of space as used by planners and developers:

> Imposing limits and controls on spatial interaction has been one of the principal aims of the urban and corporate planners during this century. The territorial segregation created through the expression of social difference has increasingly been replaced by a celebration of constrained diversity. The diversity repre-sented in shopping centres, 'megastructures, corporate plazas and (increasingly) in public parks is carefully constructed...a space of social practice that sorts and divides social groups according to the dictates of comfort and order rather than to those of political struggle...The strategies of urban and corporate planners classify and distribute various social strata and classes (other than the one that exercise hegemony) across the available territory, keeping them separate and prohibiting all contacts – these being replaced by signs (or images) of contact. (Mitchell, 1995: 120)

84

THE EVERYDAY IN LEFEBVRE'S PRODUCTION OF SPACE

Lefebvre is concerned with investigating the significance and details of everyday life. In many aspects of his works on the city and space, he examines how changes wrought by modernisation have affected the patterns and routines of daily life. What he seeks to emphasise is the loss of control and sense of belonging to a community that has accompanied the transition to a more materialistic, individualistic society. Shields considers this concern with alienation as the unifying theme throughout Lefebvre's work:

> What unites all his work – from his first to his most mature works – is his deeply humanistic interest in alienation. . . . It is not technological progress, the absence of war, or ease of life, or even length of life, but the chance for a *fully lived life* that is the measure of a civilisation. The quality of any society lies in the opportunity for the unalienated and authentic life experience that it gives all its members. Grounded in anything else, democracy falls short of what it could be. In cultural terms, this quality supersedes historically imposed measures of

beauty or elegance. In political and economic terms, it is an index of liberty.
(Shields, 2000: 2)

Lefebvre's analysis of the production of space centres on the interplay of everyday experience and interactions within historical modes of production, specifically capitalism, with the development of technologies and conceptions of space (spatial practices and representations of space). This dynamic equilibrium between three complex compounds (combinations of elements) produces space. Ownership of space is not only the exercise of monopoly rights over a physical territory. It also involves how space is conceived and represented, which reflects the dominant, hegemonic forces operative within and over it. There is then an inherent element of control and regulation of space and concomitantly of the practices that are allowed or sanctioned, permitted or prescribed within it. But, as Lefebvre emphasises, space is produced and shaped for economic production and for social reproduction, and as "[s]pace is permeated with social relations: it is not only supported by social relations but is also producing and produced by social relations" (Lefebvre, 1991: 286). There is thus a reciprocal relationship between the elements involved in its production. That is, everyday practices are not only dominated by spatial practices and the representations of space preferred or imposed by practitioners such as planners, state officials, academics, etc., but also impose their own meanings, values and understandings of space by the routine practices and techniques of everyday life.

Command over space, for Lefebvre, is thus a fundamental and ubiquitous basis of power in everyday life and in society. Those who create and define the meanings, forms and practices in space (as well as time) can set the rules by which that space is used: when, by whom, for what purposes. The ideological and political forces that constitute hegemony in society seek to control the material context of everyday social experience. In this context the control over the representations given of space and the meanings attached to them are significant for understanding how power employs and is employed in and through space, how it manifests and inscribes in space meanings and ideologies that belong to the dominant hegemony. Harvey eloquently sums up the point: "If a picture or map can paint a thousand words, then power in the realms of representation may end up being as important as power over the materiality of spatial organisation itself" (Harvey, 1990: 233). Lefebvre defines everyday life as:

made of recurrences: gestures of labour and leisure, mechanical movements both human and properly mechanic, hours, days, weeks, months, years, linear and cyclical repetitions, natural and rational time, etc.: the study of creative activity (of *production*, in its widest sense) leads to the study of reproduction or the conditions in which actions producing objects and labour are reproduced, re-commenced, and re-assume their component proportions or, on the contrary, undergo gradual or sudden modifications. (Lefebvre, 1971: 18)

Shields attempts to clarify Lefebvre's use of the term 'everyday life'[18] distinguishing between *le quotidien* (everydayness) as the banal repetitive routinisation of life under capitalism and *la vie quotidienne* (daily life) the ordinary, habitual, routine nature of day-to-day living. Lefebvre's use of *la vie quotidienne* is an attempt to 'marry' daily life to the alienated concept of everydayness. Lefebvre is proposing that there is a need to reconsider the symbiosis of the two ideas. They are not separated into one alienated, bad, everyday whilst the other is special, good, unalienated 'moments'. The two meanings overlap in that the alienated everyday has the potential for extraordinariness, and therefore his use of the concept of everyday life is to encompass this potential for unreserved participation. The aim of Lefebvre's use of the term is to highlight how consciousness can be transformed by changing the material components and everyday routines of daily life and vice versa.

Lefebvre attempts to present an understanding of modernity through this concept of 'everyday life' in which knowledge of the meanings and practices of the experience of modern urban life under capitalism is crucial. Lefebvre argues that

> everyday life and modernity, the one crowning and concealing the other, revealing and veiling it. Everyday life is a compound of insignificances united in this concept, responds and corresponds to modernity, a compound of signs by which our society expresses and justifies itself and which forms part of its ideology." (Lefebvre, 1971: 24)

Central to this concept, in Lefebvre's definition, is how ideologies are constructed and applied to and within everyday life. The importance of Lefebvre's concern with the ideological content and control of everyday life is extended to his understanding of the production of space. Knowledge of space must account for the socio-historical and the economic basis by which it is produced, and this includes an ontological perspective based upon ideology but also a focus on the means, practices and uses of space.

> Thus everyday life, the social territory and place of controlled consumption, of terror-enforced passivity, is established and programmed; as a social territory it is easily identified, and under analysis it reveals its latent irrationality beneath an apparent rationality; incoherence beneath an ideology of coherence, and sub-systems or disconnected territories linked together only by speech. (Lefebvre, 1971: 197)

Therefore, views of the city, landscapes, facades, plans, etc., that is, representations of space, become the essential condition or requirement for the superiority of ruling elites (whether as sovereigns, the local or national state, or planners) in their control over space, over the city and over people. Lefebvre highlights this visual dominance in order to demonstrate the hegemony of elite views of the city. As Lefebvre argues:

> To put art at the service of the urban does not mean to prettify urban space with works of art…Rather, this means that time-space becomes works of art and that former art reconsiders itself as source and model of *appropriation* of space and time. Art brings cases and examples of appropriate 'topics' of temporal qualities inscribed in spaces…Let us not forget that gardens, parks, and landscapes were part of urban life as much as the fine arts, or that the landscape around cities were the works of art of these cities…Leaving aside representation, ornamentation and decoration, art can become *praxis* and *poiesis* on a social scale: the art of living in the city as work of art. Coming back to style and to the oeuvre, that is, to the meaning of the monument and the space appropriated in the *fete*, art can create 'structures of enchantment'. (Lefebvre, 1996: 173)

Lefebvre also cites the selective construction of monuments and other public sculpture to represent the ideologies of the dominating histories of a specific, that is elite culture. They thus represent in material form a privileged spatial practice. Who selects what subject or historical event as worthy of public representation, and where it is located, is politically incumbent. Monuments and public art carry with them, whether implicit or explicit, meanings and messages from those who have the power, capital or authority to erect them.[19] As Harvey makes clear:

87

> Spatial and temporal practices are never neutral in social affairs. They always express some kind of class or other social content, and are more often than not the focus of intense social struggle…Time and space both get defined through the organisation of social practices fundamental to commodity production. (Harvey, 1990: 239)

But there is the possibility of other aspects of the experience of space that have the potential to undermine or subvert this planned and dominating picture. De Certeau (1984) for example presents the possibility of reconstituting the regulated 'plan' of the city through everyday practices, such as walking, that create new trajectories and routes that have the potential for empowerment. Lefebvre counterposes the bases of social needs as between the need for security, predictability and certainty with the desire for adventure, unpredictability and the freedom to explore possibilities that present themselves as open. Thus, there is a need for the organisation of work, of play, time and space for self-reflection as well as interaction. Indeed, Lefebvre emphasises the fundamental need for play as an essential quality of human well-being, something that has been overlooked or underestimated in concepts of and attempts to organise, plan and regulate the city:

> The human being has the need to accumulate energies and to spend them, even waste them in play. ...To these anthropological needs which are socially elaborated...can be added specific needs which are not satisfied by those commercial and cultural infrastructures which are somewhat parsimoniously taken into account by planners. This refers to the need of creative activity, for the *oeuvre* (not only of products and consumable material goods), of the need for information, symbolism, the imaginary and play. Through these specified needs lives and survives a fundamental desire of which play, sexuality, physical activities such as sport, creative activity, art and knowledge are particular expressions and *moments*, which can more or less overcome the fragmentary division of tasks. Finally, the need of the city and urban life can only be freely expressed within a perspective which here attempts to become clearer and to open up the horizon. Would not specific urban needs be those of qualified places, places of simultaneity and encounters, places where exchange would not go through exchange value, commerce and profit? Would there not also be a need for a time for these encounters, these exchanges? (Lefebvre, 1996: 147–8)

Lefebvre argues that the satisfaction of social needs exist outwith those spaces designed and planned for overtly commercial or production purposes, that is spaces of exchange. Lefebvre is thus alerting us to the need for a more holistic understanding of everyday life in which the production of space for purposes not specifically concerned with the production of capital, but with the reproduction of the relations of capital in which, for Lefebvre, play is an essential part. Lefebvre's argument is an appeal for the continuance of spaces within the modern city for activities that do not serve strictly productive functions:

> Fairs, collective games of all sorts, survive at the interstices of an organised consumer society, in the holes of a serious society which perceives itself as structured systematically and which claims to be technical. As for the old places of assembly, they are largely devoid of meaning: the fete dies or leaves it. That they should find a meaning again does not preclude the creation of places appropriate to the renewed fete fundamentally linked to play...The space of play has coexisted and still coexists with spaces of exchange and circulation, political space and cultural space. Projects within quantified and accounted 'social space' which lose their qualitative and differentiated spaces relate to a schizophrenia which is concealed under the veils of precision, scientificity and rationality. Thus, conceived social spaces are related to social times and rhythms that are prioritised. One understands more clearly, how and up to what point in urban reality elements distribute themselves over a period of time. It is the truth of urban time which lucidly reclaims this role. To *inhabit* finds again its place over habitat. The quality which is promoted presents and represents as *playful*. By *playing* with words, one can say that there will be *play* between the parts of the

social whole (plasticity) – to the extent that *play* is proclaimed as a supreme value, eminently solemn, if not serious, overtaking use and exchange value by gathering them together. (Lefebvre, 1996: 171–2)

Lefebvre's understanding of the importance of everyday life in the production of space has broad implications for providing a theoretical framework for analysing specific urban places whether they are for production, circulation, exchange or are formal and informal spaces of leisure and recreation, of association or collective engagement and inter-action. We need to investigate the form, structure and function of such spaces that are intimately related to everyday life but not necessarily with production per se, as in 'work', but in the reproduction of the rela-tions of production through the regeneration, the re-creation, of the labour force through preferably, the healthy use of leisure time. Cities as planned and managed spaces include such intervention in their structure and organisation and in the everyday life of their population to provide leisure and recreational opportunities. The need for such interventions became more essential as the consequences of modernisation, urbanisa-tion and industrialisation took their toll on the physical environment as well as the physical, mental and moral health of the population. As Lefebvre writes, "[t]he stress of 'modern life' makes amusements, distractions and relaxation a necessity" (Lefebvre, 1971: 53). This is neatly echoed by Harvey: "[t]he social spaces of distraction and display become as vital to urban culture as the spaces of working and living" (Harvey, 1986: 256). This has implications for a spatial reading of the urban in which everyday activities can potentially conflict with the designed intentions of urban and city planners. What is allowed, prescribed, when and where and by whom are essential questions as to the real, as opposed to the hypothetical, 'freedom' that public space implies. Conflicts in and over space are a reflection competing meanings and values invested in the use and appropriation of space by individuals and by groups. This raises questions as to the 'ownership' of public space and is pertinent in highlighting Lefebvre's plea for openness as a 'right'. Lefebvre considers that the 'right to the city' becomes more essential in modern cities as it "manifests itself as a superior form of rights: right to freedom, to individualisation in socialisation, to habitat and to inhabit. The right to the *oeuvre*, to participation and *appropriation* (clearly distinct from the right to property), are implied in the right to the city" (Lefebvre, 1996: 173–4). The right to the city is defined by Lefebvre as:

89

not a natural right, nor a contractual one. In the most 'positive' of terms it signifies the rights of citizens and city dwellers, and of groups (on the basis of social relations) constitute, to appear on all the networks and circuits of communication, information and exchange...To exclude the *urban* from groups, classes, individuals, is also to exclude them from civilisation, if not from society itself. The *right to the city* legitimates the refusal to allow oneself to be removed from urban reality by a discriminatory and segregative organisation. This right of the citizen (if one wants, of 'man') proclaims the inevitable crisis of city centres based upon segregation and establishing it: centres of decision-making, wealth, power, of information and knowledge, which reject towards peripheral spaces all those who do not participate in political privileges. Equally, it stipulates the right to meetings and gatherings; places and objects must answer to certain 'needs' generally misunderstood, to certain despised and moreover transfunctional 'functions': the 'need' for social life and a centre, the need and the function of play, the symbolic function of space. (Lefebvre, 1996: 195)

However, as Lefebvre indicates, the 'right' to the city, and therefore its public spaces, implies the potential for conflict between different groups over meaning and values as well as uses and practices. Thus, Lefebvre's plea is for knowledge not only of the production of space that includes understanding and acknowledging the ideology subsumed within concepts, plans and designs, but also the rights of the urban public to 'own' by use, attachment of meanings, symbols and understandings of space. That is, to replace the prioritisation of space for exchange with that of the use value of space. However, Mitchell makes clear, in his analysis of the role and function of contemporary public spaces, that potential conflict resides within competing and often mutually exclusive visions of what *is* public space:

90

> Whatever the origins of any public space, its status as 'public' is created and maintained through the ongoing opposition of visions that have been held, on the one hand by those who seek order and control and, on the other, by those who seek places for oppositional political activity and unmediated interaction... Public space is the product of competing ideas about what constitutes that space – order and control or free, and perhaps dangerous, interaction – and who constitutes the 'public'. (Mitchell, 1995: 115)

THE SIGNIFICANCE OF LEFEBVRE'S PRODUCTION OF SPACE

Lefebvre's central thesis in *The Production of Space* is that space is a fundamental element in the operation and organisation of society within historical modes of production. However, space must be considered as a unique factor in that it is at the same time, one of the forces of production and also the medium through which social relations occur and is the outcome of this process. It is a causal element in the relations of production but also produced by the relations that occur within and through it. Space, for Lefebvre,

> is not a thing among other things, nor a product among other products: rather, it subsumes things produced, and encompasses their interrelationships in their coexistence and simultaneity – their (relative) order and/or (relative) disorder. It is the outcome of a sequence and set of operations, and thus cannot be reduced to the rank of a simple object...Itself the outcome of past actions, social space is what permits fresh actions to occur, whilst suggesting others and prohibiting yet others. Among these actions, some serve production, others consumption (i.e. the enjoyment of the fruits of production.) Social space implies a great diversity of knowledge. (Lefebvre, 1991: 73)

Lefebvre's concept of social space encompasses a critical analysis of urban reality and everyday life, an inseparable concatenation, which simultaneously is a product and a process:

> The analysis is concerned with the whole of practico-social activities, as they are entangled in a complex space, urban and everyday, ensuring up to a point the reproduction of relations of production (that is, social relations). The global synthesis is realised through this actual space, its critique and its knowledge... At the centre, recognised here and elsewhere, is the process of *reproduction of relations of production*, which unfolds before one, which is accomplished with each social activity, including the most ostensibly anodyne (leisure activities, everyday life, dwelling and habitat, the use of space) and which has yet to be the subject of a global study. (Lefebvre, 1996: 185, 187)

His approach to understanding the production of space, 'true knowledge of space', is outlined in his triad of necessary elements. Thus, spatial practices, representations of space and spaces of representation may be said to provide a framework for understanding social spaces in the context of their production within particular societies and historical periods. His analysis takes account of the need to produce spaces for economic production *and* for social reproduction. The significance of Lefebvre's conceptualisation of the production of space lies not least in its recognition of the need to analyse spaces specifically involved in processes of social reproduction, which as Hayden argues

> ranges over different scales, including the space in and around the body (biological reproduction), the space of housing (the reproduction of the labour force), and the public space of the city (the reproduction of social relations). Here he links the physical to the social in decisive ways...Lefebvre suggests that space is a medium through which social life is produced and reproduced. (Hayden, 1997: 114)

91

Merrifield also makes a useful link between Lefebvre's analysis of the production of space and the investigation and analysis of particular places:

> The space-relations identified by Lefebvre, then take on meaning through, and are permeated by, historically defined social relations (and vice versa)...space represented the realm of flows of capital, money, commodities and information, and remained the domain of the hegemonic forces in society. From this viewpoint, place comprises the locus and a sort of stopping of those flows, a specific moment in the dynamics of space-relations under capitalism. Place is shaped by the grounding (the 'thingification' if you will) of these material flows, though it concomitantly serves to shape them too by way of social and class struggle over place necessitating, for example, that abstract space takes a particular physical and social form in place...It is the realm of dispassionate 'objects' rationally 'ordered in space'; a deracinated space where representation is simply the representation of the ruling groups, just as ruling ideas were for Marx. Here knowledge and power attempt to reign supreme and impose what they know onto lived sensual and sexual experience. Correspondingly, everyday life becomes a practical and sensual activity acted out in place...Life is place-dependent, and hence the Lefebvrian struggle to change life has to launch itself from a place platform...everyday life in place is 'the supreme court where wisdom, knowledge and power are brought to judgement'. (Merrifield, 1993: 525)

92   Lefebvre's warning then is that, "[s]o far as the concept of production is concerned, it does not become fully concrete or take on a true content until replies have been given to the questions that it makes possible: 'Who produces?', 'What?', 'How?', 'Why and for Whom?'" (Lefebvre, 1991: 111, 69). This would seem an appropriate and essential set of questions necessary for the investigation of any social space in which a complex of factors has contributed to their production, representation and the uses to which they are put. Similarly, investigating how social activities are structured and experienced there is a spatial context that also needs to be understood. As Harvey puts it:

> Symbolic orderings of space and time provide a framework for experience through which we learn who or what we are in society...The common sense notion that 'there is a time and a place for everything' gets carried into a set of prescriptions which replicate the social order by assigning social meanings to spaces and times. (Harvey, 1990: 214)

Lefebvre's contribution to the social theory of space is important because it provides a valuable framework for understanding the importance of space in the analysis of modern urban capitalism, its survival and its perpetuation. Lefebvre provides a theoretical foundation that takes into account the interplay between a number of crucial elements, a complex of dynamic interactions provides a framework, for analysing how conflicts over design, form and function become entwined with social class and spatial segregation. That is, if 'true knowledge of space' is to be achieved by a consideration of the dynamic triad of necessary elements, there is a need to investigate, illustrate and substantiate how space is produced, how it is represented in diverse discourses, as well as how everyday meanings and uses affect and are affected by it.

Lefebvre's 'Production of space' is a complex analysis of the fundamental importance of space in the survival and perpetuation of capitalism that provides essential concepts, insights and perspectives for a meaningful understanding of social space. The interlinked necessary elements of his triadic analysis of spatial practices, representation and use provides a structure for the analysis of the space of modern, increasingly urban capitalism, that is essential for incorporating an understanding of the diverse factors salient to the experience of contemporary social activities. However, a criticism of Lefebvre's analysis is that it does not provide sufficient illustrative and substantive detail of the operation, the workings, of each of his dynamic elements. It is an abstract theoretical analysis that identifies a number of macro and micro social factors without specific consideration of the implications and application of each of his elements. The significance of Lefebvre's work is that it reprioritises and radicalises the role of space in social relations and provided a theoretical and conceptual foundation from and through which other social theorists have sought to analyse and investigate the importance of space for social relations and the formations in which they are found.

93

NOTES

1 As Shields writes: "Rather than simply discussing the philosophical status of space – 'how many dimensions exist', or is space a 'thing' or 'void between things'? – Lefebvre investigates social attitudes towards space, all the while not neglecting to emphasise the integral importance of physical dimensions and spatial categories such as boundaries and regions in everyday life." (Shields, 2000: 5–6).

2 Katz and Kirkby argue that this is a fundamental feature of capitalism itself: "Since the Enlightenment, the narratives of science have been embedded in the social relations of capitalism within which projects are constructed in particular ways, unmistakably tied to the manipulation of nature. The exploitation and domination of the latter by agents of capital is continuous with the social relations through which labour is exploited and subaltern groups are dominated. Embracing the separation between society and nature, capitalist hegemony is predicated as much on the notion of external or primordial nature as it is on the decisions of class, gender, race, ethnicity and age. Our comprehension of this link is muddied by our invocation of objective science and romanticised conceptualisation of nature and society, but also by the fact that human beings exist in contradictory relation to

nature. At the basis of the contradiction lies the recognition that humans are 'of nature' but are also capable of objective reason and thus possess "second nature". (Katz and Kirkby, 1991: 263)

3 Lefebvre describes how this reconstruction of nature comes about:

And now men – the most 'cultivated' men at first, people from the towns, and then the masses – rediscover the spring. They are amazed by it. They rediscover nature, long forgotten by their ancestors and their fathers. But this spring is no longer the springtime which breaks the laws of the city. It is springtime which has already been controlled and appropriated. The life of nature no longer unfolds before their eyes, something beyond them, an absurd and ludicrous spectacle, its exuberant blossoms threatening death, a dangerous, turbulent, elemental disorder, a wild bestial frenzy. At the same time as it resumes its place in the cycle of nature, spring – though still ruled by the law of cycles – becomes subsumed in the cycle of social living. It regains a meaning, but slowly; a few ancient traditions live on – notably despite the contradiction, the consecration of the month of May to virginity. Bit by bit a symbolism will be imposed upon this new-found springtime, a system of meanings and significations it does not possess as a fact of nature. Through songs and poetry, popular or scholarly, culture re-establishes contact with nature, thus resolving a partial but deep-rooted conflict. People use these songs and poems to appropriate nature again, and to reconstitute a lost symbolism. Nature and history are not made to coincide, but they are no longer separate. Springtime is a festival again, a meeting point, a moment of accord. Nature and history have not become fused, but they are not dissociated either. (Lefebvre, 1995: 148)

94

4 Again, Lefebvre highlights and emphasises that the distinction between town and country, nature and culture, etc. can result in too overly rigid dichotomies of conceptions:

A theme which has been used and over-used, hyper-inflated and extrapolated, namely, 'nature and culture', originates from the relations between town and country and deflects it...What is important is the complex movement by which the political city uses this sacred-damned character of the ground, so that the economic (commercial city) can desecrate it...In industrial countries, the old exploitation by the city, centre of capital accumulation, of the surrounding countryside, gives way to more subtle forms of domination and exploitation, the city becoming [the] centre of decision-making and also apparently of association. However that may be, the expanding city attacks the countryside, corrodes and dissolves it. (Lefebvre, 1996: 118–19)

5 It is this double role or function of cities that Lefebvre uses as a rejoinder to criticisms of his own theoretical perspective on space and the city. For example, "...Castells does not understand space. He sets aside space. His is still a simplistic Marxist schema, as is Preteceilles'. They are very reductionist because all they see is land speculation, the price of land. They aren't wrong – what they say isn't absolutely false – but is only one part of a new and immense reality, that one more or less examines." (Lefebvre, 1985: 31).

6 The consequences for the physical, social and moral health of cities and their populations when rapid economic growth outstrips the necessary infrastructure to sustain it is a theme developed in David Harvey's work on the political economy of space (see Chapter 4).

7 Saunders notes that

The basic contradiction in the production of space is between the necessity for capital to exploit it for profit and the social requirements of those who consume; in other words, the contradiction between profit and need, exchange value and use value. The political expression of this contradiction is found in the constant political struggle between individualistic and collectivistic strategies. It is this contradiction and this struggle that lies at the heart of Lefebvre's concern with the urban question. (Saunders, 1981: 154)

8 The term production acquires a more forceful and wider significance, when interpreted according to Marx's early works (though still bearing *Das Kapital* in mind); production is not merely the making of products: the term signifies on the one hand 'spiritual' production, that is to say creations (including social time and space), and on the other material production or the making of things; it also signifies the self-production of a 'human-being' in the process of historical self-development, which involves the production of social relations. Finally, taken in its fullest sense, the term embraces re-production, not only biological (which is the province of demography) but the material reproduction of the tools of production, of technical instruments and of social relations into the bargain (Lefebvre, 1971: 31).

9 Gregory sums up Lefebvre's overall aim thus:

95

Lefebvre wants to elucidate the specificity of the capitalist mode of production of space, to understand how the production of space came to be saturated with tonalities of capitalism. He attempts to do so by sketching out, in different but overlapping texts, what he eventually called "the long history of space" ... The task of his genealogy is thus to provide a history of space that will show how this constellation of power-knowledge – this supposedly 'true space' – is an artificial construction that privileges mental space, marginalises social space and compromises lived experience. (Gregory, 1994: 359, 365)

10 Merrifield states that: "Lefebvre strove for a unity theory of space, a rapprochement between physical space (nature), mental space (formal abstractions about space) and social space (the space occupied by 'sensory phenomena, including products of the imagination such as projects and projections, symbols and utopias" (Merrifield, 1993: 522).

11 See Merrifield 1993 for a discussion of the possibilities of using Lefebvre's spatialised dialectic as a framework for investigating the relationships between space and place. As Merrifield states:

Lefebvre's maverick non-dogmatic *spatialised* reading of Marx's materialist dialectic (a project he termed *spatiology*) offers the most fruitful route for broaching the problematic of place ... that of reconciling the way in which experience is lived and acted out in place, and how this relates to, and is embedded in, political and economic practices that are operative over broader spatial scales...Consequently, space internalises conflictual and contradictory social forces and social conflict is thereby 'inscribed in place'. This conflict arises from the inextricable tension between the usage and appropriation of place for social purposes and the domination of place (and space) as a productive and commercial force through private ownership...It follows here that place is not merely abstract space: it is the terrain where basic social practices – consumption, enjoyment, tradition, self-identification, solidarity, social support and social reproduction etc. are lived out. As a moment of capitalist space, place is where everyday life is situated. And as such, place can be taken as practised space. (Merrifield, 1993: 517, 522)

12 This is a point Shields emphasises:

Because Lefebvre is referring to not only the empirical disposition of things in the landscape as 'space' (the physical aspect) but also attitudes and habitual practices, his metaphoric *l'espace* might be better understood as the *spatialisation* of social order. In this movement to space, abstract structures such as 'culture' become concrete practices and arrangement in space. Social action involves not just a rhythm but also geometry and spacing. Spatialisation also captures the processual nature of *l'espace* that Lefebvre insists is a matter of ongoing activities. That is, it is not just an achieved order in the built environment, or an ideology, but also an order that is itself always undergoing change from within through the actions and innovations of social agents. In short, all 'space' is social space. (Shields, 2000: 155)

96

13 Massey sums up the importance of the interaction of the spatial in analysing the organisation of society:

Understanding the spatial organisation of society, then, is crucial. It is central to our understanding of the way in which social processes work out, possibly to our conceptualisation of some of those processes in the first place, and certainly in our ability to act on them politically...If the spatial is not autonomous from the social, can the social be theorised autonomously from its spatial form, requirements and implications?...Part of what is fundamentally at issue here is the reassessment of our definition of necessary relations within the social sciences. (Massey, 1985: 17, 18)

14 This is a point that Shields also stresses:

Space...is treated in such a way as to render it homogenous, its parts comparable, therefore exchangeable...The subordination of space to money and capital implies a quantification which extends from the monetary evaluation of each plot of the entire space...Space now becomes one of the new 'scarcities', together with its resources, water, air, and even light. (Shields, 2000: 180)

15 As Lefebvre writes somewhat prosaically:

Metaphorically, it symbolises force, male fertility, masculine violence. Here again the part is taken for the whole; phallic brutality does not remain abstract, for it is the brutality of political power, of the means of constraint: police, army, bureaucracy. Phallic erectibility bestows a special status on the perpendicular, proclaiming a phallocracy as the orientation of space, as the goal of the process. (Lefebvre, 1991: 287)

16 Lefebvre argues that

Bourdieu provides a clarification. He explains how 'a matrix of perceptions, appreciations and actions' can at one and the same time be put to work flexibly to 'achieve infinitely diversified tasks' while at the same time being 'in the last minute' (Engel's famous phrase) engendered out of the material experience of 'objective structures', and therefore 'out of the economic basis of social formations in question'. The mediating link is provided by the concept of 'habitus' – a 'durably installed generative principle of regulated improvisations' which 'produces practices' which in turn tend to reproduce the objective conditions which produced the generative principle of habitus in the first place. (Lefebvre, 1991: 219)

It is perhaps pertinent to also reflect Bourdieu's principle in his own words:

Because the habitus is an endless capacity to engender products – thoughts, perceptions, expressions, actions – whose limits are set by the historically and socially situated conditions of its production, the conditioning and conditional freedom it secures is as remote from the creation of unpredictable novelty as it is from a simple mechanical reproduction of the initial conditionings. (Bourdieu, 1977: 95)

97

17 The definition given by Williams of hegemony as a lived process, involving resistance and conflict over meanings and values (ideology) as well as practices and expectations over the whole of the experience of life, not only a static structured system of domination between states or social classes is useful in this context.

Gramsci made a distinction between 'rule' (*dominio*) and 'hegemony'. 'Rule' is expressed in directly political forms and in times of crisis by direct or effective coercion. But the more normal situation is a complex interlocking of political, social and cultural forces which are its necessary elements... What is decisive is not only the conscious system of ideas and beliefs, but the whole lived social process as practically organised by specific and dominant meanings and beliefs. (Williams, 1977: 108–9)

18 It is worth distinguishing carefully between everyday life and the concept 'the everyday' in order to clarify its meaning. The term 'everyday life' in Lefebvre's books means 'banal and meaningless life', not daily life. In French, there is a certain interchangeability between the idea of banal activities and daily tasks. While 'everyday life' in the sense of daily tasks is an amorphous set of more or less usual and unremarkable activities, 'the everyday' always means the ordinary, banal and repetitive (Shields, 2000: 69).

19 See Deutsche (1998) for a critical discussion of the use of public art in creating a dominant urban aesthetic.

four

David Harvey: the political economy of space

David Harvey's long contribution to the analysis of space now spans three decades. Few can doubt his contribution to a critical geography in which space is prioritised as a fundamental element for understanding how capitalism has survived and prospered. Harvey's 'project' was to establish a 'historico-geographical materialism' in which he sought to develop Marx's paradigm of capitalist accumulation to include the production of space in the production and reproduction of social life. As Saunders states Harvey's focus is on "the recurrent tension... between the (geographical) problem of space and the (sociological) problem of the social processes that take place within it" (Saunders, 1981: 220). This is an important contribution to the development of an inter-disciplinary analysis of space and its application for the investigation of modern society. In this, Harvey writes that Marx's original formulation needs to be enhanced to include a spatial as well as temporal analysis of the development, perpetuation and expansion of modern capitalism:

> Historical materialism has to be upgraded, I insist, to historical-geographical materialism. The historical geography of capitalism has to be the object of theorising. (Harvey, 1985: xii)

Harvey's 'project', like Lefebvre's, is concerned with developing a theory of the production of space which acknowledges the role of space in the accumulation and circulation of capital as well as in the reproduction of labour power. That is, capital accumulation takes place in an historical and geographical context that engenders specific spatial forms. At the core of Harvey's analysis then is an account of space (and time) in which material processes and social relations are considered essential to the question of urbanisation. For Harvey, this question of urbanisation and what he calls 'the urban process' is a theme that runs throughout Harvey's considerable output. For Harvey,

> The question 'what is space?' is replaced by the question 'how is it that different human practices create and make use of distinctive conceptualisations of space?'...

An understanding of urbanism and of the social process – spatial form theme requires that we understand how human activity creates the need for specific spatial concepts and how daily social practice solves with consummate ease seemingly deep philosophical mysteries concerning the nature of space and the relationships between social processes and spatial forms. (Harvey, 1973: 14)

For Harvey, both space and time must be considered as basic categories of human existence. They cannot be separated from material processes. To understand space (and time) then, according to Harvey, one must investigate the material processes and practices that form the basis for the reproduction of social life. Every mode of production then will produce its own conceptions of space and time. Harvey asserts that a seeming consensus now exists in that it is recognised that space and time are socially constructed. It is worth emphasising, as Harvey does, what this materialist perspective means for the analysis of the role of space and time in social life. Harvey states that

different societies produce qualitatively different conceptions of space and time [therefore]...each social formation constructs objective conceptions of space and time sufficient unto its own needs and purposes of material social reproduction and organises its material practices in accordance with those conceptions. (Harvey, 1997: 256–8)

99

Space then, for Harvey, is understood as produced, shaped, moulded and used within specific epochs and societies. The forms that space takes not only represent the mode of production but symbolise the cultural aspirations of a given society at a specific time as well as the existing social order. Geographical space then for Harvey should not be separated from society but must be understood as the product of social relations and historical practices, as they become embedded and internalised within spatial forms and structures. Harvey's original focus, and one that remains throughout his work, his project of historical–geographical materialism, is to analyse the role of space under industrial capitalism. More specifically to investigate:

the way in which markets conceal social (and we should add, geographical) information and relations. We have to penetrate the veil of fetishism with which we are necessarily surrounded by virtue of the system of commodity production and exchange and discover what lies behind it. (Harvey, 1997: 262–3)

Harvey's approach is fundamentally a Marxist analysis of the role of space in the processes of the accumulation and circulation of capital, of the production of the built environment and class struggle and which are manifest in the meanings and values, as well as the spatial arrangement, organisation and form of the urban landscape. That is, it is a consideration of the spatial dimension of Marx's analysis of capitalism as a mode of production in which the built environment of the city expresses the needs of capital both for production and for the reproduction of labour power. As Smith puts it, Harvey's theoretical orientation throughout his works is rooted in a Marxist theory that:

> attempts to explain the specific economic, political and social structure of society in a given period as the result not of supposedly universal forces (for example, human nature), but as a result of historically specific and contingent processes. It is not just that competition and the market, economic growth and the profit motive are historically contingent, but that the form they take changes and develops within the history of capitalism itself. A further strength of Marxist theory is its relational perspective which treats capitalist society as a coherent (if not always consistent) whole, rather than as an agglomeration of fragments. (Smith, 1984: x)

What Harvey seeks is a spatialisation of Marx through the consideration of the production of space and specifically, the creation of the built environment of the city as necessary conditions for, and the product of the processes of accumulation, circulation and consumption of capital. Harvey's project then is to develop Marx's 'paradigm of production' to include the production of space as an essential element in the production and reproduction of social life. As Harvey puts it,

100

> Capital is a process and not a thing. It is a process of reproduction of social life through commodity production, in which all of us in the advanced capitalist world are heavily implicated. Its internalised rules of operation are such as to ensure that it is a dynamic and revolutionary mode of social organisation, restlessly and ceaselessly transforming the society within which it is embedded. The process masks and fetishises, achieves growth through creative destruction, creates new wants and needs, exploits the capacity for human labour and desire, transforms spaces, and speeds up the pace of life. It produces problems of over-accumulation for which there are but a limited number of possible solutions. (Harvey, 1990: 343)

In essence, Harvey attempts to provide a political economy of space under capitalism that has important insights for the analysis of the production, location and distribution of particular spaces in a specific era (industrial capitalism) and the rise to dominance of a form of spatial organisation and administration (urbanisation). It serves as a means for analysing the production of the urban environment as a social landscape in which the spaces of reproduction are necessarily shaped and moulded by class struggle and conflict. This is politically important and significant because as Harvey puts it, "[i]deas about environment, population, and resources are not neutral. They are political in origin and have political effects" (Harvey, 1977: 237). Harvey's concern then is to investigate the production and use of the physical and social landscape of the city that is shaped and formed within the urbanising process of capital accumulation.

Much of Harvey's work, it will be argued, supplements and illuminates Lefebvre's thesis concerning the production of space, in particular his necessary element of 'spatial practice', but differs in that whilst Lefebvre sees urbanisation as the means by which capitalism survives through the production of new and increasingly dominant urban spatial forms, Harvey argues that the creation of space is dependent on the investment priorities and demands of industrial capital. For Harvey, the production of specific spatial forms and the spatial arrangements of urban industrial capitalism are fundamental for understanding the organisation and structuring of the necessary social relations of modern capitalist society. Thus Harvey argues that capital accumulation demands urban forms that facilitate the more effective extraction of surplus value by organising the spatial form of the urban as a production centre, as a location for consumption, as facilitating the circulation of capital and for the reproduction of labour. This then is Harvey's rationale for attempting to develop a political economy of space as a means to spatialise and upgrade Marx's analysis of capitalism to provide an explanation for how it is that the urban became the key spatial node for the social relations of modern capitalism's necessary social relations, structures and processes. How it is that the urban as particular spatial forms are the product of capitalism. Harvey thus attempts to provide an understanding of the fundamental processes underlying the spatial form and organisation of modern, industrial urban capitalism. That is,

101

> Any general theory of the city must somehow relate the social processes in the city to the spatial form which the city assumes... We must relate social behaviour to the way in which the city assumes a certain geography, a certain spatial form. We must recognise that once a particular spatial form is created it tends to institutionalise and, in some respects, to determine the future development of social process. (Harvey, 1973: 23, 27)

THE SPACE OF INDUSTRIAL CAPITALISM

Crucially for Harvey, after Marx, the needs of industrial capital (to minimise circulation costs, but to maximise the availability of labour, access to markets and raw materials, etc.) promoted the concentration and 'rational' location of production, and all associated activities within large urban centres. As Harvey states,

> Vast concentrations of capital and labour have come together in metropolitan areas of incredible complexity, while transport and communication systems, stretched in far-flung nets around the globe, permit information and ideas as well as material goods and even labour power to move around with relative ease. Factories and fields, schools, churches, shopping centres and parks, roads and railways litter a landscape that has been indelibly and irreversibly carved out according to the dictates of capitalism. (Harvey, 1982: 373)

Industrial capitalism dominates urbanism by producing the space and the spatial structures necessary for the creation of surplus value that, concomitantly, leads to the construction of the built environment. Harvey's understanding of what he calls 'the urban process' and its importance for capitalism differs from Lefebvre in that despite both viewing the production of space as crucial for the survival and perpetuation of capitalism, Harvey does not prioritise the urban over the needs of industrial capital. As Harvey puts it:

> Urbanism may be regarded as a particular form or patterning of the social process. This process unfolds in a spatially structured environment created by man. The city can therefore be regarded as a tangible, built environment – an environment which is a social product. (Harvey, 1973: 196)

102

Harvey's analysis of the production of space emphasises the investment logic of industrial capital as the key causal function of urbanisation in that "[i]n certain important and crucial respects industrial society and the structures which comprise it continue to dominate urbanism" (Harvey, 1973: 311). Harvey's spatialisation of Marx seeks to address how the needs and priorities of capital accumulation have consequences for investment in and creation of the physical and social infrastructure of the urban as well as in those areas directly related to the means of production. This then leads to the creation of a 'space economy'.

> Urbanism entails the geographic concentration of a socially designated surplus product. This means a geographic circulation of surplus goods and services, a movement of people and, in the money economy, a circulation of investment, money and credit. The space economy so created is subject to all manner of substitutions, interruptions, breakdowns, shifts and growth paths. The reputation and significance of individual cities rests to a large degree upon their location with respect to the geographical circulation of the surplus. The qualitative attributes of urbanism will likewise be affected by the rise and fall in the total quantity of surplus as well as the degree to which the surplus is produced in concentratable form. (Harvey, 1973: 246)

For Harvey then the circulation and investment of surplus is fundamental to his analysis of the development of a space economy. However, to explore Harvey's analysis of the urban as the space of capitalism, it is necessary to address how he uses Marx's theory of accumulation.

ACCUMULATION AND CIRCUITS OF CAPITAL

Harvey, like Marx and Lefebvre, views capitalism as depending upon the concentration and circulation of surplus. The city is the product of these processes by which its spatial form and arrangements prioritise the role that the urban plays in processes of accumulation and circulation of surplus value. The built environment of the city and its spatial patterning under capitalism is the product of the needs of capital for accumulation and its confrontation with labour. Harvey makes clear that his understanding of the urban process is based on Marx's analysis theory of accumulation:

> Within the framework of capitalism, I hang my interpretation of the urban process on the twin themes of accumulation and class struggle. The two themes are integral to each other and have to be regarded as different sides of the same coin – different windows from which to view the totality of capitalist activity. The class character of capitalist society means the domination of labour by capital...The essential Marxian insight, however, is that profit arises out of the domination of labour by capital and that the capitalists as a class must, if they are to reproduce themselves, continuously expand the basis for profit. We thus arrive at a conception of a society founded on the principle of "accumulation for accumulations sake, production for productions sake." (Harvey, 1978: 101, 102)

Different social, economic, technological and institutional possibilities produce potentially different combinations and therefore different roles for the city as a 'node' in the space economy. Harvey's approach is an attempt to explain the connections between the production of the built environment and the capital accumulation process.

> The industrial city was a new centrepiece of accumulation. The production of surpluses through the direct exploitation of living labour in production was its trademark. This meant the geographical concentration of labour power and productive forces (epitomised in the factory system) and open access to the world market, which, in turn, meant the consolidation of money and credit. It meant, in short, the firm implantation of all those features of geographical and temporal organisation of the circulation of capital that I began by describing. The geographical patterning of labour and commodity markets, of spatial and social divisions of production and consumption, and of differentiated

103

socio-technical mixes within the labour process became much more pronounced within the urban landscape. Inter-capitalist competition and class struggle pushed the whole social dynamic of urbanisation toward the production of rational physical and social landscapes for capital accumulation. The search for profitable trade-offs between command over and creation of advantageous locations, coupled with adaptations in the socio-technical conditions of production, became a much more visible moving force within the urban process. (Harvey, 1985: 197)

Following Marx, Harvey argues that unregulated competition between capitalists results in crises of over-accumulation in the 'primary circuit' of capital (the industrial sector) and a downturn in the realisation of surplus value. As he puts it, "[t]oo much capital is produced in aggregate relative to the opportunities to employ that capital" (Harvey, 1981: 94). One way that these periodic crises of over-accumulation can be temporarily mediated to promote and achieve more beneficial conditions for the production of surplus value is for capital to invest or 'flow' into other circuits, the secondary and tertiary circuits of capital. Harvey's point is that investment in the secondary and tertiary circuits becomes advantageous for capital, that is for capitalists as a class, to invest in areas that have the potential for producing conditions that will aid accumulation and subsequent profits, as well as ensuring their reproduction as the dominant class in society. It is thus important to clarify how it is that Harvey defines and uses 'circuits of capital' as a means to investigate the development of the physical and social infrastructure that constitutes the built environment, the landscape of the urban under capitalism.

104

The primary circuit of capital for Harvey is all the means by which the capitalist seeks to capture and extract surplus value. This includes the extension of the working day or the reorganisation of work processes which increases labour's productivity. The organisation of the division of labour and investment in fixed capital items such as machinery are also included in the primary circuit of capital. The secondary circuit of capital is marked by a distinction between the 'built environment for production' of those items which function as a physical framework for production and of those commodities that act as a physical framework for consumption. The built environment is important for fixed capital (factories, offices, etc.) and for the consumption fund (housing being the best example). In both of these, the built environment represents a physical framework within which production or consumption (or both in the case of transportation facilities) is produced by geographical investment in necessary infrastructure. Investment in the physical infrastructure of the city is thus a significant feature of the secondary circuit.

Harvey emphasises that

> fixed capital in the built environment is immobile in space in the sense that the
> value incorporated in it cannot be moved without being destroyed. Investment
> in the built environment therefore entails the creation of a whole physical
> landscape for purposes of production, circulation, exchange and consumption.
> We will call the capital flows into fixed asset and consumption fund formation
> the *secondary circuit of capital*. (Harvey, 1978: 106. Italics in original)

The tertiary circuit of capital for Harvey

> comprises, first, investment in science and technology (the purposes of which is
> to harness science to production and thereby to contribute to the processes
> which continuously revolutionise the productive forces in society) and second,
> a wide range of social expenditures which relate primarily to the processes of
> reproduction of labour power. The latter can usefully be divided into investments
> directed towards the qualitative improvement of labour power from the
> standpoint of capital (investment in education and health by means of which
> the capacity of the labourers to engage in the work process will be enhanced)
> and investment in the co-optation, integration and repression of labour by
> ideological, military and other means. (Harvey, 1978: 108)

It is Harvey's thesis that the flow of capital from one circuit to another
is conditional on crises of accumulation in the primary sector due to
unregulated competition between capitalists. Thus 'capitalists as a class'
will invest in the secondary and tertiary circuits in the hope that
conditions more favourable to accumulation will result. Harvey argues
then that it is the needs and desires of industrial capital that produces
the built environment of the city as a means to achieve more efficient
and effective accumulation. However, this is not without contradictions
and difficulties, as Harvey explains:

105

> Capital represents itself in the form of the physical landscape created in its own
> image, created as use values to enhance the progressive accumulation of capital.
> The geographical landscape which results is the crowning glory of past capitalist
> development. But at the same time it expresses the power of dead labour over
> living labour and as such it imprisons and inhibits the accumulation process
> within a set of specific physical constraints. And these can be removed only
> slowly unless there is substantial devaluation of the exchange value locked up
> in the creation of these physical assets. Capitalist development has therefore to
> negotiate a knife-edge path between preserving the exchange values of past
> capital investments in the built environment and destroying the value of these
> investments in order to open up fresh room for accumulation. Under capitalism
> there is, then, a perpetual struggle in which capital builds a physical landscape
> appropriate to its own condition at a particular moment in time, only to have to
> destroy it, usually in the course of a crisis, at a subsequent point in time.
> (Harvey, 1978: 124)

These crises of accumulation result in the need to create a built environment that opens up the potential for future accumulation. However, the physical landscape created by past crises may hinder or impede future accumulation. This then is Harvey's analysis and explanation for the cyclical redevelopment, redesign and regeneration of the urban landscape. In this, Harvey is explicit in emphasising how the Marxist theory of accumulation should be used for understanding the production of features of the urban landscape:

> The understanding that I have to offer of the urban process under capitalism comes from seeing it in relation to the theory of accumulation...Whatever else it may entail, the urban process implies the creation of a material physical infra-structure for production, circulation, exchange and consumption...The reproduction of labour power is essential and requires certain kinds of social expenditures and the creation of a consumption fund. The flows we have sketched, in so far as they portray capital movements into the built environment (for both production and consumption) and the laying out of social expenditure for the reproduction of labour power, provide us, then with the structural links we need to understand the urban process under capitalism. (Harvey, 1978: 113–14)

It is on the creation of the space of industrial capitalism that Harvey focuses when he turns his attention to the built environment.

106

THE BUILT ENVIRONMENT OF THE CITY AND THE URBAN

The Marxist method of analysis applied to that of the urban is encapsulated in Harvey's assertion that "Urbanism involves the concentration of surplus (however designated) in some version of the city (whether it be walled enclave or the sprawling metropolis of the present day)" (Harvey, 1973: 237). Harvey defines the city as an urban system that "contains a geographical distribution of created resources of great economic, social, psychological and symbolic significance" (Harvey, 1973: 69). Capitalism then for Harvey creates a physical landscape, it produces space, a material, physical infrastructure for production, circulation, exchange and consumption, in its own image through the urbanisation of capital whilst social relations simultaneously become increasingly urbanised to meet the needs of capital. Harvey puts it thus

> the urbanisation of capital is primarily concerned with how labour, working under capitalist control, creates a "second nature" of built environments with particular kinds of spatial configurations...[it is]...an objectification in the landscape of that intersection between the productive force of capital investment and the social relations required to reproduce an increasingly urbanised capitalism. (Harvey, 1985: xv–xvi)

Capitalist society then according to Harvey must create a physical landscape, specifically the 'built environment', for the purposes of production and reproduction of capital and the social relations of capital. This is fundamental for the continual expansion of capitalism and the extraction of more surplus value. This is a key and repeated theme in Harvey's long analysis of the urban process and is emphasised in much of his work.[1] For Harvey, the built environment is the product of the needs of capitalism to create the most effective conditions and environment for accumulation. Thus Harvey makes the point that

> The studies on the urbanisation of capital are primarily concerned with how labour, working under capitalist control, creates a "second nature" of built environments with particular kinds of spatial configurations. I am primarily concerned with how capitalism creates a physical landscape of roads, houses, factories, schools, shops and so forth in its own image and what the contradictions are that arise out of such processes of producing space...The study of urbanisation is a study of that process as it unfolds through the production of physical and social landscapes and the production of consciousness. The study of urbanisation is not the study of a legal political entity or of a physical artefact. It is concerned with processes of capital circulation; the shifting flows of labour power, commodities, and money capital; the spatial organisation of production and the transformation of space relations; movements of information and geopolitical conflicts between territorially-based class alliances, and so on. (Harvey, 1985: xv–xvi)

107

It is the ways and means by which this creation of the built environment of the city is achieved that Harvey seeks to investigate in his analysis of the space economy. In this there is a need to understand how command over space is required for the development of a market in land.

COMMAND OVER SPACE AND THE MARKET IN LAND

It is not just those features or elements associated directly with production but the whole of the urban environment that Harvey considers essential for the success of capitalist accumulation. The built environment of the city then is viewed by Harvey as a physical framework within which production or consumption (or in some cases – such as transport facilities – both) takes place. This is, as Harvey emphasises, significant for understanding the spatiality of capitalism, how a distinct spatial form materialises as a result of the rise of industrial capitalism and the demands of accumulation that structures the landscape of the city. These structures are fixed and immobile and may act eventually as spatial barriers to the further expansion of the process of capital accumulation.

However, exchange value and use value in relation to land take on their meaning in special circumstances. Dominant institutions and individuals use space hierarchically and symbolically in that space is created, organised and manipulated to emphasise and reflect status, prestige and social relationships. However, Harvey is explicit in stressing that the city is not to be thought of as only being a human constructed spatial system that is directed at increasing capital accumulation. Whilst this, it may be argued, is its function and the built environment is the direct product of this process, it also has other affects and consequences as a social environment through and in which we live our lives and attempt to glean meaning from it. As Harvey writes,

> I think it is far more satisfactory to regard the city as a gigantic resource system, most of which is man-made. It is also an areally localised resource system in the sense that most of the resources we make use of in the city system are not ubiquitous and their availability, therefore, depends upon accessibility and proximity. The urban system thus contains a geographical distribution of created resources of great economic, social, psychological and symbolic significance... The signs, symbols and signals that surround us in the urban environment are powerful influences (particularly among the young). We fashion our sensibilities, extract our sense of wants and needs and locate our aspirations with respect to a geographical environment that is in large part created... Neither the activity of space creation nor the final product of created space appear to be within our individual or collective control but fashioned by forces alien to us. (Harvey, 1973: 68–9, 310)

These hierarchical structures of authority, status and privilege are transmitted through forms of spatial organisation and the symbols and meanings attached to them:

> The land market sorts spaces to functions on the basis of land prices and does so not only on the basis of ability to pay, which, though clearly differentiated, is by no means differentiated enough to etch clear class and social distinctions into the social spaces of the city. The response is for each and every stratum in society to use whatever powers of domination it can command (money, political influence, even violence) to try and seal itself off (or seal off others judged undesirable) in fragments of space within which processes of reproduction of social distinctions can be jealously guarded. (Harvey, 1985: 14)

It is this 'sorting of space' under capitalism that creates the necessity for the development of 'a space economy', a market in land that Harvey considers as essential to understanding the way in which capitalism has survived and prospered and by which divisions in space and specific spatial forms widen and deepen class distinctions. Capitalism, for Harvey as for Lefebvre, required not only the production of space but also the means to have command over it. The geographic concentration of the processes of accumulation demanded the spatial ordering of the means of production and necessitated the creation of an extensive space economy in which land and the improvements on it become commodities.[2] Harvey details his understanding of how this space economy came to be:

> The conquest of space first required that it be conceived as something usable, malleable, and therefore capable of domination through human action... Builders, engineers, and architects for their part showed how abstract representations of objective space could be combined with exploration of the concrete, malleable properties of materials in space. But these were all just islands of practice, light chronological nets thrown over a totality of social practices in which all manner of other conceptions of place and space – sacred and profane, symbolic, personal, animistic – could continue to function undisturbed. It took something more to consolidate space as universal, homogenous, objective and abstract in most social practices. That 'something' was the buying and selling of space as a commodity. The effect was then to bring all space under the single measuring rod of money value. (Harvey, 1985a: 13)

The production of space is therefore both political and economic and, as such, cannot be considered independently of social relations. The market in land and what is built upon it become crucial means by which the processes of capital accumulation develop, organise and create specific spatial forms. That is:

109

> Space can be overcome only through the production of space, of systems of communication and physical infrastructures embedded in the land. Natural landscapes are replaced by the built landscapes shaped through competition to the requirements of accelerating accumulation. The 'pulverisation' and fragmentation necessary to homogenise space have to take definite forms. (Harvey, 1985: 27–8)

Space, homogenised by its 'pulverisation' into pieces to be bought and sold on the market, as real estate, as private property, operates as a commodity but one that has special features. It is a container of social power but also the framework through which power is organised and maintained. It creates a tension between ownership and use of space for private or collective purposes, and the domination of space by the state, class or social power. Thus there is the potential for conflict between the appropriation of land by individuals or by groups for social purposes and the domination of land as private property, by the state, class or power interests. Harvey is clear that command over space is fundamental in the operation of power in different spheres and for different purposes.

> Command over space, as every general and geo-politician knows, is of the utmost strategic significance in any power struggle... This value of space lies at

the root of land rent. But spatial competition is always monopolistic competition, simply because two functions cannot occupy exactly the same location. Capture of strategic spaces within the overall space can confer much more than its aliquot share of control... Control over strategic land parcels within the urban matrix confers immense power over the whole pattern of development. And although the liberation of space and the annihilation of space by time erodes any permanent power that may attach to control of strategic spaces, the monopolistic element is always recreated afresh. Indeed control over the production of spatial organisation then becomes fundamental to the creation of new spatial monopolies. (Harvey, 1985a: 22)

For Harvey, the analysis of the role of space in the accumulation process, the creation of the specific spatial form of the modern city, spatial structures and arrangements and investment in the built environment reveals the means by which capitalism has survived and prospered.[3] As Harvey writes:

Capitalism has to urbanise in order to reproduce itself. But the urbanisation of capital creates contradictions. The social and physical landscape of an urbanised capitalism is far more, therefore, than a mute testimony to the transforming powers of capitalist growth and technological change. Capitalist urbanisation has its own distinctive logic and its own distinctive forms of contradiction... But urbanisation means a certain mode of human organisation in space and time that can somehow embrace all of these conflicting forces, not necessarily to harmonise them, but to channel them into so many possibilities of both creative and destructive social transformation... Capitalism has survived not only through the production of space, as Lefebvre insists, but also through superior command over space – and that truth prevails as much within urban regions as over the global space of capitalist endeavour. (Harvey, 1985: 222, 226)

But Harvey argues that the need to create specific spatial urban forms and arrangements can lead to contradictions when the changing demands of capital for the realisation and circulation of surplus requires new arrangements. Thus previous investment in the built environment can lead to the creation of 'spatial barriers' to future capital accumulation. This is represented in attempts at the wide-scale redevelopment of cities to secure a more favourable disposition to capital. For example, industrial cities fashioned in the nineteenth century predominantly for manufacturing may find their spatial form and arrangements unsuitable to capital seeking to invest in new technologies, finance, leisure or retail in the twenty-first century. Harvey argues that this is a fundamental feature of how capitalism works and how it has been perpetuated:

The elimination of spatial barriers and the struggle to 'annihilate space by time' is essential to the whole dynamic of capital accumulation and becomes particularly acute in crises of capital over-accumulation... A revolution in temporal and spatial relations often entails, therefore, not only the destruction of ways of life and social practices built around preceding time-space systems, but the 'creative destruction' of a wide range of physical assets embedded in the landscape...The Marxian theory of capital accumulation permits theoretical insights in to the contradictory changes that have occurred in the dimensionality of space and time in Western capitalism. (Harvey, 1997: 266)

Harvey's analysis of space is clearly located in a Marxist perspective that needs must also consider class struggle and conflict over the meanings and (use versus exchange) values associated with it.

CLASS STRUGGLE AND CONFLICT IN AND OVER SPACE

The dynamic of capital investment in the different circuits is not a one-way process. Urban processes themselves can have reciprocal effects on primary circuit investment and activity as well as wider social, economic and political activity. Thus, the modern city is created by the needs of capital but there are inherent conflicts and contradictions in the process. However, the dynamics of the market and the needs of industrial capital can produce the uneven development of the built environment as well as unintended and, for some, extremely negative consequences. Harvey writes that:

111

> The evolution of the urban system, whether we like it or not, can lead to large scale sensory deprivation with respect to certain phenomena (such as clean air, wilderness, etc.) and over-exposure to others (such as suburban vistas, air pollution, etc.). (Harvey, 1973: 85)

Harvey then considers urban struggles as a form of class struggle in that the nature of the built environment involves issues and questions that relate to capital investment as a form of surplus value extraction, but also to concerns within labour for a redistribution of income, resources and quality of life. Harvey identifies how these struggles occur and what these struggles are over:

> Public facilities, recreational opportunities, amenities, transportation access, and so on are all subjects of contention. But underlying these immediate concerns is a deeper struggle over the very meaning of the built environment as a set of use values for labour...Capital in general and its faction that produces the built environment seek to define the quality of life for labour in terms of the commodities which they can profitably produce in certain locations. Labour, on the other hand, defines quality of life solely in use-value terms and, in the process, may appeal to some underlying and fundamental conception of what it is to be human. Production for profit and production for use are often inconsistent.

> The survival of capitalism therefore requires that capital dominate not simply in the work process, but with respect to the very definition of the quality of life in the consumption sphere. (Harvey, 1978a: 14)

Crises of capital over-accumulation provided the impetus for investment in the built environment to ensure the efficient organisation and control of the physical and social infrastructure in the industrial city for the purposes of production, circulation, exchange and consumption. However, the produced space of capitalism is also the space of social reproduction, and therefore control over the production and organisation of space is a crucial factor for the reproduction of labour and of power relations. The state, urban developers, financiers or landowners etc. often mask their power over the processes of social reproduction behind the seeming neutrality of space. Whilst the urbanisation of capital is seen as an essential condition for its reproduction, it creates its own contradictions. Urbanisation, as the human organisation of space and time, somehow has to accommodate all the conflicting forces to maximise the transformative potential of new forms and structures in the spatial organisation of the city.

112

> The formation of physical and social infrastructures adequate to support the reproduction of both capital and labour power while serving as efficient frameworks for the organisation of production, consumption, and exchange surged to the forefront of political and managerial concerns. Such problems had to be approached with an eye to efficiency and economy because that was the way to assure growth, accumulation, innovation, and efficiency in interurban competition. Public investments also had to be organised on an increasing scale and on more and more long-term basis and in such a way as to compensate for individual capitalists under-producing collective infrastructures. (Harvey, 1985: 198)

Harvey's fundamental proposition is that urban struggles are a form of class struggles over resources and conditions. However, not all struggles between capital and labour necessarily result in conflict. The possibility for alliances between them results when the demands of the working class coincide with the economic needs and political interest of fractions of the capital class, if not the class as a whole. For example, demands for affordable housing by the working class may be supported by capitalists if lower rents lead to lesser demand for wage increases. Similarly, demands for resources such as schools, health and child care, and leisure and recreation facilities may strengthen the capitalist class if they can be sold as commodities or enhance a sense of well-being and contentment. As Harvey eloquently puts it:

> Capital, in short, seeks to draw labour into a Faustian bargain: accept a packaged relation to nature in the living place as just and adequate compensation for an

alienating and degrading relation to nature in the work place. And if labour refuses to be drawn in in spite of seduction, blandishment and dominant ideology mobilised by the bourgeoisie, then capital must impose it because the landscape of capitalist society must, in the final analysis respond to the accumulation needs of capital, rather than to the real, human requirements of labour. (Harvey, 1978a: 29)

Harvey therefore argues that struggles over the production and use of the built environment, whether houses, factories, roads, parks, cultural and educational institutions, etc. is one that is replete with contradictions and conflicts. Capital will invest in such features and facilities if it enhances accumulation whether directly in the production process or indirectly by improving the means by which the reproduction of labour produces more efficient, willing, docile and able workers. Harvey puts it this way:

Labour needs living space. Land is therefore a condition of living for labour in much the same way that it is a condition of production for capital ... Apart from space as a basic condition of living, we are concerned here with housing, transportation (to jobs and facilities), amenities, facilities, and a whole bundle of resources which contribute to the total living environment for labour ... The cost and quality of these items affect labour's standard of living. Labour, in seeking to protect and enhance its standard of living, engages, in the living place, in a series of running battles over a variety of issues which relate to the creation, management, and use of the built environment. (Harvey, 1978a: 11)

113

However, investment and interventions in the built environment that produce forms and arrangements that promote the reproduction of labour and which may result in class conflict or further the accumulation process is not necessarily carried on by individual capitalists or by capitalists acting as a class. It is the role of the state in the creation, organisation and maintenance of the spaces of production and reproduction that Harvey considers as an essential condition of the urban process. It is the state who are responsible for the creation, organisation and control of the space of the urban.

HEGEMONY, THE STATE AND THE SPACES OF PRODUCTION AND REPRODUCTION

It is the state, viewed in classical Marxist analysis "as a committee for managing the common affairs of the whole bourgeoisie" (Marx and Engels, 1848/1975: 35) and particularly the local state, which plays a prominent role in mediating struggles over the built environment by intervening on behalf of capital. Harvey echoes this perspective:

> One overwhelming feature does cry out for special attention. The state provides the single most important channel for flows of value into social infrastructures... State involvement arises in part because collective means have to be found to do what individual capitalist cannot reasonably do and in part because class struggle requires the mediations of the state apparatus if any kind of investment is to be made at all in socially sensitive areas. The involvement took on a new shape when it was recognised that such investments could be both productive (in the sense of improving the social conditions for surplus value creation) and stabilising (in the sense of managing effective demand over a long period). (Harvey, 1982: 404)

Therefore, the state rationalises the production of the built environment in "the interest of keeping the costs of reproduction of labour power at a minimum, the capitalist class, as a whole, may seek collective means to intervene in the processes of investment and appropriation in the built environment" (Harvey, 1978a: 14, 17). It is the state that assumes the mantle of fashioning the built environment by taking an active role in the appropriation of space. It does so by "planning the location of industry and population, of housing and public facilities, of transport and communications, of land uses, and so on, [it] creates an overall spatial frame to contain and facilitate the innumerable and fragmented decisions that otherwise shape urban developments" (Harvey, 1985: 31). Investment in those fundamental features of the built environment necessary for the reproduction of labour and for the more efficient accumulation of profit is pursued through the state and allows capitalists to distance themselves from direct involvement in such services. At root, according to Harvey, as a crucial factor in this process was the potential for enhancing capital accumulation:

> Individual capitalists find it hard to make such investments as individuals, no matter how desirable they may regard them. Once again, capitalists are forced to some degree to constitute themselves as a class – usually through the agency of the state – and thereby to find ways to channel investment into research and development and into the quantitative and qualitative improvement of labour power. We should recognise that capitalists often need to make such investments in order to fashion an adequate social basis for further accumulation. But with regard to social expenditures, the investment flows are very strongly affected by the state of class struggle. (Harvey, 1978a: 108)

Two themes related to Harvey's analysis of the dominating influence of industrial capital in the production of space in century city require mention. The first concerns the transformation of the 'bourgeois public sphere' from a mediating influence between society and the state. Secondly, and intimately connected to this transformation, is the role of the urban bourgeoisie as primary agents for the hegemonic interest of industrial capital. An analysis of the role and function of Habermas' 'literate bourgeois public', "as a specific domain – the public domain versus the private... specifically a part of 'civil society'" (Habermas, 1992: 2–3) provides a basis for understanding the significance of the role of the production of public space and the built environment in the city of the nineteenth century. The private sphere is composed of the family and the necessary relations for their reproduction whilst the public sphere was the space of participation, debate, informed and influential opinion formation and became a dominant conceptual division for understanding the growth and influence of the emergent urban bourgeoisie and modern industrial capitalism.[4] The distinction between private and public spheres became significant when an increasingly powerful, educated and literate urban gentry, critical of aristocratic power and privilege, used their ability to represent public opinion as their own in an era of enormous socio-economic change. As Habermas puts it:

> The bourgeois public sphere arose historically in conjunction with a society separated from the state. The 'social' could be constituted as its own sphere to the degree that on one hand the reproduction of life took on private form, while on the other hand the private realm as a whole assumed public relevance. The general rules that governed interaction among people now became a public concern, in which private people soon enough became engaged with the public authority, the bourgeois public sphere attained its political function. Private people gathering to constitute a public turned the political sanctioning of society as a private sphere into a public topic. (Habermas, 1992: 127)

115

Historically, the bourgeois public sphere emerged in the late eighteenth century with the widening of political participation and the development of ideals of citizenship.[5] That is, the rise of the bourgeois public sphere reflected the need to represent the moral and critical authority of an emergent and economically important fraction of power in urban and industrial society. The local character of state power and the local 'provincial' basis of industry, and the inter-relationships between the two, form the basis for understanding the development of processes of urban spatial formation in which the roles of the 'urban gentry' were crucial. This reflects Gramsci's understanding of hegemonic power as "the supremacy of a social group manifests itself in two ways, as 'domination' and as 'intellectual and moral leadership'" (Gramsci, 1971: 57–8). The development of self-conscious and organised bourgeois strata involved in a number of voluntary associations, societies and philanthropic endeavours was transmitted into the organisation and administration of the local state. Thus the local state, charged with addressing the problems of urbanisation and industrialisation through interventions in the built environment to produce better conditions and arrangements in the urban landscape conducive to business and 'good order' was often run by the same people whose business interests would benefit.[6] Thus the bourgeois public sphere developed its influence in civil society, as a realm of wider social relations and public participation and constituted an arena of considerable influence in the development of the ethos of municipal administration and, concomitantly, infrastructural investment in the physical and social environment of the city. The adherence of the municipal elites, those elected representatives as well as officials, throughout much of the period was based on the principle of public service, sound and prudent administration and a commitment to providing for the 'common good'. As Gramsci put it, they were "an elite of men of culture, who have the function of providing leadership of a cultural and general ideological nature for a great movement of interrelated parties (which in reality are fractions of one and the same organic party" (Gramsci, 1971: 149–50). Therefore, the urban bourgeoisie were implicated in the organisation and administration of the local state as well as in public sphere associations in that "hegemony over its historical development belongs to private forces, to civil society – which is 'State' too" (Gramsci, 1971: 261), and among these 'private forces' industrial capital dominated in the expanding urban areas.

There is then a clear connection between Harvey's thesis concerning the dominance of industrial capital in producing spatial forms and structures appropriate to the accumulation of capital and the transformation of an urban bourgeois public sphere into agents of the hegemonic organisation and administration of the city. However, it is also necessary to be mindful that the bourgeois public sphere did not exist in isolation or without pressure from other sections of the population.[7] It is in this context of competing publics that the production of the new spaces of the industrial city must be viewed. It was not just those infrastructural requirements for housing, production, consumption and circulation that need to be considered in this respect but the streets, public squares and parks, the theatres, cinemas and leisure facilities in the modern city that provided arenas for contest and conflict over cultural and ideological forms, representations and uses and provided the background for the democratisation of power.[8]

State involvement in the organisation and provision of necessary services and amenities (such as housing, health care, education, sanitation, etc.) was in part a response to campaigns for the amelioration of the moral, physical and medical dangers perceived as having potentially revolutionary consequences in the new industrial city as well as a means for making labour a more efficient, virtuous, willing and able workforce. There was an attempt to use moral persuasion through philanthropic and municipal enterprises, or as Marx puts it, to "raise the condition of the labourer by an improvement of his mental and moral powers and to make a rational consumer of him" (Marx, 1978: 516). For Harvey, after Marx,

> the 'rational' consumption of commodities in relation to accumulation of capital implies a certain balance between market purchases and household work. The struggle to substitute the former for the latter is significant because its outcome defines the very meaning of 'use values' and the 'standard of living' for labour in its commodity aspects. The construction of the built environment has to be seen, therefore, in the context of the struggle over a whole way of living and being...The bundle of resources which comprise it – streets and sidewalks, drains and sewer systems, parks and playgrounds – contains many elements which are collectively consumed. The public provision of these public goods is a 'natural' form of collective consumption, which capital can easily colonise through the agency of the state...[therefore]...The built environment requires collective management and control, and it is therefore almost certain to be a primary field of struggle between capital and labour over what is good for people and what is good for accumulation. (Harvey, 1978a: 19, 20)

Thus Harvey recognises that the built environment also includes struggle between classes who sometimes act in opposition but also sometimes in coalition to provide not only for the material necessities of life but also those required for the reproduction of labour in general. Again for Harvey it is the needs of capital that are prioritised.

117

> The socialisation and training of labour – the management of 'human capital' as it is usually called in the bourgeois literature – cannot be left to chance. Capital therefore reaches out to dominate the living process – the reproduction of labour power – and it does so because it must. (Harvey, 1978: 126)

The possibility for alliances between labour and capital exist in that consumption demands by the working class, for example for affordable housing, which may coincide with the economic and political interests of capital. Saunders makes clear the point that:

> Working class demands for a variety of consumption provisions may also be consistent with the interest of capital so long as the resources in question (schooling or health care for example) can be made available in the commodity form, and even struggles over questions concerning 'community' and the 'quality of life' may reinforce capitalist domination by attempting to re-establish in the sphere of consumption some spurious relation to nature (as in municipal parks) that the very process of capitalist production has torn asunder. (Saunders, 1981: 227)

There are elements of environmental determinism evident in some of these strategies: for example, better housing makes better workers; a better environment in the city makes healthier workers, etc. Thus the 'spatial environmental determinism' of city planners, designers and administrators was a recognition that the spatial form of a city may act on human behaviour and thus on social processes. The manipulation of the spatial environment of the city was an attempt to inhibit or destroy those activities, behaviours or processes deemed negative to an efficient capitalist accumulation process. This was done on a large scale most famously by Hausmans's reorganisation of Paris.[9] Capital therefore attempts to discipline labour in the work place and in the times and places where workers live and play, to instil the work ethic and civilising bourgeois values over all spheres of life. To this extent, Harvey's concern with explaining the production of the built environment of the city as a product of the needs of industrial capital provides an insight into how the production of social spaces in the city, that serve no immediate production, circulation or exchange end, but have a function as part of the consumption fund that is intimately involved in the process of the reproduction of labour. In this Harvey is clear that in modernity:

118

> The social spaces of distraction and display become as vital to urban culture as the spaces of working and living. Social competition with respect to life-style and command over space, always important for upper segments of the bourgeoisie, became more and more important within the mass culture of urbanisation, sometimes even masking the role of community in processes of class reproduction. (Harvey, 1985: 256–7)

The production of amenities and artefacts in the city, that is the social and physical infrastructure of the built environment, was coupled with another, not necessarily antagonistic element in the urbanisation of capital and the creation of the urban environment of the industrial city. The principle of 'gilding the ghetto' involved "a commitment to community improvement and a commitment to those institutions, such as the church and civil government, capable of forging community spirit" (Harvey, 1978: 128). Thus, a newly empowered bourgeoisie, along with architects, planners and social theorists sought rational solutions to the problems that threatened the health, order, economy etc. of the new industrial metropolises:

> [A]ll rode forth as saviours of the modern city, bursting with ideas as to what it might mean to the needs of efficiency, cleanliness, and, at least in some respects, to human needs...it is undeniable that the aggregate effect was to make cities work better, to improve the lot not only of urban elites but also of urban masses, to radically improve basic infrastructures (such as water and

energy supply, housing, sewage, and air quality) as well as to liberate urban spaces for fresh rounds of organised capital accumulation in ways that lasted for much of the nineteenth century. Compared to the best of the 'gas and water municipal socialism' of those days, one would have to say that the contemporary blasé attitude (to borrow a phrase of Simmel's concerning one of the most powerful mental attitudes to modern urban life) towards the degeneration of our cities leaves much to be desired. (Harvey, 1996: 406)

Harvey makes clear his admiration and appreciation of what was achieved in the nineteenth century by a mix of moral reform, civic solidarity and municipal organisation to improve the quality of life in the urban environment.

Was it not, after all, a central aim in the work of Olmsted and Howard, to try to bring together the country and the city in a productive tension and to cultivate an aesthetic sensibility that could bridge the chronic ills of urbanised industrialism and the supposedly healthier pursuits of country life? It would be churlish to deny real achievements on this front. The marks of what were done in those years – the park systems, the garden cities and suburbs, the tree-lined streets – are now part of a living tradition that define certain qualities of urban living that many (and not only the bourgeoisie) can and do still appreciate. But it [is] also undeniable that this ecological vision, noble and innovative though it was at the time, was predominantly aesthetic (and very bourgeois) in its orientation and was easily co-opted and routinised into real-estate development practices for the middle classes. (Harvey, 1996: 427)

119

Harvey is unambiguous in his analysis of the built environment as the product of the needs for capital to expand and enhance accumulation. However, the role of the state as well as class struggles over demands for better housing, recreational and leisure amenities, created a commitment to the provision of an urban, social and physical infrastructure that was more holistic and widespread than much of what is evident in modern investment strategies in the redevelopment of the contemporary urban environment.

CONCLUSION

Harvey's project to spatialise Marx through an emphasis on historical–geographical materialism' results in the analysis of the urban through a political-economy of space. Harvey's focus on the political–economic imperatives for the production of space, and particularly the creation, organisation and administration of the built environment as part of the process of capital accumulation and class struggle, is a significant contribution to the analysis of the role of space in capitalist urban modernity. It also offers a corrective to the 'human ecology' model of urban growth promulgated by the Chicago School in their explanation of the city. Domination by powerful individuals, groups, classes or fractions, who organise and produce space to exercise or control its use value or the activities that occur there entails the means by which new systems of land use, transportation, communication and organisation arise with and through the development of a market in land. These dimensions are not mutually exclusive of each other but exist in a relationship of dynamic inter-dependence. Harvey's argument, which he attributes to the work and ideas of Lefebvre, is that command over space is one fundamental element in an interconnecting nexus of sources of social power that also includes money and time. Therefore, whoever defines the meanings, forms and material practices of space and time (as well as money) has power over the fundamental operation of the social, political and economic conditions, organisation and operation of society. This is a point that Harvey emphasises in that:

> ideological and political hegemony in any society depends on the ability to control the material context of personal and social experience. For this reason, the materialisations and meanings given to money, time and space have more than a little significance for the maintenance of political power. (Harvey, 1990: 227)

120

Therefore, spatial and temporal practices and discourses become established that serve to achieve, preserve, perpetuate and expand the distribution of social, political and economic power. However, these practices and discourses are not unchallenged or unproblematic. Social and political struggle can, over time, alter the meaning, value and power inherent in spatial configurations, forms and structures, and thus effect social change. Harvey returns again and again to what may be called a *leitmotif* in his work: that is, the consideration of the social construction of space and time and their relationship to the social construction of place:

> Political struggles over the meaning and manner of such representations of place and identity abound, most particularly over the way in which places, their inhabitants and their social functions get located, named and discursively represented...The assignment of place within some socio-spatial structure indicates distinctive roles, capacities for action and access to power. Locating things (both physically and metaphorically) is fundamental to activities of valuing as well as identification. Placing and the making of places are essential to social development, social control, and empowerment in any social order. The processes of place construction therefore interrelate...with the social construction of space and time. (Harvey, 1996: 265)

Place in this context can be defined simply as a position or location, a geographically delineated area. It can also be considered as a thing, an object or entity that solidifies relationships of space and time in that it is the institutionalised objectification of social relations of space and time, as material practices, as forms of power and discourses that come to be embedded in the landscape. The social construction of particular places then may be considered as relatively permanent physical and social structures within the social, cultural and physical landscape. That is, they become fixed capital entities embedded in the landscape as configurations of organised social relations. However, as Harvey has pointed out places with meanings and values to people and groups may be threatened by new imperatives of capital and become transformed or destroyed in the process.

> The incentive to create the world market, to reduce spatial barriers, and to annihilate space through time is omni-present, as is the incentive to rationalise spatial organisation into efficient configurations of production (serial organisation of the detail division of labour, factory systems, and assembly line, territorial division of labour and agglomeration in large towns), circulation networks (transport and communication systems) and consumption (household and domestic layout, community organisation, and residential differentiation, collective consumption in cities)...But here, too, capitalism encounters multiple contradictions. Spatial barriers can be reduced only through the production of particular spaces...The production, restructuring, and growth of spatial organisation is a highly problematic and very expensive affair, held back by vast investments in physical infrastructures that cannot be moved, and social infrastructures that are always slow to change. (Harvey, 1990: 232)

121

In Harvey's later books (*Spaces of Hope*, 2000 and *The New Imperialism*, 2005) he reasserts the central thesis of his Marxist analysis, that the spatial relations of capitalism are not neutral, to engage with the idea of how neo-liberal globalising capitalism and the labour process are dialectically linked. He argues that all is not lost and that alternatives to the domination and command of space by free market global capital do exist. He offers some hope that in struggles against the inequities of the distinctions and dominant universality of capitalism's structuring of the spaces and places of labour, life and leisure, there is the potential for new social and spatial forms and relations to develop. In this he points to the possibilities of transforming urban landscapes by enlightened and radicalised architects, planners and designers in a more positive and perhaps a utopian direction as opposed to those urban transformations, often under the guise of regeneration, of the dictates of capital that are all too familiar in the present.

Harvey's contribution to the analysis of space is one that presents an understanding and explanation of how the modern urban landscape has been and continues to be formed under capitalism. It applies a consistent critical awareness of the importance of space, in spatial forms and arrangements, of structures and artefacts of the development of the urban for social relations. His continuing historical–geographical materialist project to upgrade Marx's paradigm of production provides a means to analyse and investigate the continuing urban processes under global capitalism that continue to influence and structure urban development and experience in the twenty-first century. The various urban regeneration schemes in cities throughout the world that provide a means for the 'gentrification' of disused industrial areas, the redevelopment of dockside and waterfronts for commercial, residential and leisure functions etc. represents an opportunity to apply Harvey's political economy of space to the problematics of contemporary cityscapes.

NOTES

1 Harvey provides a definition and description of the built environment created by the urban process:

> the totality of physical structures: houses, roads, factories, offices, sewage systems, parks, cultural institutions, educational facilities, and so on...fixed capital items to be used in production (factories, highways, railroads, offices, and so on) and consumption fund items to be used in consumption (houses, roads, parks, sidewalks, and the like). (Harvey, 1978a: 9–10)

This description and definition is emphasised elsewhere by Harvey:

> The built environment comprises a whole host of diverse elements: factories, dams, offices, shops, warehouses, roads, railways, docks, power stations, water supply and sewage disposal systems, schools, hospitals, parks, cinemas, restaurants – the list is endless.... The whole question of the spatial ordering of the built environment has then to be considered; the decision where to put one element cannot be divorced from the 'where' of others. The built environment has to be regarded, then as a geographically ordered, complex, composite commodity. The production, ordering, maintenance, renewal, and transformation of such a commodity poses serious dilemmas. The production of individual elements – houses, factories, shops, schools, roads, etc. – has to be co-ordinated, both in time and space, in such a way as to allow the composite commodity to assume an appropriate configuration. (Harvey, 1982: 233)

2 Harvey considers the creation of a space economy as a necessary development of the circulation of surplus as a product of capitalism as a mode of production:

> A space economy has to be created and maintained if urbanism is to survive as a social form. Expanded reproduction and changing scale in urbanism also

require an expanding (geographically) or intensifying space economy. The flow of goods and services throughout this space economy are a tangible expression of that process which circulates surplus value in order to concentrate more of it. (Harvey, 1973: 237–8)

3 In language reminiscent of Lefebvre, Harvey highlights the importance of urbanisation both for the survival of capitalism and for the creation of a new form of consciousness and relationship to nature.

We know that capitalism has survived into the 20th century in part through the production of an increasingly urbanised space. The result has been a particular kind of urban experience, radically different quantitatively and qualitatively from anything that preceded it in world history. Capitalism has produced a 'second nature' through urbanisation and the creation of the built environment of extraordinary breadth and intricacy. It has also produced a new kind of human nature through the urbanisation of human consciousness and the production of social spaces and a particular structure of inter-relations between the different loci of consciousness formation. . . . The urban process then appears as both fundamental to the perpetuation of capitalism and a primary expression of its inner contradictions now expressed as external constraints. (Harvey, 1985: 273)

4 Habermas provides some details of the distinction between the public and private spheres:

123

Included in the private realm was the authentic 'public sphere', for it was a public sphere constituted by private people . . . The private sphere comprised civil society in the narrower sense, that is to say, the realm of commodity exchange and of social labour; imbedded in it was the family with its interior domain (Intimsphare). The public sphere in the political realm evolved from the public sphere in the world of letters; through the vehicle of public opinion it put the state in touch with the needs of society. (Habermas, 1992: 30–1)

5 Howell gives some clarification of the historical origins and development as well as the political context for the rise and role of the public sphere:

The public sphere is a sphere which mediates between society and the state, in which the public organises itself as the bearer of public opinion. It has its origins in the late 18th century ideals of citizenship and of a wider, informed and educated public, of representative and participatory government, and above all in the new forms of political action that these enshrined. Historically then the public sphere is particular and specific to a time and a place, and also to certain social transformations. It is linked to the demand for political reform, principally on the part of an emergent but increasingly self-confident bourgeoisie, and it depended on and presumed the prior transformation of social relations, their condensation into new political arrangements and the generation of new social, cultural and political discourse around this changing environment. (Howell, 1993: 309)

6 This is a point that Gray emphasises in his analysis of the links between the local state and an increasingly dominant bourgeois public sphere. In this, for Gray, ruling class intellectuals were

[p]articularly concerned with the administrative and ideological organisation of society, they were to be found as members of statistical societies and Royal Commissions, writers and readers of the quarterly press, organisers of charity and social discipline...They played a crucial role in the organisation of hegemony...The industrial bourgeoisie constituted the *hegemonic fraction* within the power bloc – whose interests preponderate in the exercise of state power, and whose particular social relations figure in dominant ideological representations...Various overlapping intellectual and literary cadres strongly committed to utilitarianism and free trade, staffed key new branches of the State apparatus. Moreover 'divinity and economics' ran together and the laws of political economy were closely entangled with moral, and often religiously sanctioned, norms of 'rational conduct'. (Gray, 1981: 237, 239)

7 Ely stresses Habermas was at pains to recognise this point:

It is important to acknowledge the existence of competing publics not just later in the nineteenth century...but at every stage in the history of the public sphere and, indeed, from the very beginning...The emergence of the bourgeois public was never defined solely by the struggle against absolutism and traditional authority. Also, it necessarily addressed the problem of popular containment as well...Consequently, the public sphere makes more sense as the structured setting where cultural and ideological contest or negotiation among the variety of publics takes place, rather than as the spontaneous and class-specific achievement of the bourgeoisie in some sufficient sense. (Ely, 1992: 306)

8 As Habermas writes:

Laws passed under the 'pressure of the street' could hardly be understood any longer as embodying the reasonable consensus of publicly debating private persons...The competitive order no longer lent sufficient credibility to its promise that, along with the alleged equality of opportunity to accumulate private property, it also maintained open access to the public sphere in the political realm. The principle of the latter, rather, demanded the direct admittance of the labouring classes, of the uneducated masses without property – precisely through the extension of equal political rights. Electoral reform was the topic of the nineteenth century: no longer the principle of publicity as such, as had been true in the eighteenth century, but of the enlargement of the public. (Habermas, 1992, 132–3)

9 See Chapter 3 in Harvey (1985) and also Harvey (2003), Paris: capital of modernity, for a detailed study of the redevelopment of the space of Paris as a means to organise and control the population as well as represent the national prestige and imperial status of the capital and of France.

five

Michel Foucault: space, knowledge and power

Michel Foucault did not propose a general theory of space or of power. However, his well-known proposition of the emergence through a number of interrelated professions and activities in the nineteenth century of a 'disciplinary society', provides the opportunity for investigating both his use of the concept of power/knowledge and the importance of the spatial dimension in his understanding of social relations. What will be explored and given particular emphasis here are those 'disciplinary discourses' that illuminate the dispersed practices of power operative and inherent in representations of forms of space that are an integral part of Foucault's social theory. These discourses are pertinent to an appreciation of the historical origins and development of modern, predominantly urban society, in which 'disciplinary spaces' are created through the application of knowledge/power for the cultivation, instillation and propagation of 'civilised', bourgeois values. They are an important feature of Foucault's analysis of modern socio-spatial forms and the social relations of power. In particular, Foucault's assertion of the role of the medical professions as 'the first specialists of space' will be analysed to investigate the power of disciplinary discourses in the production, representation and use of space in the development of a planned, managed, policed urban society. In this, the role of space and spatial forms will be considered in relation to Foucault's understanding of what he terms the two aspects of 'bio-power': the creation of 'docile bodies' and the policing of the 'species body'. The following necessarily selective usage of Foucault's array of concepts and works is one that heeds Foucault's own advice for the treatment of 'original' thinkers:

> The only valid tribute to thought such as Nietzsche's is precisely to use it, to deform it, to make it groan and protest. And if commentators then say that I am being unfaithful to Nietzsche, that is of absolutely no interest to me. (Foucault, 1980: 53–4)

The following then is my attempt not to make Foucault (or the reader) groan and protest but to illuminate the spatiality of Foucault's analysis of modern disciplinary society. What will be considered then is how Foucault understood the role and importance of space in understanding the historical development of the spaces and practices of modern society.

POWER, KNOWLEDGE AND SPACE

'Power–knowledge' is an essential concept in Foucault's work. It is an attempt to embody the inextricably linked dynamic relationship between power and knowledge as a process. For Foucault, power is distributed through and in the construction and application of knowledge in particular and localised arenas. Concomitantly, power is established, maintained and presupposed by knowledge. As Foucault states:

> it is not the activity of the subject of knowledge that produces a corpus of knowledge, useful or resistant to power, but power–knowledge, the processes and struggles that traverse it and of which it is made up, that determines the forms and possible domains of knowledge. (Foucault, 1977: 28)

This is a point that Armstrong reiterates as crucial to Foucault's analysis:

126

> Power assumes a relationship based on some knowledge which creates and sustains it; conversely, power establishes a particular regime of truth in which certain knowledge becomes admissible or possible. (Armstrong, 1983: 10)

There is, for Foucault, a whole range of endeavours and practices in which the acquisition of knowledge and the exercise of power are inextricably and intimately interlinked. He identifies what is considered as a fundamental historical transformation in the exercise of power that was intimately related to forms of knowledge, and technologies of understanding, that were based upon the discernment of local, 'micro-terrains' of power. Power is effective through its penetration and knowledge of a variety of relationships, from the most personal and intimate to the most public and professional. How these micro-powers are constructed and effective in a number of local fields, domains or territories is essential for understanding the very existence and operation of large, centralised or global power concentrations and institutionalised arrangements.

> Once knowledge can be analysed in terms of region (a fiscal administrative, military notion), domain (juridico-political notion), implantation, displacement (what displaces itself is an army, a squadron, a population), transposition, one is able to capture the process by which knowledge functions as a form of power and disseminates the effects of power. There is an administration of knowledge,

a politics of knowledge, relations of power which pass via knowledge and which, if one tries to transcribe them, lead one to consider forms of domination designated by such notions of field (an economico-juridical notion), region (fiscal, administrative, military notion) and territory (juridico-political notion, the area controlled by a certain kind of power). And the politico-strategic term is an indication of how the military and the administration actually comes to inscribe themselves both on a material soil and within forms of discourse. (Foucault, 1980: 69)

Foucault's analysis of power then may be said to be primarily concerned with understanding how power is exercised in different historical periods, provinces, domains and spheres, and thus has a certain relevance to understanding its operation in and through space. Rather than asking what is power, who holds it and what is its source, for Foucault it is the relation of forces in the operation and exercise of power that is the focus of investigation. For Foucault, power is understood as dispersed throughout society as a heterogeneous ensemble of strategies and techniques, an open-ended 'cluster of relations' that exist in its exercise.[1] Power, is thus not the possession (legitimated in juridical relations of contracts, codes and laws) of any particular group, class or institution. Since power is presented as having many forms it cannot be derived solely from the spheres of circulation or of production, and it is not confined to key institutions such as the state. Foucault's focus is instead upon how 'micro-powers' invade our everyday lives and relationships and constitute the conditions and means of power not only for the state and its apparatus but also in a myriad of ways and forms that is not necessarily best understood in Marx's dichotomy of class conflict in which one class holds sway over another. As he states:

> I believe that anything can be deduced from the general phenomenon of the domination of the bourgeois class. What needs to be done is something quite different. One needs to investigate historically, and beginning at the lowest level, how mechanisms of power have been able to function...We must escape from the limited field of juridical sovereignty and state institutions, and instead base our analysis of power on the study of the tactics and techniques of domination... What makes power hold good...is simply the fact that it doesn't only weigh on us as a force that says no, but that it traverses and produces things, it induces pleasure, forms knowledge, produces discourses. (Foucault, 1980: 100, 102, 119)

This is a point that Foucault emphasised elsewhere:

> We must cease once and for all to describe the effects of power in negative terms, power produces; it produces reality; it produces domains of objects and rituals of truth. The individual and the knowledge that may be gained of him belong to this production. (Foucault, 1977: 194)

The exercise of power then, for Foucault, occurs in a variety of places, through a number of individuals, institutions and organisations at different times and places and in a number of forms. Therefore, despite space being seemingly relegated in importance to time in conventional social analysis, it is a crucial factor in the social, economic and political operation and organisation of society. As Foucault famously put it:

> Space was treated as the dead, the fixed, the undialectical, the immobile. Time on the contrary, was richness, fecundity, life, dialectic...[which led to it being]... either dismissed as belonging to 'nature' – that is, the given, the basic conditions, 'physical geography', in other words a sort of 'prehistoric' stratum; or else it was conceived as the residential site or field of expansion of peoples, of a culture, a language or a State. (Foucault, 1980: 70, 149)

This is a point on which Foucault is categorical: "Space is fundamental in any form of community life; space is fundamental in any exercise of power" (Foucault, 1986: 252).[2] In other words, Foucault is suspicious of 'total' explanations that sought to resolve the complexity of the social world into a single 'spirit' or 'principle', theory or ideology. He rejected any idea of general or totalising theories of power. He writes that

128

> Nothing is fundamental. That is what is interesting in the analysis of society. That is why nothing irritates me as much as these inquiries – which are by definition metaphysical – on the foundations of power is a society or the self-institution of society, etc. These are not fundamental phenomena. There are only reciprocal relations, and the perpetual gaps between intentions in relation to one another. (Foucault, 1982: 18)

Thus Foucault is critical of theories, such as Marxist conceptions of power, that give it an 'epiphenomenal' status, that consider power as unitary, sovereign or centralised, belonging to one group or class, institution or body. That is, as only immanent in class relations. However, Foucault does not dismiss entirely the contribution of Marx's work in understanding historical processes for the operation of power in modern societies. Indeed, Foucault clearly states that:

> It is impossible at the present time to write history without using a whole range of concepts directly or indirectly linked to Marx's thought and situating oneself in a horizon of thought which has been defined and described by Marx. (Foucault, 1980: 53)[3]

Therefore, the understanding that Foucault presents of the diffusion and dispersion of power throughout society by economically dominant class interests, as analysed by Marx, is one that serves their own interests. That is:

> The bourgeoisie is perfectly well aware that a new constitution or legislature will not suffice to assure its hegemony; it realises that it has to invent a new technology ensuring the irrigation by effects of power of the whole social body down to its smallest particles. And it was by such means that the bourgeoisie not only made a revolution but succeeded in establishing a social hegemony which it has never relinquished. (Foucault, 1980: 156)

Foucault's proposition is of a dispersed system of spatial sciences that emerged in eighteenth-century Europe as part of a general system of knowledge based on medical and administrative necessity as providing an explanation of the means by which this hegemony was established and maintained. What was established, according to Foucault, was

> a type of power which is constantly exercised by means of surveillance rather than in a discontinuous manner... it presupposes a tightly knit grid of material coercions...one of the great inventions of bourgeois society. (Foucault, 1980: 105)

It is an analysis that puts knowledge of, and command over space at the centre of techniques and practices for instructing individuals and populations, in institutional settings and in wider social arrangements, at work and at rest and play. It is an analysis that seeks to understand and represent the processes by which moral consent as well as methods of physical control and subservience were constructed and maintained. It is therefore an approach that provides an important understanding of how and by whom and to what end particular forms and representations of space are constructed and promulgated.

129

The development in the eighteenth century of an awareness and understanding of spatial forms was, for Foucault, an expression of how power came to be articulated and exercised. For example he states that

> Architecture begins, at the end of the [eighteenth] century, to become involved in problems of population, health and the urban question...[it] becomes a question of using the disposition of space for economico-political ends. (Foucault, 1980: 148)

It is in such assemblages, in their distribution and arrangement, of activities and people, in and around the architecture and environment of the city that the spatial dimension of the operation of power becomes concretised. Space, for Foucault, is where discourses about power and knowledge become actual relations of power rather than merely residing in abstract notions and ideologies. Foucault argues that

> in the eighteenth century one sees the development of reflection upon architecture as a function of the aims and techniques of the government of societies. One begins to see a form of political literature that addresses what the order of a society should be, what a city should be, given the requirements of the maintenance of order; given that one should avoid epidemics, avoid revolts, permit a decent and moral life, and so on... from the eighteenth century on, every discussion of politics as the art of the government of men necessarily includes a chapter or a series of chapter on urbanism, on collective facilities, on hygiene, and on private architecture... The city was no longer perceived as a place of privilege, as an exception in a territory of fields, forests, and roads. The cities were no longer islands beyond the common law. Instead, the cities, with the problems that they raised, and the particular forms that they took, served as the models for the governmental rationality that was to apply to the whole territory. (Foucault, 1986: 239, 240, 241)

Foucault echoes many early investigators of the shadow side of urban life when he states that behind these interventions lay a concern about the consequences for civilised society of the onrush of urbanisation and industrialisation.

130

> A fear haunted the latter half of the eighteenth century: the fear of darkened spaces, of the pall of gloom which prevents the full visibility of things, men and truths. It sought to break up the patches of darkness that blocked the light, eliminate the shadowy areas of society, demolish the unlit chambers where arbitrary political acts, monarchical caprice, religious superstitions, tyrannical and priestly plots, epidemics and the illusions of ignorance were fomented... The new political order could not be established until these places were eradicated. (Foucault, 1980: 153)

The control and division of space and of time thus became a fundamental means by which knowledge and power came to be exercised increasingly over all spheres of society.

> Once knowledge can be analysed in terms of regions, domains, implantation, displacements, transposition, one is able to capture the process by which knowledge functions as a form of power... [one can]... decipher discourse through the use of spatial, strategic metaphors [that] enables one to grasp precisely the points at which discourses are transformed in, through and on the basis of relations of power. (Foucault, 1980: 69, 70)

Knowledge and power thus became operative in and through a number of diverse and interlinked 'disciplines', what Foucault defined as forms of practice – "small acts of cunning endowed with a great power of diffusion" (Foucault, 1977: 139) – not as institutional structures.

For Foucault space needs to be related to the functional requirements of power; thus, what is conceptualised is the emergence of a new set of specifically spatial practices and procedures that is closely linked to the development of the city and what he terms 'governmentality'. Put simply, governmentality is the extraordinary expansion in the scope of government begun in the mid-eighteenth century and continuing to grow till today. This includes all those activities and spheres of human activity, whether as individuals or as collectivities which need to be structured, manipulated or controlled. As Foucault himself writes:

> This word [government] must be allowed the very broad meaning which it had in the sixteenth century. 'Government' did not refer only to political structures or the management of states; rather it designates the way in which the conduct of individuals or states might be directed: the government of children, of souls, of communities, of families, of the sick. It did not cover only the legitimately constituted forms of political or economic subjection, but also modes of action, more or less considered, which were designed to act upon the possibilities of action of other people. To govern, in this sense, is to structure the possible field of action of others. (Foucault, 1982: 221)

The need to create, define, manage, organise and control space for particular functions (e.g. as sites for the medical supervision of diseases, or of the education of children, or the keeping of peace and order) *131* became inseparable from a whole series of other military and 'police' duties. It is necessary to be explicit here concerning what Foucault defines, what he means by 'police'.

> At the outset, the notion of police applied only to the set of regulations that were to assure the tranquillity of a city, but at that moment the police became the very type for the government of the whole territory . . . In the seventeenth and eighteenth centuries, 'police' signified a program of government rationality. This can be characterised as a project to create a system of regulation of the general conduct of individuals whereby everything would be controlled to the point of self-sustenance, without the need for intervention. (Foucault, 1986: 241)[4]

Thus it is possible to see that for Foucault what developed was the creation and representation of spaces as well as their partitioning and manipulation as the product of specific knowledge applied to meet functional and desirable ends.

> Particular places were defined not only by the need to supervise, to break dangerous communications, but also to create a useful space . . . Hence the need to distribute and partition off space in a rigorous manner . . . Gradually, an administrative and political space was articulated upon therapeutic space; it tended to individualise bodies, diseases, symptoms, lives and deaths; it

constituted a real table of juxtaposed and carefully distinct singularities. Out of discipline a medically useful space was born. (Foucault, 1977: 143–4)

It is then in the development of such 'disciplinary discourses' applied to the developing space of modernity that Foucault proposes how and in what ways space came to be known and thus rendered useful to power.

DISCIPLINARY DISCOURSES OF SPACE

What arose from the early experience of the consequences of industrialisation and urbanisation is the perception of the need for the development of new ways and means for understanding and thus controlling and organising space and, concomitantly, the individuals and groups that inhabit it. Foucault describes how this was achieved in different ways. First, discipline begins from the organisation of individuals in space in which several techniques are applied, and which he terms 'the art of distinctions'. Sometimes space needed to be enclosed to specify that it is a place of discipline, for example in the barracks, the school, the prison or the factory. Sometimes space must be partitioned with the aim of knowing, mastering and using space so that each individual can be assigned and know their place within the enclosed order of the institution or disciplinary sphere. As Foucault puts it,

132

> Disciplinary space tends to be divided into as many sections as there are bodies or elements to be distributed. One must eliminate the effects of imprecise distributions, the uncontrolled disappearance of individuals, their diffuse circulation, their unusable and dangerous coagulation; it was a tactic of anti-desertion, anti-vagabondage, anti-concentration. Its aim was to establish presences and absences, to know where and how to locate individuals, to set up useful communications, to interrupt others, to be able at each moment to supervise the conduct of each individual, to asses it, to judge it, to calculate its qualities or merits. It was a procedure, therefore, aimed at knowing, mastering and using. Discipline organises an analytical space. (Foucault, 1977: 143)

The means of supervision of correct training could, it was argued, be most efficiently organised and administered so that "the perfect disciplinary apparatus would make it possible for a single gaze to see everything constantly" (Foucault, 1977: 173). Thus, Jeremy Bentham's design of the Panopticon for the architecture of the prison was considered the ideal apparatus for the most efficient organisation of disciplinary space. However, as Foucault makes clear, 'panopticism' represented a general diagram for the dissemination of disciplinary technologies throughout wider society. The panoptic schema as applied to the prison could and it was argued, by Bentham should, be adapted and adopted to other spheres and spaces.

> The panoptic schema, without disappearing as such or losing any of its properties, was destined to spread throughout the whole social body; its vocation was to become a generalised function. The plague-stricken town provided an exceptional disciplinary model: perfect, but absolutely violent; to the disease that brought death; life inside it was reduced to its simplest expression; it was, against the power of death, the meticulous exercise of the right of the sword. The panopticon, on the other hand, has a role in amplification; although it arranges power, although it is intended to make it more economic and more effective, it does not do so for power itself, nor for the immediate salvation of a threatened society: its aim is to strengthen the social forces – to increase production, to develop the economy, spread education, raise the level of public morality, to increase and multiply. (Foucault, 1977: 207–8)[5]

The disciplinary gaze, the 'system of surveillance', the 'Eye of Power' epitomised by the architecture of the Panopticon, thus became an essential and fundamental part of the machinery of production, a specific mechanism for the exercise of power as the division of labour increased in developing industrialised economies. It was also adopted and applied by professional experts and by bureaucratic officials to monitor and regulate all sorts of private and public spaces, behaviours and activities. Bureaucracy is the dominant mode of operation of the state and of the economy, but as with Foucault's concept of power, it is neither a class in itself nor is it the power of the state. It can serve any organisation, scheme or plan as the most efficient means of applying operative procedures for the goals and ends that are specified as useful, fortuitous or beneficial.[6] Regulation and instruction was to be achieved without recourse to physical domination:

133

> There is no need for arms, physical violence, material constraints. Just a gaze. An inspecting gaze, a gaze which each individual under its weight will end by interiorising to the point that he is his own overseer, each individual thus exercising this surveillance over and against himself. (Foucault, 1980: 155)

Foucault's analysis of power/knowledge described how "massive, compact disciplines are broken down into flexible methods of control which may be transferred and adapted" (Foucault, 1977: 211). Thus, disciplinary knowledge and techniques could be applied in the industrial era to a range of activities, people and circumstances. As Foucault puts it:

> In reality, power in its exercise goes much further, passes through much finer channels, and is much more ambiguous, since each individual has at his disposal a certain power, and for that very reason can also act as the vehicle for

transmitting a wider power. The reproduction of the relations of production is not the only function served by power...The individual, with his identity and characteristics, is the product of a relation of power exercised over bodies, multiplicities, movements, desires, forces. (Foucault, 1980: 72, 74)

In addition to the control of space, disciplinary techniques also required the control of the individual in time. For example, the instigation of the timetable from the practices of religious institutions such as the monastery and convent, and the army, could be adopted, transferred and adapted to the school, the prison, the workhouse and the factory. Thus Foucault argues that:

> The new disciplines had no difficulty in taking up their place in the old forms; the schools and poorhouses extended the life and regularity of the monastic communities to which they were often attached. The rigours of the industrial period retained a religious air. (Foucault, 1977: 149)

Thus, working, learning and paying one's dues for transgression were all regulated by and associated with the passage, monitoring and articulation of time in supervised space. In this respect, Foucault explored the concept of the 'docile-body' as the subject of the power, authority and practices of a number of disciplines that constructed an *anatomopolitics of the body*' as a means of knowing and thus of controlling bodies in space.

134

> The historical moment of the disciplines was the moment when an art of the human body was born, which was directed not only at the growth of its skills, nor at the intensification of its subjection, but at the formation of a relation that in the mechanism itself makes it more obedient as it becomes more useful, and conversely Thus discipline produces subjected and practised bodies, 'docile' bodies. Discipline increases the forces of the body (in economic terms of utility) and diminishes these same forces (in terms of obedience)...If economic exploitation separates the force and the product of labour, let us say that disciplinary coercion establishes in the body the constricting link between an increased aptitude and an increased domination. (Foucault, 1980: 137–8)[7]

What Foucault emphasises, despite acknowledging the historical precedents[8] is that the aim of disciplinary technology, wherever and in whatever form it operates, as being the moulding of a "docile body that may be subjected to, used, transformed and improved to meet a desired end" (Foucault, 1980: 198). That is, power is administered and applied in and through a variety of disciplinary technologies, that are themselves the result of knowledge, its accumulation and dispersal. This is to ensure that

> power relations can materially penetrate the body in depth, without depending even on the mediation of the subject's own representations. If power takes hold

on the body, this isn't through its having first to be interiorised in people's consciousness...(Foucault, 1980: 186)[9]

The body was thus to be exercised, drilled, trained and manipulated in time and through space by the application of disciplinary power. The movements, gestures and activities that made up the working day were correlated to a strict time-keeping which aimed to create socially, economically and politically useful, docile, orderly, punctual, responsible, obedient, fit, healthy, educated, temperate, pious and thrifty productive bodies.[10] What was created was a new 'moral geography' replete with all those 'civilising' virtues and good habits deemed appropriate for the maximisation of economic potential and for the defence of the state. Foucault's analysis goes further in that the diffusion of disciplinary discourses from institutional settings of work, punishment, schooling, the military, etc. to all social spheres and arenas identifies the means by which bourgeois hegemony tried to construct and manipulate moral consent as well as methods of physical control and subservience for its own ends. The imposition of the 'Eye of Power' to the spatial entity of the urban is, for Foucault, one of the first and most explicit examples of the operation of disciplinary discourses of space.

THE FIRST SPECIALISTS OF SPACE – THE MEDICAL DISCOURSE

Foucault is unequivocal in stressing the role of doctors from the end of the eighteenth century as being fundamentally involved in the analysis and organisation of space. The operation of medical disciplinary discourses illustrates and emphasises the exercise of knowledge and power in creating not only representations of space but useful and beneficial space. Foucault describes how doctors

at that time were among other things the first specialists of space. They posed four fundamental problems. That of local conditions (regional climates, soil, humidity and dryness): under the term 'constitution', they studied these combinations of local determinants and seasonal variations which at a given moment favour a particular sort of disease; that of co-existences (either between men, questions of density and proximity, or between men and things, the question of water, sewage, ventilation, or between men and animals, the question of stables and abattoirs, or between men and the dead, the question of cemeteries); that of residences (the environment, urban problems); that of displacements (the migration of men, the propagation of diseases.) Doctors were, along with the military, the first managers of collective space. But the military were chiefly concerned to think the space of 'campaigns' (and thus of 'passages') and that of fortresses, whereas the doctors were concerned to think the space of habitations and towns. (Foucault, 1980: 150–1)

What Foucault is proposing is that from the eighteenth century onwards medicine and politics came to be interlinked in the consideration of and necessity for action in the increasingly, populous cities. Medicine as a discipline came to be involved in processes, techniques and interventions that were closely related to political developments, aims and objectives. As Foucault writes:

> What the eighteenth century shows, in any case, is a double-sided process...in short, the progressive emplacement of what was to become the great medical edifice of the nineteenth century, cannot be divorced from the concurrent organisation of a politics of health, the consideration of disease as a political and economic problem for social collectivities which they must seek to resolve as a matter of overall policy. (Foucault, 1980: 166)

Foucault's proposition is that doctors were at the forefront of the diagnosis and treatment of the perceived problems of industrial society. New methods of surveillance for collecting information on populations came to be developed out of the need to produce, understand and control the spaces and populations of the newly industrialised and urbanising towns and cities. It cultivated new ways of seeing, the 'Eye of Power', and of calculating and ordering the social, economic and political existence of society. That is:

136

> The great eighteenth century demographic upswing in western Europe, the necessity for co-ordinating and integrating it into the apparatus of production and the urgency of controlling it with finer and more adequate power mechanisms causes 'population', with its numerical variables of space and chronology, longevity and health, to emerge not only as a problem but as an object of surveillance, analysis, intervention, modification, etc. .... Within this set of problems, the 'body' – the body of individuals and the body of populations – appears as the bearer of new variables, not merely as between the scarce and the numerous, the submissive and the restive, rich and poor, health and sick, strong and weak, but also between the more or less utilisable, more or less amenable to profitable investment, those with greater or lesser prospects of survival, death and illness, and with more or less capacity for being usefully trained. (Foucault, 1980: 171, 172)

Medical disciplinary discourses may be said to be concerned with how knowledge, techniques and practices, of populations and individuals, involved medical personnel and institutions in the development of a modern form of government in which political authorities (the local and national state) worked in alliance with experts in order to administer a variety of perceived problems. The medical profession was thus implicated in the operation of power and the exercise of political initiatives within the context of the development of a new understanding of the problems faced by the growth of cities, new technologies and the movement and behaviour of populations. That is, urbanisation and industrialisation brought with them problems and consequences that needed to be addressed not only by the state but also by the development of new techniques and methods of analysis formulated and applied by professional disciplines and charitable public bodies and organisations. This was especially true in the development of the medical disciplines and in their self-perceived roles and activities. The aim was to promote public health and private well-being within a realm that was considered inherently social as a means whereby knowledge about the population could be used to construct a more healthy, fit and able, efficient, obedient and docile population. As Foucault puts it:

> A 'medico-administrative' knowledge begins to develop concerning society, its health and sickness, its conditions of life, housing and habits, which serves as the basic core for the 'social economy' and sociology of the 19th century. And there is likewise constituted a politico-medical hold on a population hedged in by a whole series of prescriptions relating not only to disease but to general forms of existence and behaviours (food and drink, sexuality and fecundity, clothing and the layout of living space). (Foucault, 1980: 176)

Rose identifies in Foucault's various analyses of medical discourses five great apparatus of health – the medical administration of public space, the hygienic regulation of domestic life, the curative clinic, the medical staffing of the population, the instrumental mitigation of suffering – as being involved in different relations between experts and those subject to their intervention. The medicalisation of public space evolved in tandem with the intervention of medical personnel in the private life and space of the family. The social body was to be reconstructed through the intervention of town planning that would invade those areas long perceived as being the worst examples of disease, immorality and ill health with the purifying object of introducing light, air and education (both moral and hygienic). As Rose stresses, this was a concerted application of knowledge being applied to the problem of public space.

137

> This medico-administrative government of public space was not merely a matter of medical officers of health, sanitary reformers and the policing of food and drink. It also entailed the development of spatial technologies of health, in the form of a new set of relations between medicine and architecture. In the schemes of planning space, at the macro-level of the towns and the micro-level of the design of buildings – prisons, asylums, schools, homes, bathrooms, kitchens – one sees the desire to make space healthy. Architects and planners seek to enact a medical vocation organising the relations between persons, functions, objects, effluents, activities, in order to minimise all that would encourage disease and to maximise all that would promote health. The dream of the healthy body – the healthy city, the healthy home – has, perhaps done more than most to embody the medical aspiration within the territories upon which we manage our individual lives. (Rose, 1994: 64)

Foucault singles out the role of the 'medical police' as being fundamental in the construction of a social model of society and of positivist social science in just such practices as were developed and applied by the medical profession in the nineteenth century. This has for Foucault direct relevance for the development of the social sciences and particularly sociology.

> Sociological knowledge (savoir) is formed rather in practices like those of the doctors... In fact if the intervention of the doctors was of capital importance at this period, this was because it was demanded by a whole new range of political and economic problems, highlighting the importance of the facts of the population. (Foucault, 1980: 151)

Certainly, there is ample historical evidence for the fundamental role that medical personnel have played in collecting information on populations that was instrumental in advising social policy and political strategies for ameliorating urban 'problems', conditions and experiences.[11] As Foucault puts it, "the doctor becomes the great advisor and expert, if not in the art of governing, at least in that of observing, correcting and improving the social 'body' and maintaining it in a permanent state of health" (Foucault, 1980: 177).

138 In this period of the nineteenth century anatomical models were an attractive basis for social theorists, and for the formation of social policy for the new urban environment, in that they provided a familiar epistemology as well as empirical means and statistical evidence. Society was given as an organic form and thought of in medical terms: that is as a social body afflicted by illness and needing to be restored to health. Thus, medical personnel become involved with other authorities, such as the state and voluntary bodies, in relations whose concern is with issues of individual and population's health, sickness and the development of techniques for surveillance, segregation and discipline.[12] This was allied with the miasmic conception of epidemics, of which there were many in the eighteenth and nineteenth centuries, that is that stagnant air breeds disease and was primarily concerned with the spatialisation of diseases. They were understood as occurring around and circulating in certain types of social spaces and came to afflict those of certain characters, habits and behaviours who inhabited them. Thus a geographic disposition of disease could be constructed that could be applied to and analysed in relation to the geography of the town or city and the rate and level of infection could be equated with certain areas and classes. The analogy of the human body and social organisation was, in the nineteenth century, adapted and adopted to suit the new conditions that were emerging in the industrial towns and cities. The role of scientific medicine in the apparent objective, minute investigation of the urban environment is a theme that Foucault credits to the medical profession's concern with spatialisation. The investigation of the urban population became an essential part of the disciplinary programme for social policy.[13] The image of the 'social body' was a defence against representations of humans as machines and, like other anatomical models, represented society as a unified whole with groups and individuals characterised by having specialised functions. But public health was not only a matter of sanitation, it involved the moral and physical regulation of public spaces and private behaviours.[14]

For some the solution was to surgically remove the afflicted parts by increasingly sub-dividing the city's districts so as to more minutely observe, on a street and house basis, and thus make more manageable the knowledge that is acquired of them for the purposes of control and regulation. The collection, for example, of official statistics on birth, death, marriage, etc. was part of the process whereby the population came to be subject to surveillance, analysis and intervention. Strategies were varied and depended on the group or population (children, adults, parents, workers, patients, criminals, etc.) that was targeted and the specific goals that were aimed at. That is, whether the object of study and concern was a national, local or regional population; a prison or school population; the dangerous classes or the labouring classes as a whole. There was in all this the development of disciplinary social practices devised and practised by medical personnel to scrutinise, police and discipline the urban population, for their own good. Damer (2000) argues that just such practices were actively employed by the municipal housing authorities in Glasgow from the late nineteenth century to the beginning of World War Two. Through surveillance and relentless patrolling, public health officials acted as 'social hygienists' constantly supervising the moral and physical 'cleanliness' of the poor. Damer is unequivocal in his opinion that:

> The discourse of Public Health was a well-worked out exercise of hegemonic power in the class struggle, or in Foucaultian terms, 'a technology of control', or a 'mechanism of subjection'. It was indeed all about surveillance and control, but surveillance and control in the interests of one class as against another. (Damer, 2000: 18)

BIO-POWER AND SPACE

Foucault's concept of 'bio-power' illustrate how techniques of power were constructed around the medico-administrative necessity of the government of space and was concerned with the exercise and effect of relations of power on humans, as individuals and as aggregates. That is, how people could be managed, controlled and maintained to enhance their capabilities and capacities for specific purposes. Thus,

> When Foucault mentions the problems of populations, health and cities, it is clear that he is referring to our modern form of power, what he calls 'bio-power'...under regimes of 'bio-power' political intervention takes place at the level of the species as a natural population to be known and controlled. This manipulation is exercised through an ever-expanding complex of social institutions, and thereby in a widening number of building types: hospitals, prisons, workplaces, schools, street plans, housing and so forth. (Wright and Rabinow, 1982: 14)

This notion of bio-power reflects an interest in the accumulation of knowledge of individuals and populations that has a specific purpose: to maximise the health (moral and physical) of individuals and populations to ensure their maximum efficiency and productivity, to minimise the negative consequences from the development of new industrial techniques in the economy, and to limit the threat from potentially revolutionary conditions through the surveillance, management and control of individual and communal activities. Thus knowledge of individuals and populations and of the spaces they occupy and inhabit was a crucial element of the application of disciplinary discourses in the development and structuring of modern society.

The first aspect, the 'docile body', has already been alluded to. The medical professions were directly involved in developing new forms of architecture. Architecture was thus one disciplinary discourse in which knowledge of space produced spatial forms that served to concretise power relations. The sanatorium, for example, was an institution by which the beneficial and health-giving properties of fresh air and sunlight could be maximised by the construction of specific designs of buildings for those suffering from the debilitating effects of respiratory diseases such as TB. There was almost inevitably a class element to the form, design and decoration of such buildings.[15]

> The treatment of working-class patients in gorgeous palaces was not only wasteful, but confusing to the patients, for they would come to regard their cure in some way associated with the facilities and luxuries enjoyed in the institution, and return home feeling that it was impossible to keep well. Thus the architecture should be "of the simplest kind capable of being imitated in all essentials in the average home of the industrial classes"...The likely success of sanatorium treatment (for the working classes) was therefore 'inversely proportional to the magnificence of the buildings and surroundings'. (Kelynack, 'The Tuberculosis Yearbook', 1913–14: 227 in Bryder, 1988: 52)

140

In other spaces such as the prison, factory, hospital, workhouse and school, the individual movements, gestures and actions of the body were studied and controlled to produce 'better' more efficient and obedient workers, prisoners, students, patients, etc. Thus creating forms of space designed to inculcate and instruct was a fundamental feature of Foucault's thesis of the development of the 'disciplinary society'. However, concern was not only expressed or directed at the physical problems associated with urban living, such as overcrowding, poor sanitation, dirt and disease, but also with the moral impact on the working classes of poor urban environments. Children were a prime target for moral and physical training and one held up as a symbol for a future, more civilised city and society.[15] The principle of bodily discipline as a means of moral training is epitomised by official attitudes that came to prominence in the late nineteenth century of the benefits of structured rational recreation and education. The formation and operation of schools thus became a principle arena for the training, disciplining and inculcation of appropriate bodily practices for the enhancement of children's physical and moral health.[16] The emphasis was to combine the practical instruction and education of institutionalised techniques with the proselytising efforts of religious and charitable institutions in schemes that would improve not only the physical environment of the city, but also the habits, behaviours and morals of future generations. Thus, in schools the emphasis

141

> ...must be thoroughly religious, in which the heart may be addressed as well as the head – the kindly feelings brought into play – suitable air and exercise afforded in-doors and out-doors – habits of cleanliness, and obedience cultivated, and not simply kept from the street 'out of harms way', and from corrupting influence, but enabled for several hours-a-day to breathe a moral atmosphere. (Stow, 1833: 17)

The second aspect of bio-power concerns the study, control and manipulation of the 'species body', that is for Foucault, populations as aggregates of individuals. This intervention represented the increasing colonisation by power into more areas and spheres of social life and activity. The expansion of the medical disciplines and their prominent role in managing the nation's health gave them a leading role in attempts to understand and organise industrial labour and industrial society as a whole and thus influence the aims and direction of government policy. As Foucault states:

> Urban space has its own dangers: disease, such as the epidemics of cholera in Europe from 1830 to about 1880, and revolution, such as the series of urban

revolts that shook all of Europe during the same period. These spatial problems, which were perhaps not new, took on a new importance...The major problems of space, from the nineteenth century on, were indeed of a different type. Which is not to say that problems of an architectural nature were forgotten. (Foucault, 1982: 17)

Sturdy and Cooter (1998) in an explicitly, if unacknowledged Foucaultian analysis, examine how medicine, both as an institutional organisation and as a profession, was transformed through the expansion of medical disciplines and the invention, dissemination and increasing prominence of scientific procedures, techniques and skills. There was an increasing professionalism in the administration of hospital services, which saw the management of hospitals less philanthropically organised with the importation of new managers from industry and finance to promote the efficient management of hospital resources. This has a certain resonance with the contemporary National Health Service being increasingly run to meet efficiency targets as well as having to meet other 'success' parameters.

However, nineteenth century public health was primarily concerned with administrative discipline and efficiency and as such it was closely linked with the growth of local and national government intervention in the surveillance and management of the health of the populations, as opposed to individuals. A medico-administrative knowledge of national and local populations was constructed through the observation and collection of information and statistics on the population, on areas, households, etc. Dangerous classes and dangerous locations were identified as needing some form of remedial action. New techniques and practices developed and were employed by the growth of institutions and practices to ensure that a fit and healthy working class would be sufficiently able to satisfy the requirements of the nation's armed services as well as the needs of the (industrial) economy. This entailed a number of interventions by the local and national state, and by charitable and voluntary organisations, that sought to understand the population, in order to regulate and control it in the most efficient and beneficial manner.

This aspect of the government of whole populations is a complex task in which issues of national policy and political power are interconnected with individual sexual, reproductive, physical and moral behaviours and attitudes. The role of Medical Officers of Health was especially effective in promoting and achieving a number of important changes in sanitary organisation, disease prevention and treatment. Similarly, they played a vital role in the organisation and provision of a whole host of services that sought to improve the vitality and health of the urban environment and its populations. The practice and organisation of medicine and the institutions that delivered it became oriented around the goal of creating, managing and maintaining a fit, healthy and efficient industrial population.[17]

Foucault's analysis of knowledge, power and space illustrates how disciplinary discourses and techniques were developed, diffused and applied in the context of the origins and expansion of increasingly urbanised and industrialised societies. Foucault is concerned to present the operation of power not merely as intrinsically repressive, negative, prohibitive or universally dominating. Disciplinary techniques could act as a positive force in the creation, shaping or moulding of subjects through the creation, organisation and policing of particular forms of space. What is clear is that the express intention was not to exact punishment for its own sake, but to create a reflective subject who would internalise the knowledge, norms and values of bourgeois society promulgated through education and training to create more useful, orderly and civilised productive individuals and populations. Knowledge of space, and command over it, was a primary and fundamental means by which it was analysed, designed and used for the purposes of maximum functional efficiency to ensure the regulated movement and accumulation of wealth, in the burgeoning urban and industrial economy of nineteenth-century capitalist society. Thus, architecture and design were employed in an attempt to instil a sense of self-discipline, the internalisation of 'normalising values' not only in miscreants and deviants (the criminal, the undeserving poor, the delinquent, etc.), but also in the general population, and in particular the working classes. Similar to Lefebvre's analysis of planning as an ideology Foucault prioritises the development of a medical discourse, as an inherently spatial analysis for the identification of the individual body, and the body of populations as the object of study, illustrates both the power of disciplinary knowledge and its diffusion throughout society. Social discipline became a technique for the control of space and time in all spheres of society through a network of interrelated disciplines. Thus, charities, reform organisations, religious and temperance movements, housing and health organisations, as well as local and national government, were all implicated and active in this movement of disciplinary diffusion. The disciplines and their discourses invaded and colonised the private as well as the public sphere. Attempts were made to control, manage and promote the most effective, that is the most 'beneficial', use of leisure and recreation time and space, as well as that of work, prison, school, etc. Rest, purposeful distraction and exercise, of the mind and body, ensures that the worker and the family unit that maintains and

143

sustains the reproduction of the next generation of labour, is fit, willing and able to resume their economic and social duties and responsibilities. Foucault's account of disciplinary discourses is an analysis of the power inherent in dominant representations and practices of power/knowledge in and over people in produced forms of space in modern society.

CONCLUSION

Foucault's analysis of the space of the modern era emphasises how particular spaces are produced, designed, constructed, controlled and regulated by disciplinary discourses and technologies of power/knowledge. They have specific functional aims whose general goal was/is the creation and manipulation of docile bodies, whether as individuals or as agglomerations of people, as populations. Foucault's analysis of the development of a modern disciplinary society then is one in which power, knowledge and space are interlinked in the development of physical landscapes and in which architecture is a prominent means to structure relations. Dominant discourses inscribe meanings and values that seek to delimit and delineate the functional and efficient use of space for particular purposes and for identified populations and activities. However, everyday activities, of both individuals and groups, can conflict and contest the values, norms and meanings of this 'lived space' precisely because they are arenas of creative social and cultural interaction. What is deemed as appropriate activities within particular produced spaces, what these spaces mean to different people and groups at different times and how some come to represent ideals of culture and of society, is the result of processes of contestation, conflict and transgression that can undermine the authority of ordered and disciplined space. This dynamic relationship between space as a cultural and material product, between popular meanings and values and elite representations, and between everyday practices and intended uses, reinforces Lefebvre's assertion of the need to consider the lived, imaginative use of space as a fundamental element for knowledge of the role of space in modern capitalist society.

The distinction between what people actually do and the designed intentions of planners or of medical specialists of space reflects the conflict between cultural and political elites, with their dominant ideological and hegemonic influence over the use of public spaces versus vernacular traditions and the popular cultures. Foucault traces the creation and imposition of disciplinary practices and a disciplinary society as embedded in spatial practices in which control and manipulation are intrinsic to their operation. Thus space, knowledge and power are important for understanding the development of what some have come to call the development of a surveillance society in which new means and methods to monitor and police space is fundamental. Therefore, the permission and restriction given to certain political, social, leisure and recreational practices as well as some social groups over others make space a potentially contested arena where normalising values pursued through the disciplining, ordering and regulation of space against the exuberance of many popular practices and pursuits becomes a new forum for social struggle. Form, structure and function are intimately related in that social (public) spaces represent everyday and universal arenas where the production of space involves relations of power, materially inscribed on the landscape but which is subject to conflicting values, meanings and uses. In this, Foucault provides essential insights of historical and contemporary relevance for the analysis of how space is produced, moulded, shaped, designed, regulated and policed by disciplinary discourses in which representations of space reflect the operation of power in, through and over space and the activities that occur there.

NOTES

1 Matless stresses that:

Power for Foucault is enabling, exercised rather than possessed, relational and immanent, neither institution nor structure nor strength but 'a complex strategical situation' (Foucault, 1981: 92) which is constantly and locally shifting. (Matless, 1992: 46)

2 This aspect of Foucault's analysis, of the importance of space for the critical analysis of social relations and of power is emphasised particularly in human geographical analysis. For example,

relations of power are really, crucially and unavoidably spun out across and through the material spaces of the world. It is within such spaces that assemblages of people, activities, technologies, institutions, ideas and dreams all come together, circulate, convene and reconvene. (Sharp et al., 2000: 24)

3 Driver succinctly makes the point that:

Put simply, *Discipline and Punish* is about the advent of a new 'economy of power'. It is quite unthinkable without some account of the social, economic, and technical development of capitalism. (Driver, 1985: 436)

4 In similar vein, Foucault elsewhere writes of what 'police' meant in other times:

Down to the end of the *ancien regime*, the term 'police' does not simply signify, at least not exclusively, the institution of police in the modern sense; 'police' is the ensemble of mechanisms serving to ensure order, the properly channelled growth of wealth and the conditions of preservation of health 'in general'. (Foucault, 1980: 170)

5 Indeed, Foucault quotes Bentham to highlight the universal applicability of the panopticism:

Morals reformed – health preserved – industry invigorated – instruction diffused – public burthens lightened – Economy seated as it were, upon a rock, – the gordian knot of the Poor-Laws not cut, but untied – all by the simple idea in architecture. (Bentham, 'Works', 1843: 39, in Foucault, 1977: 207)

6 O'Neill presents an interesting account of how Foucault's studies of the disciplinary spaces of the prison, hospital or school complements Weber's analysis of the processes by which bureaucratic techniques for the organisation and administration of society came to be diffused and established throughout society, by presenting an analysis of the rational accounting of the body, subjectivity and behaviour. He writes:

146

It is not far fetched to consider Weber as an archaeologist of the power man exerts over himself, and thus to see him as a precursor of Foucault's conception of the disciplinary society...Modern society makes itself rich, knowledgeable and powerful but at the expense of substantive reason and freedom. (O'Neill, 1986: 43)

7 See also Bale and Philo (1998) for a discussion of the creation of docile bodies.
8 The classical age discovered the body as object and target of power. It is easy enough to find signs of the attention then paid to the body – to the body that is manipulated, shaped, trained, which obeys, responds, becomes skilful and increases its forces (Foucault, 1978: 136).
9 Foucault describes in *Discipline and Punish* how the body in its every act, gesture and movement must make the best, most and efficient use of time:

The act is broken down into its elements; the position of the body, limbs, articulation is defined; to each movement are assigned a direction, an aptitude, a duration; their order of succession is prescribed. Time penetrates the body and with it all the meticulous controls of power...In the correct use of the body, which makes possible a correct use of time, nothing must remain idle or useless; everything must be called upon to form the support of the act required...A disciplined body is the prerequisite of an efficient gesture...The principle that underlay the time-table in its traditional form was essentially negative: it was the principle of non-idleness; it was forbidden to waste time, which was counted by God and paid for by men; the time-table was to eliminate the danger of wasting it – a moral offence and economic dishonesty. Discipline on the other hand, arranges a positive economy; it poses the principle of a theoretically ever-growing use of time: exhaustion rather than use; it is a question of extract-ing, from time, ever more available moments and, from each moment, ever more useful forces . . . In becoming the target of new mechanisms of power, the body is offered up to new forms of knowledge. It is the body of exercise, rather than of speculative physics; a body manipulated by authority, rather than imbued with animal spirits; a body of useful training and not of rational mechanics, but one in which, by virtue of that very fact, a number of natural requirements and functional constraints are beginning to emerge. (Foucault, 1977: 152, 154–5)

10 E. P. Thomson identifies in the mode of production and the relations of production similar attempts at regulating the time and activities of the new urban working class.

all these ways – by the division of labour; the supervision of labour; fines, bells and clocks; money incentives; preaching and schoolings; the suppression of fairs and sports – new labour habits were formed, and a new time discipline was imposed. (Thompson, 1978: 90)

11 In Glasgow, for example, there were a number of medical personnel involved in just such a process of monitoring and surveillance of the rapidly expanding urban population: Dr Cleland in the early nineteenth century and the evangelical J. B. Russell, Medical Officer of Health for the city, in the latter decades who built upon his work. See Chalmers (1930), Cleland (1836), Russell (1886, 1895, 1905).

12 As Rose puts it:

147

medical thought and medical activity, through the rationalities that unified the inhabitants of geographical space as a social body, through the compilation of statistics of birth, death, rates and types of morbidity, through the charting of social and moral topographies of bodies and their relations with one another, played a key role in 'making-up' the social body and in locating individuals in relation to this dense field of relations bearing upon the individual body. Medicine, that is to say, has played a formative role in the *invention of the social*. Medicine was to engage itself with one of the most fundamental sets of questions that troubled and provoked governmental thought during the nine-teenth century and which inspired the invention of the basic administrative knowledge and techniques of modernity. This set of questions concerned the regulation of life in towns. Over the first half of the nineteenth century, the role of the medical police was to problematise the life of populations in towns in terms of health, and to devise a whole variety of schemes for its improvement. The diversity of tactics adopted ranged from grand schemes of architectural renewal of public space in the name of health and civility to a host of more mundane projects of social hygiene, sanitary reform and sewage arrangements, pure air and pure water, paving of streets and controls on the burial of the dead. (Rose, 1994: 55–6)

13 Poovey and Driver credit J. P. Kay with a pioneering role in this development in Britain. *The Moral and Physical Condition of the Working Classes* was a detailed investigation of urban space that combined eyewitness reports and statistical tables to represent strategies for understanding the urban population and for suggesting

remedies. Kay's analysis of the social body emphasised the significance of the 'good' parts rather than focusing explicitly on the diseased areas – those aggregations of the poor and impoverished who were already spatialised.

> The dense masses of the habitations of the poor, which streets and their arms, as though to grasp and enclose the dwellings of the noble and wealthy, in the metropolis, and in our huge provincial cities, have heretofore been regarded as mighty wilderness of building in which the incurable ills of society rankled, beyond the reach of sanative interference. (Kay, 1832/1969: 11)

14 This is a point that Kay makes explicit:

> There is...a licentiousness capable of corrupting the whole body of society, like an insidious disease, which eludes observation, yet is equally fatal in its effects. Criminal acts may be statistically classed – the victims of the law may be enumerated – but the number of those affected with the moral leprosy of vice cannot be exhibited with mathematical precision.... The social body cannot be constructed like a machine, on abstract principles which merely include physical motions, and their numerical results in the production of wealth. The mutual relations of men is not merely dynamical, nor can the composition of their forces be subjected to a purely mathematical calculation. Political economy, though its object is to ascertain the means of increasing the wealth of nations, cannot accomplish its design, without at the same time regarding their happiness, and as its largest ingredient the cultivation of religion and morality. (Kay, 1832/1969: 62, 63–4)

15 Maver details how children became the subject of not only the local states operatives and institutions, but also religious reformers and charitable organisations:

> Children became polemical devices in the crusade to create a purer environment, because they could represent such a potential metaphor for urban deprivation... While urbanisation and industrialisation drastically cut across the integrity of this idealised and intrinsically rural society, evangelical Presbyterianism was wholly positive in the conviction that it could be restored, and that the most unsavoury city centres could be rendered wholesome and healthy. The quest for purity thus took on a deeper meaning, because it represented the spiritual as well as the physical cleansing process that was deemed so vital for reversing the vitiating tendencies of urban life. (Maver, 1997: 802–3)

16 Driver also demonstrates how children were the focus of techniques and practices that led them to be isolated and removed from the spaces and institutions that were identified as having negative effects. Indeed, what is emphasised is the strict control and regulation of children's bodies in space to provide education and instruction only in what were considered positively beneficial actions and behaviours:

> It was the disciplines themselves, the techniques for division rather than association and contagion. Children were a prime target for training. They were to be rescued not only from the city streets, those crucibles of crime and

148

pauperism, but also from other 'inappropriate' institutions, such as prisons and workhouses, where they could inevitably be in contact with adults and irredeemably 'immoral' elements. Registers of conduct, systems of rewards, careful allocation of times and spaces would accomplish all that forceful confinement could, and more. The ultimate aim was self-control and self-regulation. (Driver, 1985: 434)

17 Indeed, this aim was explicitly made in 1921 in a report by the Industrial Fatigue Research Board commenting that "the word 'efficiency' is not to be interpreted as equivalent merely to productive efficiency, but as the physiological quality that results from favourable conditions of work. The word is in fact almost equivalent to 'fitness'" ('Industrial Fatigue Research Board', Annual Report, II, 1921, p. 17, cited in Sturdy and Cooter, 1998: 448).

six

legacies and prospects: spatialising contemporary modernity

The book aims to demonstrate the importance of understanding space for the analysis of the development of modern (particularly urban) social formations, practices and experience. A detailed exegesis of a number of social theories of space has been presented to demonstrate that space needs to be taken seriously as a fundamental element for understanding social reality. That is, to consider how space is perceived, conceived, represented and ultimately used and experienced is of necessity a crucial concern for sociology as well as other social sciences. Space is a determining factor in the framing of social relations and is also reciprocally interconnected in the making of space by those very social interactions that occur in space. There is then a necessity to consider the spatial dimension in the investigation of social relations, of institutions, of how power operates in and through space and how it is challenged through conflict and contestation in and over how space is or should be used, and how differences and divisions are expressed and experienced in and through space.

The implicit spatiality of Marx's critique of capitalism provided the initial foundations (in this as it could be said of all social theory) for the later development of other more explicit attempts at theorising space. Marx's influence on social theory in general and on the development of spatial analysis is I hope obvious and continues to be an inspiration to those social theorists concerned with spatialising capital in an era of global (uneven) development. Whilst it has been argued that Marx did not explicitly theorise space in his voluminous critique of capitalism, there contains within it a recognition of the importance of space for understanding social relations under capitalism in general but also specific aspects of the experience and structuring of labour, of production and reproduction, of circulation and of the expansion of capitalism on a global scale. In this, Marx's influence can clearly be seen in the seminal theory of space produced by Henri Lefebvre and David Harvey's emphasis on creating a historico-geographical materialism. Both emphasise in different ways the need to take space seriously as a factor and condition in the development, perpetuation and survival of capitalism.

Georg Simmel's inclusion as a significant and early sociological analysis of space and indeed much of Simmel's work contains within it a keen awareness of the inter-relationship between forms of sociation and the spatiality that is expressed within and through those 'webs of interaction' that constitute, for Simmel, society. Simmel provides a number of considered distinctions and categorisation of key 'aspects of space' that are to be found within later social theories and analyses. In this we can point to that of mobility (global flows and migrations), boundedness (nation states, new urban formations such as walled enclaves), fixity, proximity and distance (integration, segregation, access to services, employment, etc.) as areas in which Simmel was a sociological pioneer of space, despite his contribution being until recently relatively ignored.

Lefebvre's influence on spatial theory cannot be underestimated. It has galvanised not only human and cultural geographers in applying a spatial dialectical materialism to the analysis of the relationships between human beings and each other in socially constructed space but also a re-evaluation of our relationship with nature. Lefebvre's contribution to a number of key areas includes not only that of the urban where he may be said to have broadened Marx's concept of production to include spatial production and the role of the state in the production and perpetuation of the historical development and relations of capitalist space. His analysis of the rhythms, times and places of everyday life, of the routines and alienation inherent in the socially produced spaces of leisure and recreation, domestic life as well as those of work and the urban have also been influential for developing research on gendered space and on the spatialising of sexual and ethnic identities. Lefebvre's contribution to spatial analysis is significant not only because it provides a basis for the reinvigoration and reprioritisation of space but also because of his insistence that perceptions, conceptions, representations and uses of space are fundamental for understanding how each society in each epoch is organised, structured and depicted. For Lefebvre, the urban was *the* spatial form of modern capitalism. His analysis and prioritisation of modern capitalism and of space continues to provide inspiration for the development of empirical, substantive and theoretical work on the experience as well as the constitution of an increasingly globalising urban world.

Both Lefebvre and Harvey have in themselves become seminal influences in the reprioritisation of space as fundamental for the analysis of the perpetuation or survival of capitalism. Whilst it might be said that Harvey owes a certain debt to Lefebvre's original analysis of space, he has in his own right publicised and popularised spatial analysis to a wider interdisciplinary audience. Harvey has consistently and critically sought to develop an analysis of the development of capitalism as an intrinsically spatial phenomenon in which there is a need to explicitly address key aspects of its organisation and perpetuation. In this, his socio-spatial analysis emphasises why it is crucial to develop an understanding of the development of an economy of space in the context of urban infrastructures, social justice and of the increasing colonisation of the space of global (post-modern) capital. In this, Harvey's concerted analysis continues to conclude that the spatial arrangements and forms of the urban are not haphazard but are organised according to the dictates of the needs of capital. As such, there are spatial divisions and segregations as well as those of the social. In this we are reminded that space, like time, is money. Harvey's later work still reflects this concern with developing his project of historico-geographical materialism but applying it to the new conditions of post-modernity and globalisation.

Michel Foucault's somewhat diverse treatments of space provided an alternative perspective both to the Marxist-influenced theories of Lefebvre and Harvey as well as to Simmel's approach. It deals explicitly with questions concerning the interlinking of knowledge of space and its control by power through various disciplinary discourses. Whilst its emphasis is somewhat of a correction to overtly class-oriented analyses of space, Foucault's analysis of space is ultimately located and concerned with how space is designed, represented, policed and controlled as a factor of 'bio-power', that is to influence and mould individuals and populations according to the meanings, values, priorities, morals and ideologies of those with power. In this, Foucault's concept of governmentality is applied to space through the application of disciplinary technologies for the inculcation of good order. It is an analysis that recognises and accepts that the creation of representations of space as well as the explicit policing of space must be considered within the context of the historical development as well as experience of the institutional structures and disciplinary frameworks of capitalism. Whilst his emphasis and perspective is perhaps focused on micro-terrains of the operation of power it still provides a valuable analysis of how, why and by whom space has been used in mechanisms of control and policing. The 'eye of power', the disciplinary gaze is one that has been very influential in developing analyses of crime and policing, of urban design and architecture, of the constitution of the principles of an all encompassing surveillance society.

What can be said concerning all of these theorists is that they have taken space seriously and have attempted to produce analyses that provide some explanation for the role of space in and on social reality. Those that have been given detailed consideration represent a foundation from which a reprioritisation of space and social theory may be said to have emerged and who have had considerable influence in the development of later analyses of space both theoretically and substantively. The emphasis given to this selection of an admittedly limited number of theorists will no doubt raise questions as to who or what has been omitted. It was not the intention to provide a comprehensive overview and analysis of *all* the available perspectives that have been or are now operating in the numerous inter-disciplinary fields of social science. It was, merely, to demonstrate the vital contributions made by such foundational thinkers on space.

However this final chapter will seek to address some new developments and directions in space and social theory in which the legacy of these social theories of space can be said to be influential. Again this chapter cannot aim to be completely comprehensive but will attempt to illuminate how space and social theories of space have come to be applied in a variety of contexts to the analysis of contemporary social relations and structures, patterns of movement and flows, inequalities and experience, as well as how new approaches have been developed. This chapter then will address some new developments in spatial theory as well as indicate where the influence of those theorists addressed earlier can be discerned. In this way it is possible to emphasise how social theories of space are being used to investigate and interrogate 'new horizons' in the development of sociology. That is, the spatiality of social relations in contemporary societies are increasingly being considered as essential to the analysis of the structures, forms and experiences of a number of key and crucial areas. Space is increasingly acknowledged as an essential element or factor in the analysis of contemporary social relations, both in the form and content of their structure as well as in their expression and experience. Therefore, what will be considered below are developments in the analysis of the spatiality of the urban, of gender, ethnicity, sexuality, crime and globalisation. Whilst these are presented in somewhat discrete sections it needs to be emphasised that this is not an attempt at constructing or perpetuating exclusive boundaries or of creating and perpetuating distinctions and divisions. The overlapping and interlinking of difference and division is mapped out in the creation and experience of those spaces and places that we inhabit and which are more or less open or accessible to us. There is therefore a necessary fluidity and permeability between those sections outlined below. In this there is also no priority or status intended in the order in which they are presented.

153

NEW DIRECTIONS AND HORIZONS ON SPACE

urban space (again)

Much has already been said about spatial theory and the urban in those theories and perspectives addressed in previous chapters. However, there is a need to take account of new developments and perspectives as well as the need to recognise that the urban remains as the "prime (though not the only) sites of modernity ... a crucial site of contemporary social life" (Savage et al., 2003: iii, viii). Indeed it can be argued that urbanisation either as a process or as a reflection of more universal spatial processes continues unabated now that the majority of world's population are urban residents. It is envisaged that at continuing growth rates by 2020 the urban population will be approximately seventy-five per cent of the global population (Blowers and Pain, 1999: 249). The urban therefore remains significant not only for the analysis and investigation of contemporary social life, but for policy-makers, and for those who live or are affected by consequences of the expanding 'ecological footprint' that the urban generates. Concern with the negative impacts of urbanisation (pollution, under resourced social and physical infrastructures, ecological impact, population density, crime, inequalities, etc.) is increasingly leading to the development and expression of new urban spatial forms that reflect and express the consequences of continuing urbanisation. The expansion of capitalism in its 'new' global form has led to the expansion of urban processes and forms of development which have been extant in Western societies but are now at the forefront of processes that impact on developing and underdeveloped nations and regions. In this what is increasingly recognised is the spatial as well as social segregation and exclusion of groups and populations from social activities and opportunities.

The concern with understanding the distribution of various inequalities and opportunities has resulted in the application of spatial analysis to what has been called 'the post-code lottery' of social and health services provision. The development of an awareness of the increasing geographical divide in British society for example has been investigated by a number of researchers (see Byrne, 1999, Pacione, 1997, Philo, 1995) who have analysed how the widening geographical or spatial divide can be interpreted as indicating growing social and economic inequalities. There is evidence for an increasing social polarisation that is reflected in a spatial divide. The recognition of a North–South divide in Britain (see Mohan, 2000) which reflects divisions and differences in political affiliations and economic opportunities as well as in numerous indicators of life chances, expectancy, poverty, unemployment, etc. As David Harvey reflects:

> Evaluative schemata of places...become grist for all sorts of policy-makers mills. Places in the city get red-lined for mortgage finance, the people who live in them get written off as worthless...The material activities of place construction may then fulfil the prophecies of degradation and dereliction. Similarly, places in the city are dubbed as 'dubious' or 'dangerous' again leading to patterns of behaviour both public and private, that turn fantasy into reality. (Harvey, 1996: 321–2)

Sean Damer has pointed out (see Damer, 1989, 1990, 1992) that this 'labelling' has had serious consequences for some estates, housing schemes, cities and regions as well as countries deemed or categorised as 'black-spots', 'no-go areas' or 'danger zones'. How particular places reflect widening social and geographical inequalities impacts upon social policy-makers and political debate on identifying and designating problem areas on the basis of various social indicators such as crime, health, housing tenure, income, benefit receipts, family composition, etc. (see Atkinson and Moon, 1994). Thus an analysis of socio-spatial segregation or inclusion/exclusion is increasingly recognised and applied not only to the diverse groups, populations and communities within towns and cities but also within regions and nations.

155

An increasingly common feature of cities identified in various studies across the globe has been the development of what has been called walled enclaves or gated communities. Concerns about safety and security as well as issues surrounding identity have led to the sense of 'purified communities' (a phrase coined by Richard Sennett, 1971) in which increasingly those with the means have sought to isolate or segregate themselves from those they identify as posing some form of threat to their person, family, way of life, identity and in some cases racial purity (in apartheid South Africa the structured system of residential zoning by race was an established segregationist government policy). What has developed is the establishment of physical boundaries in which segregation takes on a spatial form so that cultural, social and economic difference is created and maintained in space. It is an attempt to establish 'walls' that differentiate and segregate those within from those without, whether this difference is based on social, economic or ethnic lines. This socio-spatial and cultural separation has obvious links to both Simmel's aspect of space as well as Marx and is an issue concerning the ability to impose and maintain such boundaries that limit those who may come and go into specific areas. Thus whilst it is clear that some impoverished communities may exclude the more well-off by virtue of perceived activities and behaviours, 'no-go' areas are increasingly found in the 'defensible space' of the gated, walled or fortified communities of the affluent. These residential areas may be in close proximity to poor areas but are literally physically walled off from them and in which only appropriate people are admitted. This is achieved through the use of surveillance cameras, uniformed (and potentially armed) private security guards. These communities are particularly associated with American cities (see Blakely and Snyder, 1997) but are also found in Europe, Canada, as well as in South America (see Caldeira's descriptions of Sao Paolo, 1996a and b), Asia (Mehrotra, 1997) and South Africa (Robinson, 1999). A further development of this idea of separate communities is the attempt to build 'ideal' new towns in which the perception of the problems of cities has led to the design and construction of exclusive and segregated urban communities (see Franz and Collins, 1999, Ross, 1999. for an analysis and critique of Disney's 'ideal' town of Celebration).

Another aspect of the application of a spatial analysis of cities is the recognition of the diversity of composition, functions and attractions to be found in different areas of every city. This applies not only to the zoning of cities in respect of residential, production, consumption function, etc that has been an integral part of the redevelopment of many cities from the mid-twentieth century. The sense of the identification of socially as well as spatially segregated distinctive neighbourhoods has led to their depiction as 'quartered cities' (see Marcuse 1989, 1995, Bell and Jayne, 2004) in which there is an emphasis on their role in structural, economic and cultural change that is suggestive of a new spatial dynamic. However, whilst the spatial inequalities that presently exist in cities can be identified as the product of past social, economic and political practices there are new spatial divisions that reflect changes in the way cities are being restructured as a regenerative response to transformations in the global economy. The marketing and image construction of cities as attractive for tourism and as venues for business, corporate and entertainment events and locations is paralleled by a recognition of the distinctiveness of particular areas or quarters as unique or important selling points. Therefore the development of urban 'gay villages' (see below), of Red Light Zones, of cultural and artistic quarters complete with museums and galleries, and of the identification of specific architectural features and cultural forms associated with specific areas of cities are all used to promote and sell the consumption of cities (see Bell and Jayne, 2004, for detailed case studies). This emphasis on specific features and areas within cities as attractions is part of the means by which the consumption of cities is increasingly tied to their commodification as spatial forms.

156

The consumption of urban culture, of place, of architecture, etc. is specifically associated and intrinsically linked to processes of urban regeneration and the development of urban economies based on tourism and visitors (see Miles and Miles, 2004). In part, this is related to municipal and national state responses to changes in the global economy in which some cities and regions with an industrial and manufacturing history have had to come to terms with new economic conditions there are increasingly area-based as well as city-wide initiatives aimed at regeneration. Whilst some of these are well known, for example the gentrified city in which former industrial and commercial buildings are transformed into high-value residential properties, other schemes are aimed at investing in the social and environmental landscape of less affluent neighbourhoods but also includes issues related to the environmental and social sustainability of cities. As part of urban renewal programmes there is recognition that the physical environment needs not only economic investment but the active participation of residents and community groups. Thus, one aspect of area or neighbourhood regeneration is to provide opportunities for community participation in the construction, maintenance and 'ownership' of local, 'natural' and/or social space. For example, the (re)development of communal green spaces, the provision of community gardening schemes, play parks, recycling and 'clean-up' projects are aimed at emphasising local knowledge, commitment and participation in the civic realm as it is 'known and owned by the people who live there. Such schemes reflect and attempt to maximise local identities, histories, communal associations and solidarities, etc. as part of strategies aimed at socially inclusive activities and projects that recognise the importance of place and the everyday spaces that are used and valued by local communities.

Whilst it would be disingenuous to propose that socio-spatial segregation is a new phenomenon these examples show how spatial analysis is increasingly being employed and applied to the perceived 'problems' of (contemporary) cities. The continuing salience of the urban as a key site for contemporary social life necessarily employs socio-spatial analyses for understanding the urban and for policy initiatives and infrastructural investment. Whether as recognition of cities as nodes in global networks of finance, production, consumption, information, etc. or in the regeneration of the urban environment and infrastructure as a response to issues relating to urban sustainability (economic, social, political, environmental, etc.) space and spatial theories are informing and shaping the analysis of the urban and the formation of social policy strategies. Spatial processes and analyses therefore are being employed for understanding, maintaining and managing the quality of life of cities

157

and their populations and for developing a more sustainable future for them. The 'problem of cities' and 'the urban question' now increasingly involves more explicit questions of space.

LANDSCAPE AND SPATIAL THEORY

As an alternative to the environmental determinism of some approaches the development of landscape as a concept (both natural and cultural) emphasises the reciprocity of influences between the environment and humans. It specifically addresses not only the impact of humans on the environment but also the aesthetic influences and impacts that the landscape has on human subjectivity. Thus the meanings that come to be invested in particular landscapes can become idealised and created through particular ways of seeing and interpreting particular forms of landscape, whether as beautiful, useful, ugly, romantic, etc.

Dennis Cosgrove is perhaps the most influential theorist who has had a profound influence in developing landscape as a central concern in interdisciplinary considerations of space and place. Influenced by John Berger's (1972) analysis of 'ways of seeing' and reading art and Raymond Williams's (1973) embedding of literary criticism in a social context in which images, representations, values and meanings are reflected in and by particular landscapes (specifically, Williams analysis of representations of the country and the city).

Cosgrove explores the cultural processes that shape landscape but also the constitutive role that landscape plays in shaping human relations, meanings and values associated with landscape. This reciprocal interrelationship reflects Cosgrove's thesis that "landscape represents an historically specific way of experiencing the world developed by, and meaningful to, certain social groups. It is ... an ideological concept" Cosgrove, 1998: 15). In a number of publications (Cosgrove, 1997, 1998, Cosgrove and Daniels, 1988) he develops this perspective of landscape as a "way of seeing – a way in which some Europeans have represented to themselves and to others the world about them and their relationships with it, and through which they commented on social relations" (Cosgrove, 1984: 1). The analysis of landscape as socially constructed and structured to reflect a dominant ideology has resonances with Marx, Lefebvre and Foucault. Thus 'landscape' not only creates and represents illusions and visions of landscapes at home (whether through gardening, estate management, design and architecture, etc. or though maps, pictures and literary descriptions) but also 'other' landscapes colonised by imperial conquest. Thus Cosgrove's analysis of landscapes as reflecting dominant representations of the world illuminates how particular meanings became associated with those landscapes and the peoples who inhabited them. There is therefore a connection here between the ideology of landscape and the relationship between culture and imperialism as explored in detail by Edward Said (see Said, 1978, 1993, 2000) in which a view of the Orient was and still is to some extent imposed on the peoples and their lands by a Western imperialist tradition and gaze. Said's concept of 'imaginative geographies' refers to the invention and construction of geographical space which delimits, structures and organises our consciousness and ways of thinking with the ultimate aim of controlling people and places. This conception of landscape as a social and cultural space is therefore a valuable extension of spatial thinking and analysis and is being applied in contemporary investigations of the neo-liberal capitalist agenda of globalisation in which representations of landscape, space, culture, people and places are increasingly associated with resources for exploitations and use in the global market.

A similar socio-spatial understanding of landscape as a 'way of seeing' has been developed by John Urry in his analysis of the development of *The Tourist Gaze* (1990). Urry's thesis is that tourism has developed as historically specific 'ways of seeing' and consuming landscapes and townscapes towards which the gaze is directed, structured and formed through signs, symbols, arrangements of features, etc. in ways that impart socially constructed experiences that reflect and reinforce particular and 'expected' understandings and meanings. This perspective of the social construction of tourist spaces for consumption and for pleasure informs our understanding of an increasingly important social and economic activity which has consequences not only for those participating in tourism as a business or as a consumer but also for those indigenous people whose cultures, landscapes, places of meaning, values and importance are being presented and represented for consumption. The 'selling' of places as commodities to be packaged and consumed requires not only an understanding and awareness of the material needs and requirements of visitors but also an appreciation of the need to satisfy aesthetic and emotional desires that are themselves promoted and advertised as attractive. Thus, in this context spaces are designed, produced and represented as something to be consumed that meets the socially constructed expectations of tourists who employ conditioned understandings of and expectations for particular experiences. In this context the application of spatial analyses to the understanding of tourism can provide insights into the potential success or failure of particular tourist economies, increasingly essential for the sustainability of many cities, regions and national economies.

159

The socio-spatial analyses propounded by Cosgrove and Urry are valuable tools in the analysis of debates concerning the conservation and protection of the 'natural' landscape in the face of 'threats' from development, pollution and urban expansion. Whether the 'value' of landscapes resides in an appreciation of their supposedly unspoilt state or as habitats of bio-diversity or as potentially productive sites for development, an understanding of the social construction of 'ways of seeing' landscapes informs those debates concerned with their protection as historically, naturally, culturally important, etc. If all landscapes are ideological then political debate, rhetoric and struggle will eventually decide their fate but one in which understanding of their socio-spatial and cultural construction is a much needed part of the process.

space and gender

It is worthwhile to recognise that much of the analyses of space detailed in the preceding chapters expressed at best as an abstract universalising tendency that ignored or left unacknowledged many social differences and divisions (except in the relationship between class, space and capitalism). However, there is much work that has recently been done to spatialise sexism and gender. Feminist analysis makes clear that women and men occupy or are positioned differently in space. Space thus has a gendered dimension that concomitantly ensures gender is spatially organised. That is, if gender is socially constructed whereby differences are maintained through a complex of social, economic and political conditions these are spatially organised and delimited to create, promote and accentuate gender roles and opportunities. Thus there is need for an explicit acknowledgement of the differences that women experience and perceive in their lives as well as the structural circumscribing of opportunities that can be illuminated via a spatial analysis of the space that women have been predominantly forced to inhabit. The 'modern gender order' (Connell, 1995) of a public/private male/female division assumes a gendering of space. This dichotomisation has a spatial dimension in that women are assumed to be or associated with particular spaces and places that confirm and maintain their subjugation and subordination. For example, the role of women as predominantly supportive or care-giving (wife, mother, carer, etc.) suggests a structured environment of spatial constraint that may be associated with the public/private sphere analysis of the emergence in industrial and urban society of the home as a predominantly gendered domain.

The domestic sphere as a privatised arena in which gender relations are constructed, structured and promulgated is an example which has increasingly drawn upon spatial analysis to investigate how architecture is used to frame space and the gender roles within it. Without engaging in the debate over the universalism or of the exclusivity of the private/public gender divide it is clear that the home and the domestic sphere has been represented as a gendered space in which the role or carer has been predominantly associated with women. Thus in the design of many modern domestic homes there is a clear delineation of function and gender role (see Fiske et al., 1987) in which not only the division of public/private, paid work/domestic labour is encapsulated in the whole of the home as a gendered ream but within the home there are recognisable divisions of space that reflect not only different functions but also areas that are concerned with activities associated with gender (e.g. the kitchen, the laundry or utility area as 'female space', the games room or study, garage and shed as 'male space'.) The house therefore can be said to be a designed gendered space. However, as Felski puts it the home is a complex space that:

> like any other space, is shaped by conflicts and power struggles. It is often the site of intergenerational conflicts, such as an adolescent sense of identity that can be predicated upon a burning desire to leave home. It can be a place of female subordination as well as an arena where women can show competence in the exercise of domestic skills. Home is often a place for displaying commodities and hence saturated by class distinctions. (Felski, 1999: 22)

161

What is clear is that the domestic sphere as represented and produced as the designed space of home is one that has a gendered association. Not only is the individual home a complex space where traditional and dominant female roles and identities have been fashioned but residential areas themselves have been portrayed and analysed as gendered spaces. The most obvious and studied example is the suburb. The suburbs whether as working-class peripheral housing estates or middle-class ideal homes were essentially planned residential areas separated from places of work. They were designed as a different kind of urban space principally for women and children's need first. With the separation of paid employment and domestic labour there is a sense of spatial separation and segregation implied in the development of suburbs that both insulates and isolates women in the domestic sphere. This aspect of the spatialising of gender roles and relations in the suburb has been the subject of analysis and contestation over how negative were the effects and consequences for women of living in such developments. Thus there has been debate over the suburb as a paradise where women are empowered to take control over their lives and to organise the gendered space of the suburban home according to their own wishes, tastes and needs. Indeed Chambers (1997) argues that women were active in creating networks of support and activities that were fundamental to the construction of community life in such residential areas. However, the dominant vision of suburbia as less positive for women experience is, as Silverstone (1997) puts it, reflective of the utopian idealisation of the space and time of domestic, suburban life.

> Suburban culture is a gendered culture...The suburban home has been built around an ideology and a reality of women's domestication, oppressed by the insistent demands of the household, denied access to the varied spaces and times, the iteration of public and private that marks the male suburban experience and which creates for them, the crucial distinctions between work and leisure, weekday and weekend. In particular, post-war suburbanisation was buttressed by a concerted effort by public policy and media images to resocialise women into the home, and into the bosom of the nuclear family. (Silverstone, 1997: 7)

Whilst the role of women in the new spaces of the city such as suburbs has been considered as an extension of the public/private, work/domestic gendering of space what also needs to be considered is the possibility or not of women's roles as well as movement in the public sphere. Thus studies of the freedom or constraint of women in the space of the city needs a consideration not only of those areas traditionally viewed as 'women's spaces' (shopping centres, department stores, etc.), but also the increasing potential for leisure and recreation opened up by the developing urbanisation of society. Elizabeth Wilson (1991) . for example has argued that the anonymity and excitement of late nineteenth and early twentieth century city living was a crucial element on the rise of feminist politics. This was due to urban living giving a certain freedom from the control of the patriarchal family home and which brought new opportunities for association and interaction to women who took advantage of new urban spaces and forms to develop new associations, identities and activities. Thus, the streets, theatres, cinemas, dance halls, parks, etc. all provided opportunities for women outwith the functionalised or economically determined gendered space of the private and the home. Public space becomes inhabited and colonised by women taking advantage of new social and spatial opportunities. Thus the strict dichotomy implied in much of the analyses of gendered space has been contested in that throughout the period when women were supposed to be ensconced in private domestic spaces they were also involved in a variety of public and political campaigns outside the home. These included the abolition of the slave trade, the temperance movement, social hygiene campaigns, religious and charitable organisations such as the Salvation Army as well as the suffrage movement itself. In addition,

162

whilst the domestic ideology of the home was applied to middle-class women, for many working-class women the outside world of paid employment, in factories, mills, shops, as paid servants, etc. was an obvious and necessary public role. In more recent times the occupation of public space by women in pursuit of political aims whether as peace protestors at Greenham Common or in the numerous Reclaim the Streets/Night marches from the 1970's onwards that have periodically occurred in many cities in the US, UK, Europe and South America.

In respect of women inhabiting and occupying public spaces whether the streets, the department stores, arcades and railway stations increasingly women have come to challenge those spaces most associated with male pursuits and activities. The public house is one such example of a traditionally gendered everyday space of consumption, 'a home form home' for men (see Hey, 1986). Whilst women may have served traditionally as barmaids it is not until relatively recently that the public house has increasingly if perhaps somewhat grudgingly not only allowed and accepted women as clientele but actively encouraged them as consumers in their own right. The 'snug' or lounge where women were traditionally 'kept' away from the eyes of male drinkers and where women would not view the mysterious habits of 'the male at drink' is now almost gone from most public drinking establishment in the United Kingdom, Europe and America. What has occurred is a gradual opening up and acceptance of women as consumers in their own right and this has led to more female-friendly drinking establishments. Whilst it would be too much to say that pubs are safe places for women to drink on their own, liberation of pubs and other licensed premises as more visible spaces through the replacement of opaque glass with clear, better lighting and security staff, has ensured that the pub is both more anonymous and more welcoming, easier to assess visually and socially and therefore less excluding to women. The design and regulation of the pub as a social space is now more gender balanced if not exactly neutral. So much so that there is now concern expressed at the anti-social behaviour and alcohol consumption of young women as they take advantage of the more 'open' public spaces of drinking establishments.

Whilst some analyses focus on the separation (spatial, social, economic, etc.) of women from work into a domestic spatial sphere (including the design, organisation and decoration of 'the home') there is also a sense of the structured spatialisation of women's experience and opportunity in general. The development of socialist and Marxist feminist analyses of capitalism view the interdependence of economic development, gender relations and space as fundamental. This serves to produce an analysis of the urban and the region as key spatial units for

163

the survival and perpetuation of patriarchy under capitalism. The urban provides a scale for analysis that identifies the (private) spatial separation of suburban homes from the (public) world of paid employment as a crucial and key element in the perpetuation of divisions in gender roles through the reproduction of labour power.

Doreen Massey has been a crucial figure in the assertion of the construction of gender relations as key to the spatial organisation of social relations. In *Space, Place and Gender* Massey (1994) investigated how the different working-class gender models of masculinity and femininity were characterised and promulgated by a rigid sexual division of labour so that muscular masculinity was matched by a house-bound femininity. However she is also concerned to expand the spatial analysis of gender roles to investigated how regional difference in gender relations have been strategically used in industry (see Massey, 1984, 1991, 1994). Similarly, she has analysed the masculine gender associations attributed to high technology, scientific and technical work versus feminised domestic, caring and supportive labour. Thus the location of industries that seek to take advantage of suburban 'housewives' as relatively low paid part-time workers is one key element in the analyses of the many new service sector and call centre employers. In this she has investigated what she terms temporal and spatial flexibility that perpetuates gender inequalities in employment and asserts the need for a spatial analysis that does not relegate feminism to a 'little local difficulty' amidst the broader and by implication more important dimensions of post-modernity (see Massey, 1991).

Conceptualising gender relations as intrinsic to the spatial organisation of modern capitalism opens the door to the inclusion and investigation of women in and of space. If space is a determining as well as a determined fundamental condition or aspect of experience, as all the theorists considered previously argue, then there exists the potential for the analysis of a variety of contexts, situations, experiences, etc. where the confluence of gender and space are essential elements. Whilst women at home, at work and in the varieties of recreational opportunities that now exists in the developed world are increasingly publicly acknowledged and debated at the level of media speculation and scrutiny as well as in political debate and social policy dictums (young women's sexuality, public inebriation, behaviour, safety, etc.) there also is a need for studies of the spatiality of non-Western women both in the West and also in comparative studies of other socio-spatial and cultural formations. Therefore, social construction of gender relations across ethnicities, religions, sexualities, nationalities, etc. is an increasingly fruitful and important aspect of post-colonial feminist research on space and gender.

164

As debates concerning the visibility or otherwise, the participation or exclusion, of the role and representation of non-Western women in Western societies are likely to continue the need for the comparative analysis of gender and space is ever more imperative.

spatialising sexuality

The spatialising of sexuality can be conceptualised as the analysis of the ways in which space can be seen to both reflect as well as structure the performativity of sexual identities. This is particularly influenced by Foucault's theories on disciplinary discourses and power/knowledge informs the study of the spatiality of the construction of sexuality and identity. That is, to investigate the ways in which the organisation of space informs the construction and organisation of sexualities. For example, the feminist critique of how the gendered sexuality of women's bodies are shaped and disciplined by (self) surveillance and by external domination reflects an awareness and acknowledgement of not only how women are expected to look and act in public but also which spaces are more or less open to women at particular times of the day and night. Thus public space, as argued previously has been very much a gendered space.

165

However, public space assumes, prioritises and provides for the performance of and acceptance of heterosexuality. The expression of heterosexuality is not only allowed or permissible it is in certain places actively encouraged. One thinks of not only the explicit heterosexuality of strip bars and lap-dancing clubs but also what one might call the 'banal heterosexuality' of everyday life in romantic candle-lit dinners-for-two, in the hand-holding, kissing, cuddling, etc. of mixed sex couples that is accepted and condoned in most public spaces. Similarly, the commodification of (hetero)sexual imagery (albeit with the potential for consumption and appropriation by the homosexual gaze) is used to advertise and sell all sorts of products. How space is used therefore in managing sexual identities is a topic that has received recent analysis. In particular, the experience of gay men and lesbians and other sexual minority groups takes place within the general assumption of heterosexuality as the norm. This has implications for the management of minority sexual identities in both time and space. As Bell and Valentine write

> To avoid a rupture of their 'identity' many lesbians use time-space strategies to segregate their audiences. This includes establishing geographical boundaries between past and present identities, separating different activity spheres and

hence identities in space, expressing a lesbian identity only in formal 'gay spaces', confining their 'gay' socialising to homes or informal 'gay spaces', expressing their lesbian identity only in public places at specific times, and altering the layout and decoration of private spaces to conceal clues about their sexual identity from specific people. (Bell and Valentine, 1995a: 147)

One can appreciate why this concealment of sexual identity is a necessary safety and security measure when one considers how homophobia has regularly led to the persecution of homosexuals by the police and courts as well as the violence experienced by homosexuals caught 'in the open' spaces of public parks and toilets.

Whilst everyday space may be said to be heterosexual space there have been significant changes in the expression as well as acceptance of gay identities. For example, the campaign for 'gay rights' has led to the colonisation and inhabitation of the streets and public spaces of many cities during gay festivals and marches that has seen an increasing public profile given to gay identities. Most major European and American cities have annual events, marches and festivals but perhaps the best known are the Gay Mardi Gras held in San Francisco and in Sydney and Berlin's Love Parade. Gay men and lesbians may be said to have taken advantage of the anonymity of the city to escape the conventionalism that bound morality to a narrow definition of acceptable sexuality and identity. It offered a place to escape and to eventually forge new spaces where identities and lifestyles could be developed and perpetuated in feelings of security and solidarity through the concentration of like-minded individuals. There is thus a growing literature on the importance of gay bars, clubs and what has become known as 'gay villages' in many cities for the establishment and performance of gay sexual identities (see Adler and Brenner, 1992, Bell and Valentine, 1995b, Castells, 1983, Chauncey, 1995, Fitzgerald, 1986, Knopp, 1992, Lauria and Knopp, 1985). In contrast to gated communities or walled enclaves that are physically and socially separated and segregated residential areas gay villages such as that in the Castro area of San Francisco and surrounding Canal Street in Manchester are primarily areas of the city that are social centres for gay people, primarily men to meet and spend leisure time. The creation and economic success of such gay social spaces in the form of clubs, pubs, cafes, etc. has not only created 'safe spaces' for gay identities to be publicly expressed but has also led to the rejuvenation of many previously run-down inner city areas. So much so that the economic impact of 'Gay Villages' whether in Amsterdam (Europe's self styled gay capital) Manchester, San Francisco or Brighton is recognised and actively encouraged by local state authorities to maximise the economic benefits from the 'Pink Pound/Dollar/Euro' (see Bruce, 1997).

This specifically gay space has challenged prejudice as well as providing opportunities for the expression, the public performativity, of gay identities. Most major cities now contain such areas and spaces that are visible, vibrant and commercial.

It is therefore connected to the social division of sexuality and the spatial division of public sexual identity in that the *Gay Village* appears as a defined and represented area where through concentration of numbers a minority sexuality can or are allowed to freely associate without the over-arching fear of discrimination, conflict and violence that has been directed to other openly 'different' groups in society both in the past and present. There is then a concentration of venues, facilities, businesses, activities and social life in which there is 'safety in numbers' and a freedom in space to express and perform ones sexual identity in public.

There is then a developing research profile that focuses on the spatialisation of sexuality and how space informs and determines the expression and performance of sexuality. However, questions arise as to how and in what ways particular spaces and places associated and represented as 'gay' or straight are organised and structured to permit or deny access on grounds other than sexual identity. For example, many gay clubs and bars are found in areas of towns and cities in which gentrification has occurred and consequently may be prohibitive for those homosexuals without the income or who reside in close proximity to be able to access or use. Similarly, issues concerning the potential conflict between 'straight' and 'gay' communities and neighbourhoods as well as cultural, ethnic and gender differences need to be considered when analysing the experience and reality of such examples of the socio-spatial integration, segregation or concentration of the space of sexuality. However, some argue that these gay spaces are 'colossal closets' (Hindle, 1994) where gay identity can be publicly expressed but within very strict and limited spatial parameters.

167

'race' and space

One contemporary aspect of race and space concerns debates and analyses of immigration. Whilst it may be a truism to state that immigration is by definition the movement of people in space, from one country, region, etc. to another there is a more critical aspect that needs to be considered. Whilst claims are made to the permeability of nation state boundaries in this era of global capitalism and it is true that for some mobility is increasingly easy and convenient, for others it reflects not only the spatial division of the planet into a 'rich North/poor South' hemispheric dichotomy but also one increasingly underscored by policies of exclusion based on ethnicity or race. The development, for example of the supranational geography of the European Union (EU) exemplifies problems associated with the 'legitimacy' of some immigrants versus others. Thus the notion of economic migrants carries racial over-tones when applied to poor, non-white/European workers/families seeking employment in the EU as opposed to those who travel the globe as part of an international army of labour to meet the needs of multi-national corporations for skilled technicians, administrators and managers. The development of concerted and coordinated measures to keep out the 'hordes' of illegal immigrants is one that is regularly used in political and media campaigns in both Europe and America. The depictions of 'Fortress America' and 'Fortress Europe' are not only about creating physical barriers or impediments to movement but are also portrayed against a backdrop of racial and ethnic stereotyping in which international legal obligations to 'asylum seekers' are increasingly obfuscated within the parameters of an enclosed, bounded and defended national or supranational territory.

In the same ways that cities have been discussed previously as divided or segregated by gender, sexuality and class so too can a spatial analysis be applied to racial/ethnic segregation/integration. Whilst the ecological model of cities in the analysis of the Chicago School (see Zorbaugh, Park, Burgess et al.) provided some explanation for the spatial distribution and mobility of successive waves of urban immigrants it lacked the sophistication and critical acuities applied by later political economy approaches to the competition for urban space, services, employment, etc. (see Harvey, 1978a,b, 1982, 1985a,b, Castells, 1977). However, it did acknowledge how different neighbourhoods and areas reflected not only a socio-economic spatial segregation but also the development of the ethnic or racial spatialisation of urban populations. The physical organisation of cities can be said to be structured by underlying processes of differentiation and segregation in which different areas reflect inequalities and are manifest in the spatial structuring and organisation of the city. Thus most cities in the Western world have identifiable areas in which some form of racial/ethnic segregation has become representative or reflective of structured inequalities. Whilst this may have deleterious effects in creating negative associations of identifiable areas there is also the sense in which such concentrations of ethnic minorities in geographical space allows for both a sense of safety and security and also the development of communities and networks of neighbourhood support that have positive benefits. The development of businesses, community groups and centres, art and cultural events and projects, as well as the provision of formal and informal social service provision is accommodated by the inhabitation of geographically distinct areas.

The long-term effects of cycles of economic restructuring which has affected those traditional manufacturing industries that attracted immigrants to their former colonial 'mother countries' has left many communities in a state of economic stagnation or permanent depression. The associated processes of economic decline, lack of investment in certain aspects of the urban infrastructure as well as the effects of institutional racisms in many sectors of the local and national state has created concentrations of urban deprivation are represented in the development of 'racialised' ghettoes. In most American cities for example, it is not difficult to identify the socio-spatial segregation of the poor black and Latino inhabitants from their wealthier white counterparts. The representation of those areas/communities/neighbourhoods as afflicted by poverty, family breakdown, health and educational inequalities, as well as crime, drugs and violence more often than not takes on racial overtones.

The periodic urban revolts that erupt in many European and American cities are most often associated with and correspond to some form of racial and spatial segregation. In Britain the Broadwater Farm riot of 1985 and those in Oldham, Burnley and Bradford in 2001, as well as more recently in cities and towns across France in 2005 took place predominantly in those suburban and peripheral estates that have become or racially and socio-economically segregated. This spatial segregation reinforces the alienation and exclusion of those who are left isolated and ill-served on such estates. The intervention of the state at local and national level as well as the changing priorities of international capital has led not only to the restructuring of economies but also to the marginalisation of whole regions as well as estates and towns within countries. In much of this those who are most likely to suffer from other forms of inequality besides economic occupy the worst housing. There is then a need to understand and analyse such urban problems as racial and class inequalities as they are expressed and experienced in space. A further aspect of the analysis of race and space that informs this consideration of the spatial segregation of the urban environment is reflected in the legacy of colonialism that has become inscribed on the landscape of many cities. There are any number of streets and buildings that are named after places colonised in previous eras, as well as monuments and statues, buildings and architecture that represent this colonial past. How such streets and cities are negotiated amid such symbolic representations of domination and subservience reflects the sense that in many ways the processes and forms of exploitation and stratification is writ large on the landscape of urban modernity.

crime and space

Issues concerning crime and deviance from social, moral or legal norms have been of paramount concern within all societies in all epochs. The organisation, regulation and control of space have necessarily been central aspects of the effective policing and administration of activities and behaviours. The structuring of the activities of detection, of surveillance and of the administration of punishment to transgressors has been organised within geographically distinct areas such as the nation state, the region, city, division and district. Such spatialisation of crime and punishment has therefore been an intrinsic aspect of the maintenance of law as well as the good moral order of societies.

Contemporary concerns with law and order and maintaining peace and security both within national boundaries and societies (socio-spatial cultural, political and economic formations) as well as in this climate of concern with global security in the era of the '*War on Terrorism*' raises issues concerning the expansion of the control and surveillance of space at both micro and macro levels. As global economic concerns require and allow more mobility on the part of an international labour force as well as more commonly expressed and accepted mobility of international capital there are paradoxical elements to the restriction and permission of the movement of people both within national boundaries and internationally across regions and continents. There is a thus both a permeability of national, regional and international boundaries that allows as well as prevents or impedes movement and mobility.

At the global level we are increasingly faced with more and more surveillance and the control of movement through space. Certainly since *9/11* there have been obvious concerns with increased security that has expanded the sense of the need to make nations 'fortresses' as well as the constitution of coordinated intelligence and security measures, one such example being the establishment in the United States and elsewhere of measures concerned with 'homeland security'. This has led to more stringent security measures being applied to individuals as they attempt to move from one nation, country, region, etc. to another as increasing conditions and controls are placed on those who wish or need to travel whether for business, pleasure or for other reasons. Thus it may be said the most secure and 'safe' spaces are those that are associated with movement and mobility, such as air travel, given the levels of surveillance, identity checks, baggage searches, monitoring, etc. Whilst concerns with terrorism are the leitmotif for the implementation of new and enhanced security measures that are more or less universal the implications are clearly evident for a more patrolled, monitored and policed space of travel.

Debates concerning the demise of the political and social integrity of the nation state as a bounded geographically distinct territory through the increasing fluidity and mobility of globalisation *may* have some salience (see Urry, 2000) but there is also the sense that the nation state or regional trading and economic zone is becoming more an operative and integrated defensible space. Certain groups, nationalities and ethnicities thus become subjected to more scrutiny and restriction than others as 'threats', potential or otherwise, are analysed and responses formulated to mitigate them. Whether these threats are from the incursions of unwanted economic migrants or asylum seekers or whether they are from those deemed to be military or ideological adversaries and combatants, the defensible geographical and spatial realm is an ongoing political and social reality.

The control of internal national space by security and policing institutions and personnel has led to the development both of a political will as well as technological developments. The debate concerning the introduction of 'smart' bio-metric identity cards and passports in the United Kingdom, Europe and the United States that contain not only fingerprints, iris scans, DNA details, medical history, National Insurance and Health Service Numbers but also personal information, financial status, etc. implies a more subjected, controlled and policed space in the future. Access or egress, movement or mobility in certain areas and times of day, night, season, etc. may increasingly be subjected to electronic confirmation of status, suitability, credentials or even perhaps wealth, nationality, ethnicity or religious persuasion. The opportunity of accessing retail outlets such as shopping centres and malls for example, may become dependent on card-scans that confirm economic or judicial status; access to entertainment or public spaces may at times be permissible only to certain defined groups; residential or business premises may allow or deny access only to 'authorised' or acceptable individuals; travel restrictions may be denied to certain groups or individuals on the basis of information contained on identity cards.

The issue of crime inevitably raises questions as to control of desirable and undesirable activities, groups and individuals, etc. and is of prime importance for any society that seeks to describe itself as democratic. The organisation, ordering and control of movement and association in space implies a political and moral ordering of societies, of 'good' and 'bad', of allowed, permitted, sanctioned activities and people versus those deemed illicit, inappropriate, deviant or dangerous, etc. Thus the monitoring and control of space is a concern not only for the future as debates concerning the introduction of such new technologies continue. How they are applied and how they may or may not be used to create

171

or maintain inequalities are key issues in the analysis of how open and inclusive/exclusive our democratic societies are and can be allowed to be. The stigmatisation and subsequent monitoring of groups, activities, areas, etc. reflects a potentially negative consequence of fear of crime that may negate the more positive aspects of the surveillance of public spaces. The sense of safety and security implied or promised by knowing that we are being continuously watched over may be undermined by the fear of how such information may be used against you. The baby may indeed be thrown out with the bathwater if ones freedom of movement and association is limited by the fear of constant surveillance by an anonymous and potentially politically malicious 'Big Brother' technology.

However, in terms of crime at local or national levels the development of new monitoring and surveillance technologies has led to the application of sophisticated electronic measures to the policing of an increasing number of public and social spaces. It is now exceedingly common for not only state security services to employ wide-ranging CCTV equipment at marches, demonstrations, sensitive defence facilities, etc. but increasingly whole town and city centres are subjected to the 'electronic eye' of private and public authorities monitoring of the activities and behaviours of the public. This is an electronic extension of Foucault's concept of the 'Eye of Power' and the development of Panopticism more extensive and far reaching than originally described. There are a number of studies of the extent of the spread of such surveillance (Lyon, 1988, 1994, 2001, Staples 1997) and their potential consequence for civil and political liberties as well as those that question its effectiveness in curtailing criminal activities (Armitage, 2002, Crang, 1996, Ditton et al., 1999, Helms, 2003, McCahill, 2002). The expansion of cameras and surveillance equipment into many more spheres and spaces of everyday life are areas in which the control and organisation of space through technological measures is being investigated. However, not only are streets, shopping centres, car parks, airports, motorways, shops, etc. now commonly 'covered' by cameras but they are also finding their way into schools, cloakrooms and toilet facilities, pubs and clubs, etc. We are increasingly invited to install monitoring and security devices not only outside our homes but also inside to ensure that those we entrust to look after our children can be observed in the performance of their childcare duties. Our children are now the most monitored, surveilled, scrutinised and observed generation that have existed. There are fewer and fewer places where they can explore themselves and their surroundings, make and break friendships, etc. out-with the prying eyes of the adult world. Whilst this may provide a façade of security, increasingly there are concerns about privacy and human rights from a constant monitoring of individuals who have not given permission to be filmed and who have no control over how such footage may subsequently be used. Similarly, what kind of people and society are being created who are expected to live their lives almost entirely under observation is a fundamental concern for the development and perpetuation of so-called 'open-societies'.

The planned design and control of spaces as an attempt to mould, shape or determine the behaviour and activities that occur within it has implications for how public space is used, by who and for what purposes. Recently expressed concerns with public space have focussed explicitly on the supposed anti-social behaviour of youth and with issues especially centred on young people's use of space (the gathering in numbers on street corners, outside shops, in bus shelters, railway stations, parks, pedestrian walkways and underpasses, etc.) This aspect of the crime and the policing of space have involved the police and local authorities supported by new legislation that effectively implements curfews and exclusion zones on certain groups in certain spaces. The increasing use of such measures and of the electronic tagging of convicted offenders reflects new policing strategies that involve the delimiting of space and of the restriction of individuals movement in it.

An extension of these measures to restrict movement and access to public space is the regulation and curtailment of legitimate protest. The construction of what are effectively exclusion zones around events and institutions such as the Houses of Parliament in the United Kingdom as well as the recent G8 summit in Gleneagles, Scotland that sought to impose spatial limits on the rights of public association and for alternative political views and agendas to be seen and heard. Dissent from the political mainstream is now subjected to the surveillance and regulation of the space to protest where and when it may be most effectively and appropriately expressed. Whilst more research is needed to assess the effectiveness of the surveillance and marginalisation of predominantly young people it seems clear that such strategies will increasingly be used to make some social spaces no-go areas for some groups. Such issues relate specifically to the segregation and characterisation of spaces by disciplinary discourses that apply moral and political judgments to acceptable and appropriate behaviours and the 'correct' use of public space.

173

globalisation and space

The current interest in and analysis of globalisation in its multifarious forms is one that takes place with an overt recognition and acknowledgment of its spatiality. There are a number of seminal analyses of globalisation that reflect this awareness of the spatial context of globalisation. There is not the time or space here to provide a detailed critique of this inherent spatiality but what can be provided is a very brief illumination of how spatial analysis is fundamental to the understanding of globalisation. In some respects this spatiality has a foundation or may be said to be influenced by Marx's understanding of the expansion of capitalism to a global mode of production that began this book and that continues to inform much of the critique of neo-liberal capitalism today. Indeed there is an increasing awareness of the prescience and salience of Marx's analysis for the globalisation of capital (see Renton, 2001) and yet unforeseen features have come to the fore and been analysed and considered as fundamental or characteristic of its new phase. It is the spatiality of globalisation that will be briefly addressed below.

beck and global risk society

Ulrich Beck in his numerous writings on Risk Society (see Adam et al., 2000, Beck, 1992, 1995, 1999, Beck and Willms, 2004, Beck et al., 1994) expounds the thesis that amongst other things the 'new' risks created by the inherent processes of modern industrial capitalism have produced a 'manufactured uncertainty' as a state of being in late (reflexive) modernity. These risks that Beck associates particularly with radiation, environmental pollution, food and water toxicity, etc. are manifestly different from previous risks in that not only are they the cumulative products of industrial processes and technological developments (the appliance of science) they have the potential for catastrophic harm to be done to all life on the planet. As Beck puts it:

> The gain in power from techno-economic 'progress' is being increasingly overshadowed by the production of risks. In an early stage, these can be legitimated as 'latent side effects'. As they become globalised, and subject to public criticism and scientific investigation, they come so to speak, out of the closet and achieve a central importance in social and political debates...At the centre lies the risks and consequences of modernisation, which are revealed as irreversible threats to the life of plants, animals, and human beings. Unlike the factory-related or occupational hazards of the nineteenth and the first half of the 20th centuries, these can no longer be limited to certain localities or groups, but rather exhibit a tendency to globalisation which spans production and reproduction as much as national borders, and in this sense brings into being supra-national and non-class specific global hazards with a new type of social and political dynamism. (Beck, 1992: 13)

Beck's analysis of these new global risks emphasises that they are no longer limited by geography, that is, affect only those places where they

174

initially are produced. Global risks recognise no national or regional borders. For Beck these generated risks and their potential consequences are of global importance because of the potential catastrophic dangers produced by such risks as radiation, environmental degradation, global warming, etc. They are not only unlimited in space but also in time. Future generations will suffer the consequences as well as those that produce them. Whilst Beck's analysis has its critics, not least for his triumphing of an incipient non-class based sub-politics to challenge the dominant discourses of global risk society, his identification of qualitatively and quantitatively new risks that require global solutions provides some insight into the new geographies of power that are developing around such perceived risks. Those global organisations such as the United Nations, The International Monetary Fund, the Group of Eight of the most powerful economies, etc. are increasingly being called upon to agree on global treaties and protocols for not only monitoring and regulating trade but also to attempt to deal collectively with such issues as the prevention of biological pandemics (Avian Flu, AIDS, etc.), nuclear non-proliferation, climate change, etc. There is, as Beck has been keen to popularise a resistance to the dominant discourses of economic globalisation that has resulted in a rise of a plethora of movements, groups and organisations that are increasingly operating on a global scale and utilising technologies and new modes of operation to counteract the ideologies as well as the policies of global institutions and transnational corporations. It is no surprise then that the first section of Naomi Klein's popular anti globalisation manifesto *No Logo* is entitled *No Space*. Recognition of the assault on personal, political and community space by corporate capitalism as well as an awareness of the need to organise and resist on a global (spatial) level. Such slogans as '*Think Global: Act Local*' reflect an awareness of and acceptance of political allegiances not circumscribed by traditional spatial, national and class boundaries as well as the potential power inherent in individuals personal and everyday life.

175

John Urry – flows and migration

For John Urry the New World Order is one in which global 'mobilities' and flows have undermined the valency of traditional societal boundaries and bonds. The central concept of sociology has been the way in which society has been defined, understood and applied in analyses within an over-arching context of nation states and systems of nation states. Therefore sociology must come to terms with the demise of its central concept and discover a future that is not limited by such socio-spatial concepts and objects of analysis. Urry writes in *Sociology Beyond Societies* (2000) that:

> Each 'society' is a sovereign social entity with a nation-state that organises the rights and duties of each societal member or citizen. Most major sets of social relationships are seen as flowing within the territorial boundaries of the society. The state is thought to possess a monopoly of jurisdiction or governmentality over members living within the territory or region of the society. Economy, politics, culture, classes, gender and so on, are societally structured. In combination they constitute a clustering, or what is normally conceptualised as a 'social structure'. Such a structure organises and regulates the life chances of each member of the society in question. (Urry, 2000: 8)

Urry postulates that the world we now live in has fundamentally changed through aspects of technological, economic, political and cultural, etc., developments. He sites Mann's description of the contemporary world as evidence of such change:

> Today, we live in a global society. It is not a unitary society, nor is it an ideological community or a state, but it is a single power network. Shock waves reverberate around it, casting down empires, transporting massive quantities of people, materials and messages and finally, threatening the ecosystem and atmosphere of the planet. (Mann, 1993: 11)

176

For Urry, the consequences of a non-unified global society lies in the exceptional levels of global interdependence that have come to exist across all spheres and levels of social relations. However the unpredictable shock waves that spill out 'chaotically' from one part to the system as a whole can have an effect on all, not least in that they create a mass mobility of peoples, things and dangerous human wastes. For Urry then there are not just 'societies' but now massively powerful 'empires' roaming the globe.

This has serious implications for Urry's thesis that sociology needs to reconstitute itself without society as its object of analysis. In particular, if there is not a bounded society then how is it possible to establish the functional requirements that have to be met, in order that each 'society' continues? At what level or scale must these be constituted and organised if the societal level of the state no-longer provides the functional as well as socio-spatial basis or framework for provision. This is also true in terms of societal regulation: at what level and across what areas jurisprudence, policing, regulation and justice being organised and administered and perhaps of equal importance by whom. Within the post 9/11 context of the war against (global) terror new political and military arrangements and justifications are being put in place alongside portable and flexible jurisdictions for incarcerating and holding to account those suspected of terrorist offences or affiliations. Urry asks pertinent questions concerning what entity is being regulated and how can its function be specified if there are no longer discrete boundaries to what we call society? Such a perspective entails an awareness of the importance of a spatial analysis to the development and perpetuation of the processes and experiences of globalisation as new global flows and networks have generated a new functional requirement for states to regulate. Thus Urry argues that

> shifts towards global networks and flows transforms the space of each state. It is this space which states have to striate and they are therefore involved in increasing efforts at 'social regulation'. Such regulation is both necessitated, and is only made possible, by new computer-based forms of information gathering, retrieval and dissemination. What states increasingly possess are exceptional information flows, especially databases, which enable performance indicators to be implemented and monitored across extensive geographical areas, within and beyond the boundaries of the nation state. (Urry, 2000: 198)

Castells – timeless time and the space of flows

Urry's conceptions of the new global world order of flows, mobilities and networks of power shares familiarities with Manuel Castells' analysis of globalisation as constituting a new type of society, that of the Global Network society. In his three volumes on *The Information Age* and elsewhere Castells makes the claim that new information technologies combined with the economic crisis of capitalism, the demise of the communist states and the emergence of new social movements such as feminism and environmentalism have led to the development of a new type of society, that of the network society. The impact of these processes is to rapidly transform societies, economies and cultures across the globe. Without going into the details of Castells' thesis he employs spatial concepts and metaphors to explain how this has happened and occurs. For example, Castells refers to flows of capital, information, organisational interaction, images, sounds, symbols, technology which have come to gradually replace a space of localities "in whose form, function and meaning are self contained within the boundaries of physical space" (Castells, 1996: 423). For Castells, space becomes inseparable from time in that what occurs is a 'space of flows' which produces 'timeless time'. Time is compressed and broken so that things happen instantaneously and the progressive linearity of past events and practices is broken by the discontinuity of the processes by which we use the internet and other Information and Communication Technologies.

177

For Castells then, "We have entered a new technological paradigm centred around micro-electronics based, information/communication technologies and genetic engineering" (Castells, 1998: 5). He further argues that we now live in a new economy characterised by three fundamental features: it is informational, global and networked. A key aspect of Castells argument concerning this new networked and global economy is the concept of the 'space of flows' where

> the meaning and function of the space of flows depend on the flows processed within the networks, by contrast with the space of places, in which meaning, function and locality are closely interrelated. (Castells, 1998: 17)

The 'space of flows' for Castells operates as networks of electronic communication and is related to the development of a hierarchy of cities ('world cities') and places that become strategic hubs or nodes in the world markets of information. These world cities also become the location for the elites that comprise the power holders who are more able not only to access essential knowledge networks but to be more mobile themselves to take advantage of opportunities as they occur in other areas, spheres, regions, cities, etc. For Castells then space is crucial to his conceptualisation of a paradigm shift to the Network Society.

178

Giddens – time space distantiation

Anthony Giddens also considers what he recognises as the transformation of social interaction through the reordering or 'uncoupling' of space and time. Giddens use of the term 'time–space distantiation' to refer to the lifting of social interactions out of their immediate settings and stretching them over potentially vast spans of time–space (Giddens, 1990). Giddens like Castells is concerned with the implications for social change of new conceptions and constructions of time and space in that time–space transformations are crucial to modern societies as time and space become extended beyond the confines of place. Giddens argues that the standardisation of time combined with place being removed from particular locales result in social life becoming 'disembedded'. This is particulary important in that as Giddens states:

> Place is best conceptualised by the means of the idea of locale, which refers to the physical settings of social activity as situated geographically. In pre-modern societies, space and place largely coincide, whence the spatial dimension of social life are, for most of the population, and in most respects, dominated by 'presence' – by localised activities. The advent of modernity increasingly tears space away from place by fostering relations between 'absent' others, locationally distant from any given situation of face-to-face interaction. (Giddens, 1990: 18)

Giddens uses the term 'time–space distanciation' to describe how social relations are lifted out of their immediate interactional settings and stretched over what are often vast spans of global time–space. This disembedding is accompanied by re-embedding in new forms of local, face-to-face interaction. According to this analysis, our senses of not only community but also identity are shaped profoundly by the reconfiguration of space and time associated with new electronic media technologies, as well as the structural and institutional settings that impact on our identities, opportunities and life chances as 'global citizens'.

POST-MODERNISED SPACE

It would be remiss in a discourse such as this on new directions in social theory and space not to mention Ed Soja's contribution to the repriori-tisation of space, namely his attempt to locate spatiality at the centre of social theoretical thought. Soja's contribution to what he asserts is a spatially focused post-modern social theory can be found detailed consistently in his three major works (Soja, 1989, 1996, 2000). It has three main propositions. The first is that the (global) capitalist mode of production is being restructured in ways that prioritise space over time rather than what had previously been the case. The second is that space is fundamental to the constitution (that is the establishment, structure and organisation) of social life. Third, space need to be taken seriously if we are to make sense of society, in whatever form. There is then in Soja's work a concern to expose the critical role of space in social life. Whilst Soja shares this with many theorists he argues that space *must* be central to each and every element of social theory. In *Postmodern Geographies* (1986) he argues that space has been subsumed and ultimately denied by the overarching focus on times so much so that

179

> historicism as an overdeveloped historical contextualisation of social life and social theory that actually submerges and peripheralises the geographical or spatial imagination . . . [Soja] . . . identifies historicism with the creation of a critical silence, an implicit subordination of space to time that obscures geographical interpretations of the changeability of the social world and intrudes upon every level of theoretical discourse, from the most abstract ontological concepts of being to the most detailed explanations of empirical events. (Soja, 1989: 15)

What Soja argues is acknowledgement of the necessity for a spatial mode of theorising that undermines this dominance of historicism. That is he wants to apply "a triple dialectic of space, time and social being: a transformative re-theorisation of the relations between history, geography and modernity" (Soja, 1986: 12). Whilst Soja syncretically includes in his analysis a number of theorists it is Lefebvre that has had the most influence. It is Soja's application of the *trialectic* of Lefebvre's theory of the production of space that leads him to assert that the contemporary era or post-modern epoch is one in which a fundamentally restructured capitalism can only be understood by an astute awareness of the critical role of space. As he states:

> We must be insistently aware of how space can be made to hide consequences from us, how relations of power and discipline are inscribed into the apparently innocent spatiality of social life, how human geographies become filled with politics and ideology. (Soja, 1986: 6)

This has an obvious resonance with Lefebvre's analysis, after Marx, of spatial fetishism. He goes on to apply and explore the emerging post-Fordist social space of Los Angeles as an empirical example of "flexible systems of production, consumption, exploitation, spatialisation and social control" (Soja, 1986: 221). Whilst his analysis of Los Angeles has been influential in promoting a post-modern geographical imagination it is less developed and critical than that provided by Mike Davis (see Davis, 1990, 1998, 2000). Soja appears to rest on an economic base that as Gregory states gives "a morphology of landscape that...is rarely disturbed by human forms" (1994: 301). Nonetheless Soja has been highly influential in attempting to present human geography and space within the mainstream of social theory and offers an account of space that has been widely read and achieved success in publicising a variety of spatial theorists.

CONCLUSION

The aim of this chapter has been to highlight the way in which those theories of space considered previously have been developed and applied in a variety of different contexts. There is little doubt that space and spatial theories are beginning to have a more fundamental role in the analysis of contemporary social life. As the boundaries between disciplines become more blurred this will become more apparent and accepted. The analysis of globalisation and the continuing relevance of the urban as a/the crucial 'space' of contemporary social relations and activity of the majority of the worlds population in (post/late/reflexive) modernity ensures that the need to understand and theorise space will be increasingly applied. To ignore space is to deny the inherent spatiality of the construction, experience, organisation and perpetuation of all the spheres and activities that constitute social life. We live in spaces, not necessarily always of our own choosing, but nonetheless ones that resonate and reflect our status and opportunity. We live and work, move and settle, play and reproduce in space and how we think and understand space is important to how and who we are. New directions and horizons in sociology are intrinsically spatial terms, of movement and direction, of location and perception. To move forward and increase the scope and sphere of perspective requires an appreciation of the meanings and understandings of, in and for space.

181

bibliography

Adam, B., Beck, U. and Loon, J. V. (eds) (2000) *The Risk Society and Beyond: Critical Issues in Social Theory*, London, Sage

Adler, S. and Brenner, J. (1992) 'Gender and space: lesbians and gay men in the city' *International Journal of Urban and Regional Research*, 16, 24–34

Allen, J. (2000) 'On Georg Simmel: proximity, distance and movement' in Crang, M. and Thrift, N. (eds) (2000) *Thinking Space*, London, Routledge

Allen, J. (2003) *Lost Geographies of Power*, Oxford, Blackwell

Allwood, J. (1977) *The Great Exhibitions*, London, Studio Vista

Amin, A. (1999) 'Spatialities of globalisation' *Environment and Planning A* 34, 3385–99

Amin, A. (2002) 'Ethnicity and the multicultural city: living with diversity' *Environment and Planning A* l 3:6, 959–80

Anderson, B. (1983) *Imagined Communities: Reflections on the Origin and Spread of Nationalism*, London, Verso

Anderson, R. J., Hughes, J. A. and Sharrock, W. W. (eds) (1987) *Classic Disputes in Sociology*, London, Allen and Unwin

Armitage, R. (2002) 'To CCTV or not to CCTV?' *A Review of Current Research into the Effectiveness of CCTV Systems in Reducing Crime*, London, NACRO

Armstrong, D. (1983) *The Political Anatomy of the Body*, Cambridge, Cambridge University Press

Armstrong, D. (1994) 'Bodies of knowledge/knowledge of bodies' in Jones, R. and Porter, C. (eds) (1994) *Reassessing Foucault: Power, Medicine and the Body*, London, Routledge

Armstrong, T. J. (1992) *Michel Foucault: Philosopher*, London, Harvester, Wheatsheaf

Atkinson, R. and Moon, G. (1994) *Urban Policy in Britain*, Basingstoke, McMillan

Bale, J. and Philo, C. (eds) (1998) *Body Cultures: Essays on Sport, Space and Identity*, London, Routledge

Barnes, T. and Gregory, D. (eds) (1997) *Reading Human Geography*, London, Edward Arnold

Baudrillard, J. (1994) *The Illusion of the End*, Stanford, Stanford University Press

Beck, U. (1992) *Risk Society*, London, Sage

Beck, U. (1995) *Ecological Politics in an age of Risk*, Cambridge, Polity Press

Beck, U. (1999) *World Risk Society*, Cambridge, Polity Press

Beck, U. and Willms, J. (2004) *Conversations with Ulrich Beck*, Polity Press, Cambridge

Beck, U., Giddens, A. and Lash, S. (1994) *Reflexive Modernisation*, Oxford, Polity Press

Bell, D. and Jayne, M. (eds) (2004) *City of Quarters*, Aldershot, Ashgate

Bell, D. and Valentine, G. (1995a) 'The sexed self – strategies of performance and sites of resistance' in Pile, S. and Thrift, N. (1995) *Mapping the Subject: Geographies of Cultural Transformation*, London, Routledge

Bell, D. and Valentine, G. (eds) (1995b) *Mapping Desire: Geographies of Sexualities*, London, Routledge

Benjamin, W. (1999) *The Arcades Project*, London, Harvard University Press

Benko, G. and Strothmayer, U. (eds) (1997) *Space and Social Theory*, Oxford, Blackwell

Bennett, D. (ed.) (1998) *Multicultural States: Rethinking Difference and Identity*, London, Routledge

Bennett, T., Martin, C. G. and Mercer, C. (eds) (1981) *Culture, Ideology and Social Process*, Milton Keynes, Open University Press

Bentham, J. (1843) *Works*, Vol. 4, J. Bowring (ed.), Edinburgh

Berger, J. (1972) *Ways of Seeing*, London, Penguin

Bhabha, H. K. (ed.) (1990), *Nation and Narration*, London, Routledge

Blakely, E. J. and Snyder, M. (1997) *Fortress America*, Washington, The Brookings Institution

Blowers, A. and Pain, K. (1999) 'The unsustainable city' in Pile, S. Brook, C. and Mooney, G. (eds) (1999) *Unruly Cities: Order/Disorder*, London, Routledge/ Open University Press

Bottomore, T. (1956) *Karl Marx: Selected Writings on Sociology and Social Philosophy*, London, McGraw-Hill

Bourdieu, P. (1977) *Outline of a Theory of Practice*, Cambridge, Cambridge University Press

Brenner, N. (2000) 'The urban question as a scale question: reflections on Henri Lefebvre, urban theory and the politics of scale', *International Journal of Urban and Regional Research*, vol. 24: 2, June 2000

Bruce, I. (1997) 'Gay sites and the pink dollar' in Murphy, P. and Watson, S. (1997) *Surface City Sydney at the Millennium*, Sydney, Pluto Press

Bryder, L. (1988) *Below the Magic Mountain – A Social History of Tuberculosis in 20th Century Britain*, Oxford, Oxford University Press

Burgess, R. E. with McKenzie, R. D. and Wirth, L. (1925/1984) *The City: Suggestions for Investigation of Human Behaviour in the Urban Environment*, IL Midway Reprint, University of Chicago Press

Burke, P. (ed.) (1992) *Critical Thought Series 2: Critical Essays on Michel Foucault*, London, Scolar Press

Byrne, D. (1999) *Social Exclusion*, Buckingham, Open University Press

Caldeira, T. P. R. (1996a) 'Building up walls: the new pattern of spatial segregation in Sao Paolo' *International Social Science Journal*, 48:1

Caldeira, T. P. R. (1996b) 'Fortified enclaves: the new urban segregation' *Public Culture* 8:2, 329–54

Calhoun, C. (ed.) (1992) *Habermas and the Public Sphere*, Cambridge, MA, MIT Press

Castells, M. (1977) *The Urban Question*, London, Edward Arnold

Castells, M. (1983) *The City and The Grassroots*, London, Arnold

Castells, M. (1996) *The Information Age: Economy, Society and Culture Vol. I: The Rise of the Network Society*, Oxford, Blackwell

Castells, M. (1997) *The Information Age: Economy, Society and Culture Vol. II: The Power of Identity*, Oxford, Blackwell

Castells, M. (2000a) *The Information Age: Economy, Society and Culture Vol. III: End of Millennium*, Oxford, Blackwell

Castells, M. (2000b) 'Materials for an explanatory theory of the network society' *British Journal of Sociology* 51(3), 5–24

Castells, M. (2000c) 'Information technology and global capitalism' in Giddens, A. and Hutton, W. (eds) (2000) *On the Edge*, London, Jonathan Cape

Caygill, H. (1998) *Walter Benjamin: The Colour of Experience*, London, Routledge

de Certeau, M. (1984) *The Practice of Everyday Life*, London, University of California Press

de Certeau, M. (2000) *The Certeau Reader*, Oxford Malden, MA, Blackwell Publishers

Chadwick, E. (1842/1965) *Report on the Sanitary Condition of the Labouring Population of Great Britain*, Edinburgh, Edinburgh University Press

Chalmers, A. K. (1930) *The Health of Glasgow (1818–1925)*, Glasgow, Corporation of Glasgow

Chambers A. J. (1997) 'A stake in the country: women's experience of suburban development' in Silverstone, R. (ed.) (1997) *Visions of Suburbia*, London, Routledge

Chapman, T. and Hockey, J. (1999) *Ideal Homes? Social Change and Domestic Life*, London, Routledge

Chatterjee, P. (1993) *The Nation and its Fragments: Colonial and Post Colonial Histories*, Princeton, Princeton University Press

Chauncey, G. (1995) *Gay New York: The Making of the Gay Male World 1890–1940*, London, Harper Collins

Clarke, A. J. (1992) 'Tupperware suburbia: sociality and mass consumption' in Colomina, B. (ed.) (1992) *Sexuality and Space*, New York, Princeton Architectural Press

Cleland, J. (1836) *Statistical Facts Descriptive of the Former and Present State of Glasgow*, Glasgow, Bell and Bain

Cohen, G. (1978) *Karl Marx's Theory of History*, Oxford, Oxford University Press

Connell, R.W. (1995) *Masculinities*, Cambridge, Polity Press

Coser, L. (ed.) (1965) *Georg Simmel*, Englewood Cliffs, New Jersey, Prentice-Hall

Cosgrove, D. (1997) 'Spectacle and society: landscape as theatre in premodern and postmodern cities' in Groth, P. B. and Bressi, T. W. (eds) (1997) *Understanding Ordinary Landscapes*, London, Yale University Press

Cosgrove, D. (1998) *Social Formation and Symbolic Landscape*, London, University of Wisconsin Press

Cosgrove, D. and Daniels, S. (1988) *The Iconography of Landscape*, Cambridge, Cambridge University Press

Cousins, M. and Hussain, A. (eds) (1984) *Michel Foucault*, London, Macmillan

Cox, J. (2000) 'Reasons to be cheerful: theories of anti-capitalism' *International Socialism*, 89, Winter

Cox, K. (ed.) (1978) *Urbanisation and Conflict in Market Societies*, London, Methuen

Crang, M. (1996) 'Watching the city: video, resistance and surveillance' *Environment and Planning A*, 28

Crang, M. and Thrift, N. (eds) (2000) *Thinking Space*, London, Routledge

Damer, S. (1989) *From Moorpark to Wine Alley: The Rise and Fall of a Glasgow Housing Scheme Edinburgh*, Edinburgh University Press

Damer, S. (1990) *Glasgow, Going for a Song*, London, Lawrence and Wishart

Damer, S. (1992) 'Last exit to blackhall: the stigmatisation of a glasgow housing scheme' University of Glasgow, Centre for Housing Research, Discussion Paper, no. 37

Damer, S. (2000) 'Patrolling the poor: the social practice of Council House Management in Glasgow, 1885–1939' *Urban Studies*, 36/11, 2000

184

Dandeker, C. (1990) *Surveillance, Power and Modernity*, Cambridge, Cambridge University Press

Daniels, S. (1989) 'Marxism, culture and the duplicity of landscape' in Peet, R. and Thrift, N. *New Models in Geography Vol. 2*, London, Unwin Hyman

Davis, M. (1990) *City of Quartz*, London, Verso

Davis, M. (1994) *Beyond, Blade Runner: Urban Control – The Ecology of Fear*, Westfield, NJ, Open Magazines Pamphlet Series

Davis, M. (1998) *Ecology of Fear*, New York, Metropolitan Books

Davis, M. (2000) *Magical Urbanism*, London, Verso

Deutsche, R. (1991) 'Boys town' *Environment and Planning D Society and Space*, 9, 5–30

Deutsche, R. (1998) *Evictions: Art and Spatial Politics*, London, MIT Press

Deutsche, R. (1999) *Evictions: Art and Spatial Politics*, London, MIT Press

Dimendberg, E.(1998) 'Henri Lefebvre and abstract space' in Light, A. and Smith, J. M. (eds) *Philosophy and Geography II: The Production of Space*, Oxford, Rowman and Littlefield

Ditton, J., Short, E., Phillips, S., Norris, C. and Armstrong, G. (1999) The Effect of Closed Circuit Television on Recorded Crime Rates and Public Concern about Crime in Glasgow, Edinburgh, Stationary Office

Donnelly, M. (1992) On Foucault's uses of the notion of 'Biopower' in Armstrong, T. J. (1992) *Michel Foucault Philosopher*, London, Harvester Wheatsheaf

Douglas, M. (1993) 'The idea of home: a kind of space' in Mack, A. (ed.) *Home: A Place in the World*, New York, New York University Press

Dreyfus, H. and Rabinow, P. (eds) (1982) *Michel Foucault: Beyond Structuralism and Hermeneutics*, Chicago, Universisty of Chicago Press

Driver, F. (1985) 'Power, space and the body: a critical assessment of Foucault's discipline and punish' *Environment and Planning D*: 3

Driver, F. (1992) 'Geography and power: the work of Michel Foucault' in Burke, P. (ed.) (1992) *Critical Thought Series 2: Critical Essays on Michel Foucault*, London, Scolar Press

Driver, F. (1994) 'Bodies in space: Foucault's account of disciplinary power' in Jones, C. and Porter, R. (eds) (1994) *Reassessing Foucault: Power, Medicine and the Body*, London, Routledge

Duncan, J. and Duncan, J. (1988) '(Re)reading the landscape' *Environment and Planning D: Society and Space*, 6: 117–26

Duncan, J. and Ley, D. (eds) (1993) *Place/Culture/Representation*, London, Routledge

Durkheim, E. (1915/1976) *The Elementary Forms of Religious Life*, London, Allen and Unwin

Durkheim, E. (1933/1964) *The Division of Labour in Society*, New York, The Free Press

Durkheim, E. (1950) *The Rules of Sociological Method*, New York, The Free Press

Durkheim, E. (1957) *Professional Ethics and Civic Morals*, London, Routledge and Kegan Paul

Durkheim, E. (1993) *Suicide*, London, Routledge

Ely, G. (1992) 'Nations, publics and political culture: placing habermas in the nineteenth century' in Calhoun, C. (ed.) (1992) *Habermas and the Public Sphere*, Cambridge, MA, MIT Press

Engels, F. (1882/1969) *The Condition of the English Working Class*, Glasgow, Grafton Books

England, K. V. L. (1991) 'Gender relations and the spatial structure of the city' *Geoforum* 22(2), 135–47

Felski, R. (1999) 'The invention of everyday life' *New Formations*, 39, 15–31

Fischer, E. (1970) *Marx in His own Words*, Harmondsworth, Penguin

Fiske, J., Hodge, B. and Turner, G. (1987) *Myths of Oz: Reading Australian Popular Culture*, Sydney, Allen and Unwin

Fitzgerald, F. (1986) *Cities on a Hill*, New York, Pantheon

Flyberg, B. (1998) 'Habermas and Foucault: thinkers for civil society?' *British Journal of Sociology* 49:2, 210–33

Foucault, M. (1973) *The Birth of the Clinic: An Archaeology of Medical Perception*, London, Tavistock

Foucault, M. (1977) *Discipline and Punish*, London, Penguin

Foucault, M. (1979) 'Governmentality' *Ideology & Consciousness* 6, 5–21

Foucault, M. (1980a) *Power/ Knowledge – Selected Interviews and Other Writings (1972–1977)*, London, Harvester Wheatsheaf

Foucault, M. (1980b) 'Body/power' in Gordon, C. (1980) *Power/Knowledge – Selected Interviews and Other Writings (1972–1977)*, London, Harvester Wheatsheaf, 55–63

Foucault, M. (1980c) 'The eye of power' in Gordon, C. (1980) *Power/Knowledge – Selected Interviews and Other Writings (1972–1977)*, London, Harvester Wheatsheaf, 146–65

Foucault, M. (1980d) 'The politics of health in the eighteenth century' in Gordon, C. (ed.) *Power/Knowledge – Selected Interviews and Other Writings (1972–1977)*, London, Harvester Wheatsheaf, pp. 166–82

Foucault, M. (1980e) 'Questions on geography' in Gordon, C. *Power/Knowledge – Selected Interviews and Other Writings (1972–1977)* London, Harvester Wheatsheaf, 63–77

Foucault, M. (1980f) 'Two lectures' in Gordon, C. *Power/Knowledge – Selected Interviews and Other Writings (1972–1977)* London, Harvester Wheatsheaf, 78–108

Foucault, M. (1981) *The History of Sexuality*, vol. 1, London, Penguin

Foucault, M. (1982a) 'Interview with Michel Foucault on space knowledge and power', *Skyline*, March

Foucault, M. (1982b) 'The subject and power' in Dreyfus, H. and Rabinow, P. *Michel Foucault: Beyond Structuralism and Hermeneutics*, Chicago, University of Chicago Press

Foucault, M. (1984) 'Of other spaces' in *Architecture-Mouvement-Continuite*, October 1984, republished in *Diacritics*, Spring 1986, translated by Jay Miskowiec

Foucault, M. (1986) 'Space, knowledge and power' in Rabinow, P. (ed.) *The Foucault Reader*, Harmondsworth, Penguin

Fox, N. J. (1998) 'Foucault, Foucauldians and sociology' *British Journal of Sociology*, 49, September, 415–33

Franz, D. and Collins, C. (1999) *Celebration, USA: Living in Disney's Brave New Town*, New York, Henry Holt and Co.

Freiburg, J. W. (ed.) (1979) *Critical Sociology: European Perspectives*, London, John Wiley and Sons

Frisby, D. (1983) *The Alienated Mind*, London, Heineman

Frisby, D. (1984/2002) *Georg Simmel*, London, Routledge

Frisby, D. (1986) *Fragments of Modernity*, Cambridge, MA, MIT Press

Frisby, D. (1989) 'Simmel on leisure' in Rojek, C. *Leisure for Leisure*, London, MacMillan

186

Frisby, D. (1992) *Simmel and Since*, London, Routledge

Frisby, D. (1994a) 'The foundation of sociology' in *Georg Simmel: Critical Assessments*, vol. 1, London, Routledge

Frisby, D. (1994b) 'The flaneur in social theory' in Tester, K. (1994) *The Flaneur*, London, Routledge

Frisby, D. (1997) 'Introduction to the texts' in Frisby, D. and Featherstone, M., *Simmel on Culture*, London, Sage

Frisby, D. (1999) 'Culture, memory and metropolitan modernity' *The Contemporary Study of Culture*, Vienna, Turia and Kant

Frisby, D. (2001) *Cityscapes of Modernity*, London, Blackwell

Frisby, D. and Featherstone, M. (1997) *Simmel on Culture*, London, Sage

Frisby, D. and Sayer, D. (1986) *Society*, London, Tavistock

Fyfe, N. R. and Bannister, J. (1996) 'City watching: closed circuit television surveillance in public places' *Area* 28(1), 37

van Gennep, A. (1960) *Rites of Passage*, Chicago, University of Chicago Press

Giddens, A. (1984) *The Constitution of Society: Outline of Theory of Structuration*, Cambridge, Polity Press

Giddens, A. (1990) *The Consequences of Modernity*, Cambridge, Polity Press

Giddens, A. and Hutton, W. (eds) (2000) *On the Edge*, London, Jonathan Cape

Gilbert, A. (1994) *The Latin American City*, London, The Latin American Bureau

Gilloch, G. (1996) *Myth and Metropolis – Walter Benjamin and the City*, Cambridge, Polity Press

Gordon, C. (1980) *Power/Knowledge – Selected Interviews and Other Writings (1972–1977)*, London, Harvester Wheatsheaf

Gottdiener, M. (1984) *The Social Production of Urban Space* (2nd edn 1994), Texas, University of Texas Press

Gottdiener, M. (1985) *The Social Production of Space*, Austin, University of Texas

Gottdiener, M. (1987) 'Space as a force of production' *International Journal of Urban and Regional Research* 11, 404–16

Gottdiener, M. (1993) 'A Marx for our time: Henri Lefebvre and the production of space' *Sociological Theory*, 11(1)

Gottdiener, M. (1994) *The New Urban Sociology*, New York, McGraw-Hill

Gottdiener, M. (1997) *The Social Production of Urban Space*, Austin, Texas University Press

Gottdiener, M. (2000) 'Lefebvre and the bias of academic urbanism: what can be learnt from the 'new urban analysis'? *City*, 4:1

Gottdiener, M. and Feagin, J. (1988) 'The paradigm shift in urban sociology' *Urban Affairs Quarterly*, 24: 163–87

Gramsci, A. (1971) *Selections from the Prison Notebooks*, London, Lawrence and Wishart

Gray, R. (1981) 'Bourgeois hegemony in Victorian Britain' in Bennett, T., Graham, C. M. and Mercer, C. (eds) *Culture, Ideology and Social Process*, Milton Keynes, Open University Press

Greenbie, B. B. (1981) *Spaces: Dimensions of the Human Landscape*, London, Yale University Press

Gregory, D. (1994) *Geographical Imaginations*, Oxford, Blackwell

Gregory, D. and Urry, J. (1985) *Social Relations and Spatial Structures*, London, Macmillan

Gregory, D., Martin, R. and Smith, G. (1994) *Human Geography-Society-Space and Social Science*, Minneapolis, University of Minnesota Press

Groth, P. B. and Bressi, T. W. (eds) (1997) *Understanding Ordinary Landscapes*, London, Yale University Press

Habermas, J. (1992) *The Structural Transformation of the Public Sphere*, Cambridge, The Polity Press

Habermas, J. (1996) 'Georg Simmel on philosophy and culture: postscript to a collection of essays', *Critical Inquiry* 22, Spring 1996

Harvey, D. (1973) *Social Justice and the City*, London, Edward Arnold

Harvey, D. (1977a) 'Population resources and the ideology of science' in Peet, R. (ed.) *Radical Geography*, London, Macmillan

Harvey, D. (1977b) 'The geography of capitalist accumulation: a framework for analysis' in Peet, R. (ed.) *Radical Geography*, London, Macmillan

Harvey, D. (1978a) 'The urban process under capitalism: a framework for analysis' *International Journal of Urban and Regional Research* 2, 101–31.

Harvey, D. (1978b) 'Labour, capital and class struggle around the built environment in advanced capitalist societies' in Cox, K. (ed.) *Urbanisation and Conflict in Market Societies*, London, Methuen

Harvey, D. (1982) *The Limits to Capital*, Chicago, The University of Chicago Press

Harvey, D. (1985a) *The Urbanisation of Capital*, Oxford, Basil Blackwell

Harvey, D. (1985b) *Consciousness and the Urban Experience*, Oxford, Basil Blackwell

Harvey, D. (1989) *The Urban Experience*, Oxford, Blackwell Publishers

Harvey, D. (1990) *The Condition of Postmodernity*, Cambridge, Blackwell

Harvey, D. (1996) *Justice, Nature and the Geography of Difference*, Oxford, Blackwell

Harvey, D. (1997) 'Between space and time: reflections on the geographical imagination' in Barnes, T. and Gregory, D. (eds) *Reading Human Geography*, London, Edward Arnold

Harvey, D. (2000) *Spaces of Hope*, Edinburgh, Edinburgh Univeristy Press

Harvey, D. (2001) *Spaces of Capital: Towards a Critical Geography*, Edinburgh, Edinburgh University Press

Harvey, D. (2003) *Paris, Capital of Modernity*, London, Routledge

Harvey, D. (2005) *The New Imperialism*, Oxford, Oxford University Press

Hayden, D. (1997) 'Urban landscape history: the sense of place and the politics of space' in Groth, P. B. and Bressi, T. W. *Understanding Ordinary Landscapes*, London, Yale University Press

Helms, G. (2003) *Towards Safe City Centres? Remaking the Spaces of an Old-Industrial City*, Glasgow, Glasgow University

Hey, V. (1986) *Patriarchy and Pub Culture*, London, Tavistock

Hindle, P. (1994) 'Gay communities and gay space in the city' in Whittle, S. (ed.) *The Margins of the City: Gay Men's Urban Lives*, Aldershot, Arena

Howell, P. (1993) 'Public space and the public sphere: political economy and the historical geography of modernity' in *Environment and Planning D – Space and Society*, 11

Hubbard, P., Kitchin, R. and Valentine, G. (eds) (2004) *Key Thinkers on Space and Place*, London, Sage

Hutnyk, J. (1996) *The Rumour of Calcutta: Tourism, Charity and the Poverty of Representation*, London, Zed Books

Janicaud, D. (1992) 'Rationality, force and power' in Armstrong, T. J. (ed.) *Michel Foucault: Philosopher*, London, Harvester Wheatsheaf

Johnston, L. and Valentine, G. (1995) 'Wherever I lay my girlfriend that's my home: the performance and surveillance of lesbian identities in domestic environments' in Bell, D. and Valentine, G. (eds) *Mapping Desire: Geographies of Sexualities*, London Routledge

Jones, C. and Porter, R. (eds) (1994) *Reassessing Foucault: Power, Medicine and the Body*, London, Routledge

Katz, C. and Kirkby, A. (1991) 'In the nature of things: the environment and everyday life' *Transactions of the Institute of British Geographers*, 16

Kay, J. P. (1832/1969) *The Moral and Physical Condition of the Working Class*, Manchester, Morton

Kay, J. P. (1839) 'The training of pauper children' in the *Fifth Annual Report of the Poor Law Commissioners for England and Wales British Parliamentary Papers*, 1839, vol. XX

Keith, M. and Pile, S. (eds) (1993) *Place and the Politics of Identity*, London, Routledge

Kelton, T. and Valentine, G. (eds) (1998) *Cool Places: Geographies of Youth Cultures* London, Routledge

Klein, N. (2000) *No Logo*, London, Flamingo

Knopp, L. (1990) 'Some theoretical implications of gay involvement in an urban land market' *Political Geography Quarterly* 9, 337–52

Knopp, L. (1992) 'Sexuality and the spatial dynamics of capitalism' *Environment and Planning D Society and Space* 10:6, 651–70

Kofman, E. and Lebas, E. (1996) 'Introduction: lost in transposition – time, space and the city' in Lefebvre, H. (1996) *Writings on Cities*, Oxford, Blackwell

Landes, J. B. (ed.) (1998) *Feminism, the Public and the Private*, Oxford, Oxford University Press

Lash, S. and Urry, J. (1994) *Economies of Signs and Space*, London, Sage

Lauria, M. and Knopp, L. (1985) 'Towards an analysis of the role of gay communities in urban renaissance' *Urban Geography* 5(3), 152–69

Lechner, F. J. (1991) 'Simmel on social space' *Theory, Culture and Society* 8, 195–201

Lefebvre, H. (1947) *The Coming of the French Revolution*, Princeton, Princeton University Press

Lefebvre, H. (1968a) *Dialectical Materialism*, London, Jonathan Cape

Lefebvre, H. (1968b) *The Sociology of Marx*, Allen Lane

Lefebvre, H. (1969) *Napoleon*, London, Routledge and K. Paul

Lefebvre, H. (1970) 'Du Rural a l'Urbain' *Anthropos*

Lefebvre, H. (1971) *Everyday Life in the Modern World*, London, Allen Lane The Penguin Press

Lefebvre, H. (1972) *La Pensee Marxiste et la Ville*, Paris, Gallimard

Lefebvre, H. (1976) *The Survival of Capitalism*, London, Allison and Busby

Lefebvre, H. (1977) 'Reflections on the politics of space' in *Radical Geography* Peet, R. (ed.) London, Methuen and Co.: 339–52. Also in *Antipode* 8 no. 2 (1976) 30–7

Lefebvre, H. (1978) 'Les Contradictions de L'Etat Moderne La Dialectique de L'Etat', vol. 4, 1978

Lefebvre, H. (1979) 'Space social product and use value' Ch. 12. in Freiburg, J. W. (ed.) (1979) *Critical Sociology: European Perspectives*, London, John Wiley and Sons

Lefebvre, H. (1987) 'An interview with Henri Lefebvre' *Environment and Planning D: Society and Space* 5, 27–38

Lefebvre, H. (1991a) *Critique of Everyday Life*, London, Verso

Lefebvre, H. (1991b) *The Production of Space*, Oxford, Blackwell

Lefebvre, H. (1995) *Introduction to Modernity*, London, Verso

Lefebvre, H. (1996) *Writings on Cities*, Oxford, Blackwell

Levine, D. N., Carter, E. B. and Gorman, E. M. (1976a) 'Simmel's influence on American sociology I' *The American Journal of Sociology* 81:4 (January 1976), 813–45

Levine, D. N. Carter, E. B. and Gorman, E. M. (1976b) 'Simmel's influence on American sociology II' *The American Journal of Sociology* 81:5 (March 1976), 1112–32

Lewis, M. (1994) 'A sociological pub crawl around gay Newcastle' in Whittle, S. (ed.) (1994) *The Margins of the City: Gay Men's Urban Lives*, Aldershot, Arena

Leyshon, P. and Thrift, N. (1997) *Money/Space*, London, Routledge

Light, A. and Smith, J. M. (eds) (1998) *Philosophy and Geography II: The Production of Space*, Oxford, Rowman and Littlefield

Lyon, D. (1988) *The Information Society*, London, Polity

Lyon, D. (1994) *The Electronic Eye*, London, Polity

Lyon, D. (2001) *Surveillance Society*, Open University Press, Buckingham

Mack, A. (ed.) *Home: A Place in the World*, New York, New York University Press

MacNaughten, P. and Urry, J. (eds) (1998) *Contested Natures*, London, Sage

MacNaughten, P. and Urry, J. (eds) (2001) *Bodies of Nature*, London, Sage

Mann, M. (1993) *The Sources of Social Power, Vol. 2*, Cambridge, Cambridge University Press

Marcuse, P. (1989) 'Dual city: a muddy metaphor for a quartered city', *International Journal of Urban and Regional Research* 13, 697–708

Marcuse, P. (1995) 'Not chaos, but walls: postmodernism and the partitioned city' in Watson, S. and Gibson, K. (eds) (1995) *Postmodern Cities and Spaces*, Oxford, Blackwell

Marx, K. (1846/1964) *The German Ideology*, London, Lawrence and Wishart

Marx, K. (1847/1936) *The Poverty of Philosophy*, London, Lawrence

Marx, K. (1852/1977) *The Eighteenth Brumaire of Louis Bonaparte*, Moscow, Progress

Marx, K. (1853) *The Future Results of British Rule in India London*, Friday July 22 1853 in New York Daily Tribune August 8 in Renton, D. (ed.) 2001 *Marx on Globalisation*, Lawrence and Wishart, London, pp. 90–6

Marx, K. (1858/1973) *The Grundrisse*, Harmondsworth, Penguin

Marx, K. (1859/1970) *A Contribution to the Critique of Political Economy*, Moscow, Progress Publishers

Marx, K. (1867/1976) *Capital Vol. 1*, Harmondsworth, Penguin Books

Marx, K. (1877/1957) *Capital Vol. II*, Moscow, Progress Publishers

Marx, K. and Engels, F. (1848/1971) *The Communist Party Manifesto*, Moscow, Progress Publishers

Marx, K. and Engels, F. (1848/1975) *The Manifesto of the Communist Party*, Peking, The Foreign Language Press

Massey, D. (1984) *Spatial Divisions of Labour*, New York, Methuen

Massey, D. (1985) 'New directions in space' in Gregory, D. and Urry, J. (eds) (1985) *Social Relations and Spatial Structures*, London, Macmillan

Massey, D. (1991) 'Flexible sexism' *Environment and Planning D Society and Space* 9, 31–57

Massey, D. (1992) 'A place called home' in *New Formations 17*, London, Lawrence and Wishart

Massey, D. (1994) *Space Place and Gender*, Cambridge, Polity Press

Massey, D. (2005) *For Space*, London, Sage

Matless, D. (1992) 'An occasion for geography: landscape, representation and Foucault's corpus' *Environment and Planning D*, 10 (1), 1992

Maver, I. (1997) 'The quest for purity in the nineteenth century Scottish city' *Paedagogica Historica, International Journal of the History of Education*, XXXIII, 1997

McCahill, D. (2002) *The Surveillance Web: the Rise of Visual Surveillance in an English City*, Cullompton, Willan

McCann, E. J. (1999) 'Race, protest and public space: contextualising Lefebvre in the US city' *Antipode* 31:2, 163–84

McClellan, D. (1973) *Marx's Grundrisse*, St Albans, Paladin

McClellan, D. (1980) *The Thought of Karl Marx* (2nd ed), London, Macmillan

McClintock, L. (1997) *Imperial Leather, Race, Gender and Sexuality in the Colonial Contest*, London, Routledge

McDowell, L. (1983) 'Towards an understanding of the gender division of urban space' *Society and Space* 1, 59–72

McDowell, L. (1997) *Capital Culture: Gender at Work in the City*, Oxford, Blackwell

McDowell, L. (1999) 'Beyond patriarchy: a class based explanation of women's subordination' *Antipode* 18:3, 311–21

McGrane, B. (1989) *Beyond Anthropology: Society and the Other*, New York, Colombia University Press

Mehrotra, R. (1997) *One Space, Two Worlds*, London, Faber and Faber

Merrifield, A. (1993) 'Place and space: a Lefebvrian reconciliation' *Transactions of the British Institute of Geographers* 18

Merrifield, A. (1997) 'Between process ad individuation: translating metaphors and narratives of urban space' *Antipode* 29:4, 417–36

Merrifield, A. (no date) 'Public space: integration and exclusion in public life' *City*, 5/6: 57–72

Miles, S. and Miles, M. (2004) *Consuming Cities*, Basingstoke, Palgrave

Mitchell, D. (1995) 'The end of public space: people's park, definitions of the public and democracy' *Annals of the Association of American Geographers* 85:1, 120

Mitchell, R., Dorling, D. and Shaw, M. (2000) *Inequalities in Life and Death Bristol*, Policy Press/Joseph Rowntree Foundation

Mith, S. J. (1987) 'Design against crime? Beyond the rhetoric of residential crime prevention' *Journal of Property Management* 5, 146–50

Mohan, J. (2000) *A United Kingdom?* London, Arnold

Moscovici, S. (1993) *The Invention of Society*, Oxford, Polity Press

Murphy, P. and Watson, S. (1997) *Surface City: Sydney at the Millennium*, Sydney, Pluto Press

Newman, O. (1972) *Defensible Space*, New York, McMillan

Nicholson-Lord, D. (1987) *The Greening of the Cities*, London, Routledge and Kegan Paul

Norris, C., Moran J. and Armstrong, G. (eds) (1998) *Surveillance, Closed Circuit Television and Social Control*, Aldershot, Ashgate

Ollman, B. (1971) *Alienation*, Cambridge, Cambridge University Press

O'Neill, J. (1986) 'The disciplinary society: from Weber to Foucault' *British Journal of Sociology* 37 (1)

Pacione, M. (ed.) (1997) *Britain's Cities*, London, Routledge

Pain, I. (1991) 'Space, sexual violence and social control progress' in *Human Geography*, 15:4, 415–31

Pearce, J. (1996) 'Urban youth cultures: gender and spatial forms' in *Youth and Policy*, 52, 1–11

Peet, R. (ed.) (1977) *Radical Geography*, London, Methuen and Co.

Peet, R. (1998) *Modern Geographical Thought*, Oxford, Blackwell

Peet, R. and Thrift, N. (eds) (1997) *New Models in Geography Vol. 2*, London, Unwin Hyman

Philo, C. (1992) 'Foucault's geography' in *Environment and Planning D: Society and Space* 10, 137–61

Philo, C. (ed.) (1995) *Off the Map: The Social Geography of Poverty in the UK*, London, Child Poverty Action Group

Philo, C. and Bale, J. (eds) (1998) *Body Cultures: Essays on Sport, Space and Identity*, London, Routledge

Philo, C. and Kearns, G. (eds) (1993) *Selling Places: The City as Cultural Capital, Past and Present*, Oxford, Pergamon Press

Pile, S. and Thrift, N. (1995) *Mapping the Subject: Geographies of Cultural Transformation*, London, Routledge

Pile, S., Brook, C. and Mooney, G. (eds) (1999) *Unruly Cities: Order/Disorder*, London, Routledge/Open University Press

Pollock, G. (1988) 'Modernity and the spaces of femininity' in *Visions and Difference: Femininity and Histories of Art*, London, Routledge

Poovey, M. (1993) 'Anatomical realism and social investigation in early 19th century Manchester' *Differences: A Journal of Feminist Cultural Studies* 5:3, 1–30

Pratt, G. and Hanson, S. (1988) 'Gender class and space' in *Environment and Planning D Society and Space* 6, 15–35

Rabinow, P. (ed.) (1984) *The Foucault Reader*, Harmondsworth, Penguin

Renton, D. (ed.) (2001) *Marx on Globalisation*, London, Lawrence and Wishart

Robinson, J. (1999) 'Divisive cities: power and segregation in cities' in Pile, S., Brook, C. and Mooney, G. (eds) *Unruly Cities*, London, Routledge, Open University Press

Rojek, C. (ed.) (1989) *Leisure for Leisure*, London, MacMillan

Rojek, C. (1993) *Ways of Escape*, Basingstoke, McMillan

Rose, G. (1993) *Feminism and Geography*, Minneapolis, University of Minneapolis Press

Rose, N. (1994) 'Medicine, history and the present' in Jones, C. and Porter, R. (eds), (1994) *Reassessing Foucault: Power, Medicine and the Body*, London, Routledge

Ross, A. (1999) *The Celebration Chronicles: Life Liberty and the Pursuit of Property Values in Disney's New Town*, New York, Ballantine Books

Rotenberg, P. (1995) *Landscape and Power in Vienna*, London, John Hopkins University Press

Russell, J. B. (1886) *The Vital Statistics of Glasgow*, Glasgow, MacDougall

Russell, J. B. (1895) *The Evolution of the Function of Public Health Administration*, Glasgow, William Hodge and Co

Russell, J. B. (1905) *Public Health Administration in Glasgow*, Glasgow, Corporation of Glasgow

Said, E. (1978) *Orientalism*, London, Kegan Paul

Said, E. (1993) *Culture and Imperialism*, London, Chatto and Windus

Said, E. (2000) 'Invention, memory and place' *Critical Inquiry* 26: 175–92

Saunders, P. (1981) *Social Theory and the Urban Question*, London, Hutcheson

Saunders, P. (1985) 'Space, the city and urban sociology' in Gregory, D. and Urry, J. (1985) *Social Relations and Spatial Structures*, London, Macmillan

Savage, M., Warde, A. and Ward, K. (2003) *Urban Sociology, Capitalism and Modernity* (2nd edn) Basingstoke, Palgrave Macmillan

Scott, J. C. (1985) *Weapons of the Weak: Everyday Forms of Peasant Resistance*, London, Yale University Press

Sennett, R. (1971) *Uses of Disorder*, London, Allen Lane

Sharp, J., Philo, C., Routledge, P. and Paddison, R. (2000) *Entanglements of Power: Geographies of Domination/ Resistance*, London, Routledge

Shaw, M., Dorling, D. and Gordon G. D. (1999) *The Widening Gap*, Bristol Policy Press

Shields, R. (1997) 'Spatial stress and resistance: social meaning of spatialisation' in Benko, G. and Strothmayer, U. (eds) (1997) *Space and Social Theory*, Oxford, Blackwell

Shields, R. (2000) *Lefebvre, Love and Struggle*, London, Routledge

Silverstone, R. (ed.) (1997) *Visions of Suburbia*, London Routledge

Simmel, G. (1950) 'The stranger' in Wolff, K. H. (1950) *The Sociology of Georg Simmel*, New York, Free Press

Simmel, G. (1959a) 'The problem of sociology' in Wolff, K. H. (1959) *Georg Simmel*, Columbus, Ohio, Columbus Ohio State University Press

Simmel, G. (1959b) 'How is society possible' in Wolff, K. H. (1959) *Georg Simmel*, Columbus, Ohio, Columbus Ohio State University Press

Simmel, G. (1978/2004) *The Philosophy of Money*, London, Routledge

Simmel, G. (1997a) 'The adventure' in Frisby, D. and Featherstone, M. (eds) (1997) *Simmel on Culture*, London, Sage

Simmel, G. (1997b) 'The Alpine journey' in Frisby, D. and Featherstone, M. (eds) (1997) *Simmel on Culture*, London, Sage

Simmel, G. (1997c) 'The sociology of space' in Frisby, D. and Featherstone, M. (eds) (1997) *Simmel on Culture*, London, Sage

Simmel, G. (1997d) 'The metropolis and mental life' in Frisby, D. and Featherstone, M. (eds) (1997) *Simmel on Culture*, London, Sage

Simmel, G. (1997e) 'Bridge and door' in Frisby, D. and Featherstone, M. (eds) (1997) *Simmel on Culture*, London, Sage

Simmel, G. (1997f) 'The Berlin trade exhibition' in Frisby, D. and Featherstone, M. (eds) (1997) *Simmel on Culture*, London, Sage

Simonsen, K. (2005) 'Bodies, sensations, spaces and time: the contribution from Henri Lefebvre' *Geografiska. Annaler 87 B 1*, 1–14

Smart, B. (ed.) (1995) *Michel Foucault: Critical Assessments (2)*, London, Routledge

Smith, M. (2001) 'Repetition and difference: Lefebvre, Le Corbusier and modernity's (im)moral landscape' *Ethics, Place and Environment 4:1*, 31–44

Smith, N. (1984) *Uneven Development: Nature, Capital and the Production of Space*, Oxford, Blackwell

Soja, E. W. (1980) 'The socio-spatial dialectic' *Annals of Association of American Geographers 70*, 207–25

Soja, E. W. (1989) *Postmodern Geographies – The Reassertion of Space in Critical Social Theory*, London, Verso

Soja, E. W. (1996) *Thirdspace: Journeys to Los Angeles and Other Real-And-Imagined Places*, Oxford, Blackwell

Soja, E. W. (1999) 'Keeping space open' *Annals of Association of American Geographers 89*, 348–53

Soja, E. W. (2000) *Postmetropolis*, Oxford, Blackwell

Soja, E. W. and Hadjimichalis, C. (1974) 'Between historical materialism and spatial fetishism: some observations on the development of marxist spatial analysis' *Antipode* 11, 3–11

Spigel, L. 1(992) 'The suburban home companion: television and the neighbourhood ideal' in Colombina, B. (ed.) *Sexuality and Space*, Princeton, Princeton Architectural Press

Staples, W. (1997) *The Culture of Surveillance*, Cambridge, Cambridge University Press

Stow, D. (1833) Infant training: a dialogue explanatory of the system adopted in the Model Infant School, Glasgow

Stratton, J. and Ang, I. (1988) 'Multicultural imagined communities' in Bennett, D. (ed.) (1998) *Multicultural States: Rethinking Difference and Identity*, London, Routledge

Sturdy, S. and Cooter, C. (1998) 'Science, scientific management and the transformation of Medicine in Britain, c.1870–1950' *History of Science, 36 (part 4)*

Taylor, I., Evans, K. and Fraser, P. (1996) 'Out on the town: Manchester's gay village' in *A Tale of Two Cities: Global Change, Local Feeling and Everyday Life in the North of England – A Study in Manchester and Sheffield*, London, Routledge

Tenbruck F. H. (1959) 'Formal sociology' in Wolf K. H. (1959) *Georg Simmel*, Columbus, Ohio, Ohio State University Press

Tester, K. (1994) *The Flaneur*, London, Routledge

Teyssot, G. (1995) 'Heterotopias and the history of space' in Smart, B. (ed.) *Michel Foucault: Critical Assessments (2)*, London, Routledge

Thompson, E. P. (1967) 'Time, work-discipline and industrial capitalism' *Past and Present*, 38, 58–67

Thompson, E. P. (1978) *The Making of the English Working Class*, London, Penguin

Thrift, N. (1996) *Spatial Formations*, London, Sage

Tonnies, F. (1955) *Gemeinshaft and Gesellschaft*, London, Routledge and Kegan Paul

Tucker, R. C. (1978) *The Marx–Engels Reader* (2nd edn), London, Norton and Co.

Turner, V. (1977) *The Ritual Process*, Ithaca, New York, Cornell University Press

Unwin, T. (1992) *The Place of Geography*, Harlow, Essex, Longman

Urry, J. (1987) 'Nature and society: the organisation of space' in Anderson, R. J., Hughes, J. A., Sharrock, W. W. (eds) *Classic Disputes in Sociology*, London, Allen and Unwin

Urry, J. (1990) *The Tourist Gaze*, London, Sage

Urry, J. (1995) *Consuming Places*, London, Routledge

Urry, J. (2000) *Sociology Beyond Societies*, Routledge, London

Valentine, G. (1989) 'The geography of women's fear' *Area* 21, 385–90

Wakefield, A. (2003) *Selling Security: The Private Policing of Public Space*, Cullompton, Willan

Watson, S. and Gibson, K. (eds) (1995) *Postmodern Cities and Spaces*, Oxford, Blackwell

Watt, P. (1998) 'Going out of town: youth race and place in the South East of England' *Environment and Planning: Society and Space*, 16, 687–703

Watt, P. and Stenson, K. (1998) 'The street: it's a bit dodgy around there–safety, danger, ethnicity and young peoples use of public space' in Kelton, T. and Valentine, G. (eds) (1998) *Cool Places: Geographies of Youth Cultures*, London, Routledge

Webster, C. (2001) 'Gated cities of tomorrow' *Town Planning Review* 72:2

Wekerle, G. (1984) 'A woman's place is in the city' *Antipode* 16(3), 11–19

Werlen, B. (1993) *Society, Action and Space*, London, Routledge

Whittle, S. (ed.) (1994) *The Margins of the City: Gay Men's Urban Lives*, Aldershot, Arena

Williams, R. (1973) *The City and the Country*, London, Hogarth Press

Williams, R. (1976) *Keywords*, London, Fontanna

Williams, R. (1977) *Marxism and Literature*, Oxford, Oxford University Press

Wilson, E. (1991) *The Sphinx in the City: Urban Life, the Control of Disorder and Women*, London, Virago Press

Wirth, L. (1938) 'Urbanism as a way of life' *American Journal of Sociology* 44:1, 1–24

Wolff, K. H. (1950) *The Sociology of Georg Simmel*, New York, The Free Press

Wolff, K. H. (1958) *Essays on Sociology*, Ohio State University Press, Columbus, Ohio

Wright, G. and Rabinow, P. (1982) 'Spatialisation and power', *Skyline*, March, 1982

Zieleniec, A. J. L. (2002) Park space: leisure, culture and modernity – a Glasgow case study, Glasgow, Glasgow University, unpublished PhD thesis

Zieleniec A. J. L. (forthcoming in 2007) 'Night and day: the use and practice of public parks – a Glasgow case study' in Stahl, G. and Kinik, A. (2007) *Night and the City*, London, Verso

Zorbaugh, H. W. (1929/1983) *The Gold Cost and The Slum: A Sociological Study of Chicago's Near North Side*, Chicago, IL Midway Reprint, University of Chicago Press

Zukin, S. (1995a) *The Culture of Cities*, Oxford, Blackwell

Zukin, S. (1995b) *Landscapes of Power: From Detroit to Disney World*, Oxford, Blackwell

195

index

199